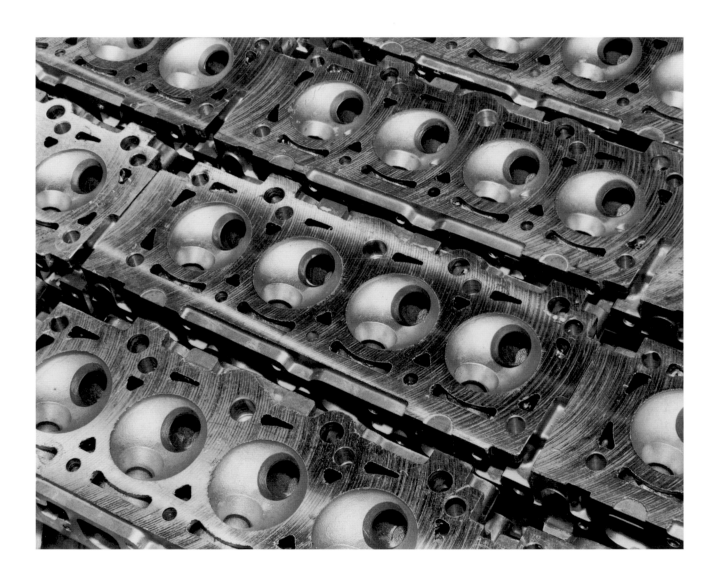

RIVER ROUGE

FORD'S INDUSTRIAL COLOSSUS

JOSEPH P. CABADAS

MOTORBOOKS
INTERNATIONAL

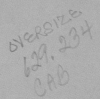
First published in 2004 by Motorbooks International, an imprint of MBI Publishing Company, Galtier Plaza, Suite 200, 380 Jackson Street, St. Paul, MN 55101-3885 USA

Motorbooks International titles are also available at discounts in bulk quantity for industrial or sales-promotional use. For details write to Special Sales Manager at Motorbooks International Wholesalers & Distributors, Galtier Plaza, Suite 200, 380 Jackson Street, St. Paul, MN 55101-3885 USA.

ISBN 0-7603-1708-9

Edited by Dennis Pernu
Designed by Chris Fayers

Endpapers: Mustang mufflers *(front)* and tailpipes *(back)* are stacked in one railroad gondola and steel wheels in another as they wait their turn to be taken into the Rouge Complex's Dearborn Assembly Plant. *Ford Photomedia*

Front cover: A retractable hardtop Ford Skyliner 500 and other Fairlane models are about ready to come off the final line at Dearborn Assembly in March 1957. For nearly two decades, the Fairlane was Ford's most luxurious and highest priced model. The cars took their name from Henry Ford's Fair Lane mansion, located about 4 miles upstream from the factory complex. *Ford Photomedia.*

Frontispiece: Cylinder heads wait to be used in the new 1.3-liter and 1.6-liter overhead-cam, four-cylinder engines for the 1981 Ford Escort and Mercury Lynx. Produced at the Dearborn Engine Plant that had just undergone expansion and renovation, the engines were made to meet ever-increasing federal fuel-economy standards. *Ford Photomedia*

Title pages: The Rouge Complex, called the Fordson Plant when this aerial photo was made in 1927, takes shape. Two large ore freighters (possibly the *Henry Ford II* and the *Benson Ford*) are visible, one in the boat slip and the other docked west of the turning basin. To the right of two transfer cranes over the storage bins, smoke can be seen rising from at least four of Powerhouse No. 1's eight 333-foot-tall smokestacks. Meanwhile, a splotch of black smoke obscures the coke ovens closer to the river. With the end of Model T production earlier that year, the complex underwent a massive retooling to manufacture 1928 Model As. *Lindsay Brooke Archives*

Table of contents: Employees Steve Imre *(on ladder)* and Kelly Albert post a sign on March 22, 1956, proclaiming the Dearborn Glass Plant had accumulated more than 6 million accident-free man-hours since December 1954, setting a world record for the glass industry. *Dearborn Historical Museum*

Back cover, left: Clouds of white steam spew from the Rouge Complex's quenching tower on December 13, 1932, in this photo taken from the ornate Dix Road Bridge. Red-hot coke, fresh from the ovens, was soaked with water to prevent it from burning up. Also visible are the coal and coke conveyors crisscrossing the complex. *Dearborn Historical Museum*. **Back cover, right:** Nighttime falls on the Ford Rouge Center's latest addition, the Dearborn Truck Plant, which began full operations in June 2004. The plant represents the hopes and dreams of Chairman William Clay Ford Jr. and Ford workers that the Rouge will survive well into the twenty-first century. *Ford Photomedia*

Printed in China

Contents

Preface:
Ties That Bind

"Youngest Oldtimer: Joseph Cabadas, rigger on the Coke Ovens, at least deserves honorable mention in the Rouge Youngest-Oldtimer Contest. He was 14 years old when he joined the Company better than 20 years ago. Born Nov. 13, 1913, Cabadas entered the Ford Trade School on Jan. 2, 1928. He and his wife, Genevieve, and their three sons live at 18260 Harmon, Melvindale."

—Ford Rouge News, *November 12, 1948*

Creating this book was a yearlong effort of researching, conducting interviews, and even just contemplating the many people and events that have linked me to Henry Ford's famed River Rouge Plant in Dearborn, Michigan.

I am not the man who was noted in the *Ford Rouge News.* He was my grandfather, who lived the Rouge experience. I learned about his life only secondhand, because he died in 1970, when I was three years old.

Like many of you, my ancestors emigrated to the United States to seize their piece of the American dream. My paternal grandfather's family came from Spain around the time of the First World War. After stopping to work in the coal mines of West Virginia, the Cabadas (pronounced kah-*bah*-dus or kah-*bay*-dus) family came to Detroit for the promise of one of Ford's well-paying jobs. At age 14, my grandfather enrolled in the Henry Ford Trade School, which taught the "practical" skills needed to work in one of his factories before going on to a job at "Ford's."

Detroit had numerous ethnic enclaves, and people tended to stick with their own kind. My grandfather, however, married a Polish woman and raised a family of three sons in the tiny community of Melvindale, just across the Rouge River from the vast factory complex where he worked. Other than the residents of Dearborn's "South End" and a portion of southwest Detroit, the people of Melvindale live as close as you can get to the industrial behemoth and the other heavy industries that grew up around the plant. Not only would you experience the smells and dust from the Rouge, but adding to Melvindale's ambiance was the underground blasting in Detroit's salt mine, which made the ground shake.

During World War II, my grandfather left the Rouge to enlist in the army air forces, while Grandma left her three sons with a neighbor to work as a "Rosie the Riveter" at Ford's Willow Run bomber plant.

After the war, my grandfather worked his way up to the position of millwright. According to Ford Motor Company historian Bob Kreipke, "A millwright was the catchall person that moved things when needed. If you had to rebrick a furnace, the millwrights came in. If you had to

move an assembly line, the millwrights worked with the electricians and sweepers. They are responsible for maintaining the infrastructure at the plants and never do the same job day to day. Millwright was a sought-after job. They never stayed in one place, and never got bored."

The Cabadases were almost a stereotypical autoworker's family. Grandpa was able to live the middle-class life, as the union negotiated ever higher wages. Not only did he have a bungalow with a second kitchen in the basement and a La-Z-Boy recliner, he also purchased a wooden Chris-Craft runabout and started building a summer vacation cottage—out west, along a manmade lake near the Michigan International Speedway in Brooklyn, rather than "up north."

My father's older brother also worked for a time at the Rouge, until he completed his college education and eventually became an engineer at Ford. My own father, though, raised his family through the economic doldrums of the 1970s, when getting a factory job to earn easy money was no longer a birthright. Despite any economic hardships we faced, I was still able to go to college—which just happened to be the Dearborn campus of the University of Michigan. Since I had high enough grades to earn a partial scholarship, a special award ceremony was held in a castle-like mansion on the campus called The Henry Ford Estate–Fair Lane.

Growing up in Dearborn Heights, a Detroit suburb just west of Dearborn, I knew all about Henry Ford and his experiment with vertical integration at the Rouge Plant, where the company turned raw materials into cars. I was taught that although Ford popularized automobiles with the Model T he hadn't invented the car, despite "popular misconceptions."

Still, I learned much about Ford and the Rouge, first in college, then as a reporter for the *News-Herald*, covering the cities of Melvindale and Allen Park in Detroit's Downriver region. In 1997, I

The author's grandfather, Jose Cabadas, is shown as he appeared in the *Ford Rouge News* in 1948, when he was a rigger on the coke ovens. *Ford Photomedia*

Above: A 1948 Ford F-5 truck pulls a flatbed loaded with nine "white metal" 1949 Ford bodies. The car bodies are being taken from the Pressed-Steel (Stamping) Building to the Dearborn Assembly Plant, where they will be finished, painted, trimmed, and moved to the final assembly line. The F-Series trucks were Ford's first postwar vehicles, but the cars were what saved the company from financial crisis. *National Automotive History Collection*

Right: Molten steel burns from orange- to white-hot in 5-ton ingot molds inside one of the Rouge Steel mills in the early 1980s. Henry Ford built the Rouge, in large part, because he wanted to have his own integrated steelworks running alongside a massive auto plant. By 1982, however, Ford Motor Company had turned its steel division into a separate enterprise, in preparation for selling it. *Ford Photomedia*

started working at a weekly automotive paper, *U.S. Auto Scene*, and was put on the Ford beat. My editor, Peter Salinas, told me to go find something to write about.

My first task was to blindly call someone in Ford's public relations department. I picked someone with a fairly high-sounding title and told him what I was doing. "You're just fishing for stories, aren't you?" he asked.

I told him, "Yes."

"Be more specific," he said.

"Well, I want to know more about what's going on at the Rouge Plant, since it's in the area I cover."

"We don't call it the Rouge Plant," the director said in a chilly tone. "It's the Rouge Complex. We have several plants on the complex."

So much for easy introductions. Yet I plunged into the job, covering a variety of stories, including financial reports, activities of employee clubs, car reviews, history, car races, you name it. That experience helped me when MBI Publishing contacted me in 2002 to coauthor a book with Byron Olsen, *The American Auto Factory*. That book looked at the history of the entire industry from the 1890s to the present and eventually won recognition from the Library of Michigan and then the gold medal for general history in 2003 from the International Automotive Media Awards.

In the book you're holding, I focus on just one place, the Rouge, and try to give you a sense of the place and the people who worked there. Yet, as I wrote this history book, I was reminded of a quote Henry Ford reportedly uttered during a libel trial against the *Chicago Tribune*: "History is bunk. It's tradition."

Ford meant that the way history was taught in the early 1900s was bunk, because it concentrated merely on the dates of battles and on royalty and great men, Bob Kreipke said. Ford wasn't hostile to the past. Within months of the conclusion of the trial, after all, Ford started on his project to build the Henry Ford Museum & Greenfield Village, dedicated to preserving Americana that was fading away—ironically, because the automobile gave people unprecedented freedom of movement.

"He knew the value in preserving history and past accomplishments," Kreipke wrote. "He bought his early cars back because he wanted to save them for history purposes, but he didn't want to live in the past and was still inventing things into his seventies."

Ford was also a pioneer in photo documentation, Kreipke points out, having created Ford Photographic in 1919 to build a lasting visual record of the company. Without that foresight, even seemingly mundane historical documents, such undertakings as this book, wouldn't be possible.

In addition to Henry Ford's vision, this book was made possible because I was able to stand on the shoulders of those who went before me in writing about the company, its people, and the Rouge Plant.

Acknowledgments

A book such as this could be put together only with the help and efforts of a host of other people. Writers such as Allan Nevins and Frank Hill, Robert Lacey, Ford R. Bryan, and David Halberstam have covered the story of Ford Motor Company and the Rouge Complex, leaving some pretty tall shoulders to stand on. Then there are the countless unnamed photographers who worked for Ford, the *Detroit News*, the *Detroit Times*, and other publications, who took the pictures that make up the other half of this book.

More immediate are the Ford workers, officers, and retirees, plus the car, train, and boat aficionados and photographers who lent me their ears and told me their stories.

I would like to thank my editor, Dennis Pernu, and others at MBI Publishing Company for helping guide this concept into a book.

I also have to give my heartfelt thanks to my wife and family for tolerating the long hours I put into researching and assembling this work.

I also owe a great deal of thanks to the following, in alphabetical order: Andrew G. Acho; Ishmael Ahmed and the staff of ACCESS; Susan Arneson, Larry Raymond, and the staff of Albert Kahn Associates; retired Dearborn Fire Chief Michael Birrell; Kenneth Borg; John E. Bowen and the staff of the Benson Ford Research Center; Jim Bright; Lindsay Brooke; Ford retirees Elijah "Smiley" Buxton Jr., Samuel Cain, Oscar "Oz" Hov-sepian, Al "Boss Hog" Morris, Albert Stevenson, and Joe Toth; my uncle, Eugene Cabadas; Ford B. Cauffiel, founder of Cauffiel Machinery Corporation; Penny Cauzillo; William Chapin; Dr. David Cole of the Center for Automotive Research; John Coletti of Ford SVT; Nancy Darga of MotorCities National Heritage Area; Michael W. R. Davis, fellow author and historian, for all his suggestions; Gary Dell; Dan Erikson, Sam Varnhagen, and Randy Jacobs of Ford Photomedia; Tom Featherstone and the staff at the Walter Reuther Library; Edsel B. Ford II; Anne Marie Gattari; David L. Good; Michelle Graham and the staff of Ford Archives; Curt Gross and the staff of the Dearborn Historical Museum; Steve Hamp and the staff of The Henry Ford; Phyllis Holmes; Jeff Holyfield at CSM Energy; Tom Hoyt; professors Charles Hyde and Jerald A. Mitchell, Wayne State University; Bob Kreipke, Ford historian; Professor David Lewis, University of Michigan;

This W. F. & John Barnes machine on the fly-cutting valve line in 1948 can perform four operations at a time. It is an early form of automation. *Dearborn Historical Museum*

Ed Lewis; Robert E. Lindsay; Jerry Mattias; William McDonough and Margaret Sanders; Ron Movinski; Ernest Novak Jr.; Tim O'Brien, Ford vice president, real estate; David O'Connor, Ed "Skip" Piotrowski, and Dennis Cole for setting me straight about the Ford Railroad; Brian Olind; Jim Paglino; Jon Pepper; Peter Pestillo, chairman of Visteon; Donald Petersen, retired Ford chairman; John Polacsek of the Dossin Great Lakes Museum; Leslie Price; Neil Ressler; Jay Richardson; Francine Romine; Jack Rourke; Jim Sanderson; Nick Sharkey; Phil Smith; Jerry Sullivan, president of UAW Local 600; Dr. Paul Tahari of the University of Michigan Trauma Burn Center; Michelle Valuet; Rob Webber; Donn Werling, retired director, Henry Ford Estate–Fair Lane; Larry Weis; Michael Whitty, professor, University of Detroit-Mercy; Jay Woodworth; Tom Yates; and Glenn Zielinski.

Introduction:
Rebirth of an Icon

"The Rouge Center and the F-Series will play a central role in our product-led recovery plan and will transform the icon of 20th century manufacturing into the icon of 21st century lean, flexible, and sustainable manufacturing. The Dearborn Truck Plant will be the flagship of next-generation lean and flexible plants. It will be capable of building up to nine different models off of three different vehicle platforms."

—*William Clay Ford Jr., press conference, December 3, 2002*

Ninety years ago, Henry Ford conceived the idea of building a vast factory complex that could refine raw materials, such as lumber, coal, iron ore, and limestone, and make them into vehicle components that would, in turn, be assembled into cars. That vision, called vertical integration, was radical for its time, yet it became reality when the River Rouge Plant was born.

In its heyday, the Rouge was nearly 2 miles long and three-quarters of a mile wide and employed more than 100,000 people. With ore freighters, trains, and trucks coming and going, and smoke and steam rising into the sky from its smokestacks, it was the symbol of well-paying jobs and economic prosperity. The Rouge, and Detroit's auto industry in general, drew immigrants from around the globe. It has been claimed, for example, that because of the Rouge, Dearborn is now home to North America's largest concentration of Muslims.

The Rouge was named after the Rouge River, a reddish-looking waterway in southeastern Michigan. The first European to lead an expedition up the river was probably Detroit's founder, Antoine de la Mothe Cadillac, hence its French name. The plant has also been called the Fordson Plant, the Rouge Plant, the Rouge Complex, and, most

This aerial shot of the Ford Rouge Plant, taken in August 1955, shows the factory complex in its prime. In the center foreground is the Rotunda, the Visitors Center for factory tours, with a plastic dome over its central courtyard. Left of the Rotunda is the Administration Building, the company's headquarters. Between the Administration Building and the complex are Interstate 94, a Rouge train yard, and the automotive and steelmaking factories. The boat slip is also visible, along with the two coke-oven gas towers that stand at its entrance like sentinels. Beyond is the river that gave the famed complex its name. *Ford Photomedia*

Right: Henry Ford and son Edsel examine a model of the Rouge Plant on May 12, 1937, at the Engineering Building. During the uptick in the Depression-era economy that year, Ford reinvested millions in Rouge factories, expanding its workforce to its late-1920s levels. Henry appears to be pointing to the western side of "B" Building, near the spot where wheels would be placed on cars. *Ford Photomedia*

Below: This map of the Rouge Plant was part of an exposé on Ford's automotive operations in the August 19, 1940, issue of *Life*. *National Automotive History Collection*

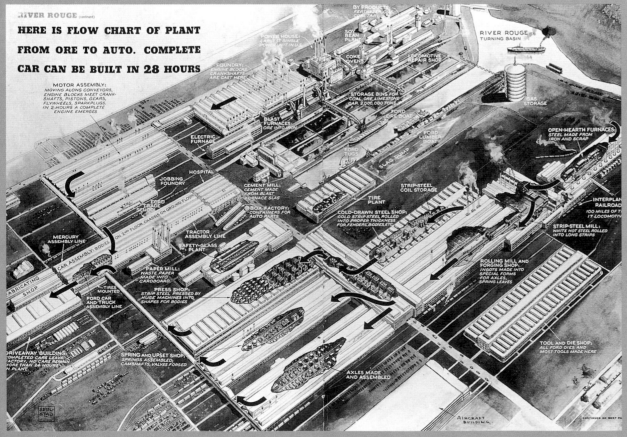

recently, the Ford Rouge Center, yet it has always been known as the icon of vertical manufacturing.

It was also the nexus of Ford Motor Company's operations. Sawmills in Michigan's Upper Peninsula supplied wood, mines in Michigan and northeastern Minnesota provided iron ore, Kentucky and West Virginia were the sources of coal, and raw rubber came from Ford's plantations in Brazil. Many smaller hydroelectric-powered Ford factories along Michigan's Rouge, Huron, and Raisin rivers, built components, and the Rouge Plant supplied automotive sheet metal, glass, batteries, engines, frames, and finished parts to other factories around the world.

In many ways, the Rouge Complex used to operate as one plant, which is why many Detroiters still simply refer to it as "the Rouge." Still, the extent of the vertical integration there, like Henry Ford's role in the development of the automobile, has often been distorted. Even in its prime, the Rouge never produced every single component for any car from scratch. Many smaller Ford factories built components—such as those called "Village Industries," plants along Michigan's Rouge, Huron, and Raisin rivers that ran on hydroelectric power. The company also relied on numerous outside suppliers for parts.

In fact, it could be argued that General Motors, not Ford, created vertical integration. GM's manufacturing centers in Flint and Lansing rivaled the Rouge's employment levels, but its factories were never as well promoted to the public. For nearly six decades, the Rouge was Ford's manufacturing showpiece, hosting tens of thousands of people on free public tours, during which the automaker displayed the might of its industrial power.

Auto magnates, not just the public, came to learn the Rouge's manufacturing lessons. Among them was Kiichiro Toyoda, the founder of Toyota, whose descendants improved on the Ford model. The Rouge also inspired Adolph Hitler to conceive the Volkswagen (the "people's car") before the outbreak of World War II. Later, in the early 1950s, Eiji Toyoda, nephew of Kiichiro, came to the Rouge, again to probe its secrets. Toyoda passed along what he learned to Taichi Ohno, Toyota's vice president and manufacturing genius, who created the Japanese automaker's widely acknowledged quality and manufacturing standards.

U.S. presidents from Herbert Hoover to Bill Clinton have used the Rouge as a campaign stop. International dignitaries, from Prince Nobuhito Takamatsu, a relative of Japanese Emperor Hirohito, to South African President Nelson Mandela came to see its power. Its visual impact has inspired such entertainers as Charlie Chaplin and the child actors of Our Gang. In one short, William Thomas, who played the character Buckwheat, said, "Da Rouge Plant is otay."

Some Rouge workers and their offspring achieved fame in their own right. Late Detroit Mayor Coleman A. Young worked there in the late 1930s, before being fired for his union organizing activities. Berry Gordy Jr., founder of Motown Records, lasted a day working in its hot, dangerous foundry. And the father of rock star Bob Seger made his living there.

Many of the vehicles produced at the Rouge became icons themselves, including the 1928 Model A, the Ford V-8s of the 1930s, the Ford-produced Jeeps of World War II, the 1949 Ford, the two-seat Thunderbird, and the Mustang.

The River Rouge Plant hosted many of Ford's milestones. For example, the twenty millionth Ford car was a 1931 Model A Fordor Town Sedan that rolled off the Rouge's Dearborn assembly line on April 14, 1931. The country was free-falling into the darkest days of the Great Depression, and the Model A led a convoy of twenty other new cars on a nationwide publicity tour.

Likewise, there was a large celebration on April 29, 1959, when the fifty millionth Ford, a white 1959 Galaxie, was finished at the Rouge. The event brought out Chairman Henry Ford II and his top lieutenant, Executive Vice President Ernest R. Breech, before a large crowd of workers, tourists, and children. Onstage with the Galaxie were a 1903 Model A and the Levacar, a futuristic concept hovercraft. The automaker was recovering from its disastrous effort to launch the Edsel brand and revamp Mercury, while the country was recovered from a recession. The Galaxie then embarked on a journey from New York City to Seattle, to re-create the 1909 Transcontinental Contest originally won by Model T race car No. 2.

Fast-forward 44 years, and the three hundred millionth Ford, a red 2004 Mustang GT convertible, was driven off the line by Chairman William Clay Ford Jr., great-grandson of both Henry Ford and tire magnate Harvey Firestone, to the cheers of Dearborn Assembly workers. The Rouge was undergoing great changes, and the automaker faced an uncertain future.

Despite these high points, the factory complex has also been home to darker visions of humanity. In 1932, a protest by the unemployed ended in bloodshed. The Rouge was home to Henry Ford's anti-Semitic *Dearborn Independent* newspaper. And it was the battleground between Ford and the UAW. Yet the automotive dreams it has inspired have overshadowed its flaws for most of its existence.

Time, however, was not kind to the Rouge. With the decline of the domestic American auto companies in the 1970s, 1980s, and 1990s, the Rouge's rust-colored, aluminum-clad buildings and belching smokestacks fit the image of the Rust Belt and the "old economy" as the country became enamored with high-tech industries and a growing environmental movement. The Rouge looked more and more like an antiquated industrial wasteland, surrounded by junkyards of rusting cars and worn-out neighborhoods. The river from which it took its name was viewed as an open sewer.

The automaker allowed much of the Rouge's decline to occur by deliberately diversifying its operations away from the complex, beginning in the 1950s. When Ford's officers realized that vertical integration had failed, the complex was torn in two, and in the 1980s, its steelmaking operations—its original reason for existence—were spun

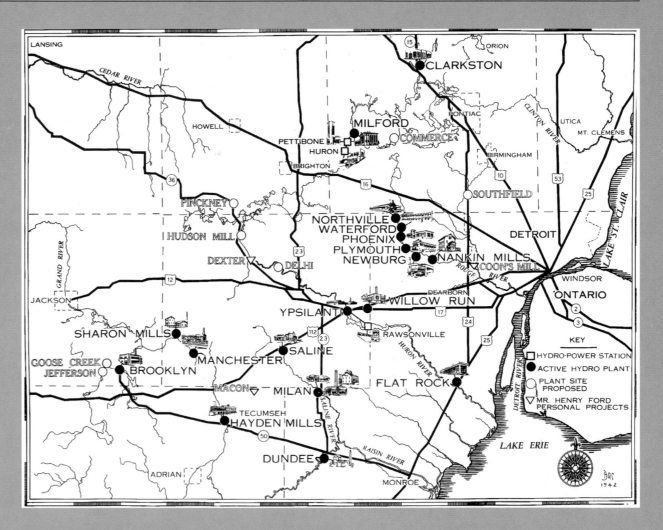

off into a separate company. Its automotive factories began operating as separate entities, with little coordination between one plant and the next. The Rouge's car assembly operations looked like they were headed for extinction.

The Ford Rouge Center's renaissance began quietly in the late 1990s, as the company developed plans for extensive renovations. This renewal wasn't publicly discussed until after the tragic powerhouse explosion on February 1, 1999, which claimed the lives of six men, permanently injured two dozen workers, and destroyed one of the plant's most notable landmarks.

Within months of the explosion, Chairman William Clay Ford Jr. announced a $2 billion facelift that included a new, ecologically friendly assembly factory with a grass roof. The goal was to turn the icon of twentieth-century manufacturing into an icon of the twenty-first century. But Bill Ford, as he likes to be called, and Ford Motor Company were about to face a firestorm of controversy and intense competition that pushed the automaker, according to outside financial analysts, toward bankruptcy.

This 1942 map shows the Rouge Plant in relationship to Ford's Village Industries and several Ford-owned factories, including the Willow Run bomber plant, in southeastern Michigan. The Village Industries were an experiment by Henry Ford to provide farmers an opportunity to earn money in local workshops when they didn't have to plow and harvest their fields. Ultimately, Ford's effort was not profitable, and Henry Ford II sold off most of the village factories right after World War II, although the Northville Mill remained as a Ford plant until 1981. *Ford Photomedia*

Many milestone events have been celebrated at the Rouge. At near right is the twenty millionth Ford car ever produced: a 1931 Model A Fordor Town, with Henry Ford at the wheel and his son Edsel in the front passenger seat. *Walter P. Reuther Library, Wayne State University*. For the completion of the fifty millionth Ford, a white '59 Galaxie *(far right)*, a large audience gathered to hear Henry Ford II, pictured at the microphone. *Ford Photomedia*. With the completion of the three hundred millionth Ford *(below)*, Chairman William Clay Ford Jr., great-grandson of Henry Ford, drove this crimson 2004 Mustang GT convertible off the line. *Ford Photomedia*

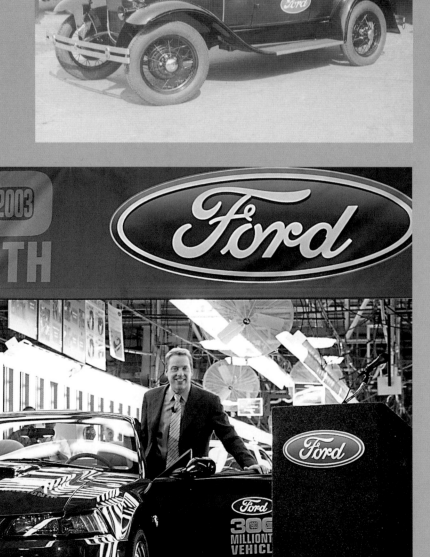

By September 1999, the media were reporting that Ford Explorers were rolling over due to tread separation problems on their Firestone Wilderness AT tires. The National Highway Traffic and Safety Administration subsequently linked the tires and Explorers to 271 highway deaths and hundreds of injuries. Two resulting recalls and lawsuits had Ford and Bridgestone-Firestone officers openly feuding and cost the automaker billions of dollars.

Meanwhile, the economic downturn that began in 2000 and deepened after the terrorist attacks of September 11, 2001, greatly hurt the automaker. Its Internet consumer outreach strategy and diversification plans started by President and CEO Jacques "Jac the Knife" Nasser spectacularly crashed, while internal dissension caused by Nasser's policies forced the company's board to fire him.

One must remember, though, that the River Rouge Plant was born during equally tumultuous times. Yet it seemed quiet enough when Henry Ford gathered several of his closest executives on a July morning in 1915 to tell them of his decision, which would not only radically change the farming community then called Springwells but would also shape global events.

They met on Miller Road, well past the outskirts of Detroit. Joining Ford was Charles Sorensen, a Danish immigrant who had started as a wood patternmaker and was now a rising star at the Highland Park plant; Sorensen's boss, P. E. (Pete) Martin; William B. Mayo, the self-taught engineer who designed Highland Park's power plant; real estate agent Fred Gregory; and John R. Lee, who ran the company's "Sociological Department."

Nearby lay the main branch of the Rouge River. It was not impressive looking. The Rouge was shallow, barely spanning 100 feet at its widest

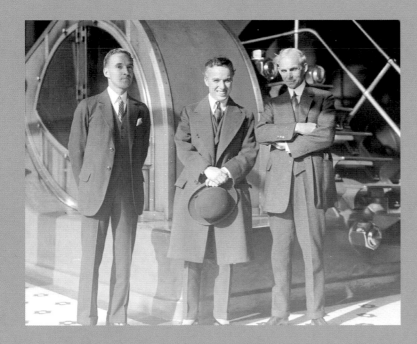

points, but it was the most important river for draining the large flat land to the north and west of Detroit. Ford knew the land well, because he had grown up on his father's farm, some 3 miles north.

"Although production was scarcely fully under way at Highland Park, Mr. Ford foresaw the time when that supposedly last word in manufacturing magnitude would be outgrown," Charles Sorensen recounted in his autobiography, *My Forty Years with Ford.* Highland Park had little room for expansion, and besides, Ford wanted his new plant to have access to the rivers, nature's shipping highways. The only other potential site for a new factory, a 400-acre plot along the Detroit River, was deemed too small.

The Rouge property was marshy. Still, it had access not only to water but to railways and roads. To the north was the Michigan Central Railroad; to the east, the Pere Marquette Railroad; and to the south, Dix Avenue. The financially challenged Detroit, Toledo & Ironton Railroad also had a line that passed nearby. The Rouge River meandered to the south and west of the site and linked up to the Detroit River. For centuries, American Indians and, later, French, English, and American settlers had used it for travel and commerce, but it was navigable only by the smallest of boats.

Ford told Gregory to assemble a group of real estate agents to get options on the land in one day. He further instructed Gregory not to use his name, fearing it would cause the farmers to inflate their asking prices. Gregory accomplished his task, and Ford paid $700,000 for the Rouge's nearly 1,200 acres, roughly 2 square miles.

At least one person doubted a factory would ever be built at the site. Gregory's teenage daughter, Mary Louise, had accompanied her father to the spot in the fall of 1914, when Ford had asked him to start

looking for a new factory location. Gregory told her that the small, muddy farm and pastureland that easily flooded would someday be home to "a big factory almost as far as you can see." She didn't believe him. As events unfolded in the next few years, Henry Ford had many obstacles to overcome, but he also had plenty of experience in outlasting his critics and misfortunes.

Chapter One

The Legend Is Born

"Before I was twenty-four, I pinned my flag on Henry Ford and his 'car for the multitude,' which was then still a dream. I saw that dream materialize and change the face of America. It was the greatest industrial adventure in history—from a backyard machine shop to a billion-dollar world-wide enterprise and creation of a magic name."

—Charles E. Sorensen, My Forty Years with Ford, *1956*

Henry Ford had long been a tinkerer, having grown up on his father William's farm in Springwells Township, where he had been known to dismantle and then try to reassemble watches. Born July 30, 1863, during the middle of the American Civil War, Henry was William and Mary (Ligott) Ford's oldest surviving child—an older sibling had died at birth. He was joined by siblings John, Margaret, Jane, William, and Robert before his mother died in childbirth when he was 13.

Filled with wanderlust, Henry went to Detroit in 1879 at age 16 and briefly worked at the Michigan Car Company, building streetcars. He then apprenticed at the James Flower & Brothers Machine Shop before joining the Detroit Dry Dock Company, where he learned to fix engines, before returning to the family farm.

On New Year's Day 1885, he met a farmer's daughter named Clara Jane Bryant at a dance in the township of Greenfield, near Springwells. Ford was enthralled with the 19-year-old woman, and three years later the couple married. Although his father gave him land for his own homestead, by September 1891 Henry and Clara moved to Detroit and rented a domicile at 570 West Forest Avenue, where their only son, Edsel, was born on November 6, 1893. The next year, they rented a duplex on Bagley Avenue.

The national economy was bad around 1890 as a "panic" or recession set in. Detroit Mayor Hazen S. Pingree allowed the impoverished to raise vegetables in city parks, vacant lots, and even on the lawn of city hall. The gardens became known as "Pingree's Potato Patches." But Ford found work as a night fireman at the Edison Illuminating Company. Promoted to night-shift engineer at the Willis Station, he began earning $125 per month.

In his spare time, Ford built a gasoline engine and dreamed of building a horseless carriage. But he was not the first to create a gasoline-powered automobile. Karl Benz of Germany publicly unveiled his first car, the three-wheeled Motorwagen, in 1885. In the United States, brothers Charles and Frank Duryea ran their first one-cylinder horseless carriage in 1893 and won America's first automobile race in 1895 in Chicago.

Ford wasn't even the first to build a car in Detroit—railroad mechanic Charles Brady King, an officiator at the 1895 Chicago race, took that honor. Coincidentally, King became a friend of Ford's through a mutual acquaintance, Oliver Barthel, and they visited each other as they worked on their respective automobiles. At about 11 p.m. on March 6, 1896, amid snow flurries, 32-year-old King drove his 3-horsepower, four-wheeled mechanical marvel out of John Lauer's machine shop on the east side of St. Antoine Street, near the Detroit River.

Toiling in a brick shed behind his house, Ford was joined by fellow Edison employees Edward "Spider" Huff, James Bishop, and George Cato in constructing a boxy vehicle with a 4-horsepower, two-cylinder engine, a single bench seat, four bicycle-like tires, and a tiller to steer with. The vehicle, which they called a Quadricycle, was constructed mostly out of scrap parts from the Edison power station. King, however, provided two used valves off his own engine and obtained the 10-foot chain that transmitted power from the motor to the wheels.

Early on June 4, the Quadricycle was ready for its first run, but the machine was too big to fit through the shed's door. Ford chopped a larger opening with an ax, sending splinters and bricks flying. With Clara wishing her husband well, Ford headed out on his first of many auto excursions.

In August, his supervisor, Alexander Dow, took Ford to the annual convention of Edison Illuminating Companies in New York, where he introduced his underling to the partially deaf Edison and said that Ford had created a car that ran on gasoline. Edison encouraged Ford to continue his work.

Back in Detroit, Mayor William C. Maybury, a friend of Ford's father, provided the seed money to build another car, and Ford sold the

Highland Park's assembly lines are quiet in this picture taken sometime between 1914 and 1915. The development of the continuously moving line drastically cut the time it took to build a Model T from 12½ man-hours in early 1913 to 1½ man-hours by April 1914. *Lindsay Brooke Archives.* **Inset:** Ford could build more cars faster and more cheaply than the competition. As company coffers bulged, Ford more than doubled its daily wage, to $5 on January 5, 1914 *(inset)*, while simultaneously reducing the workday to 8 hours. Henry Ford's legend as a "friend of the working man" grew as a result. *Ford Photomedia*

'GOLD RUSH'
IS STARTED
BY FORD'S
$5 OFFER

Thousands of Men Seek Employment in Detroit Factory.

Will Distribute $10,000,000 in Semi-Monthly Bonuses.

No Employe to Receive Less Than Five Dollars a Day.

(TIMES-STAR SPECIAL DISPATCH.)
DETROIT, Mich., January 7.—
Henry Ford in an interview to-

Right: In this shed behind his rented duplex at 58 Bagley Avenue in Detroit, Henry Ford and friends worked on his first automobile. When it was completed, early on the morning of June 4, 1896, Ford realized it was too wide to fit through the doorway and used an axe to knock out several rows of bricks. *Ford Photomedia*

Far right: Henry Ford holds the tiller of his first horseless carriage, the 1896 Quadricycle. This photo was taken on Broadway in New York City in 1910, while the company was appealing a court decision in the Selden patent case, which threatened to put it out of business. The boxy vehicle with its four bicycle wheels had a two-cylinder engine and could travel up to 20 miles per hour. *Walter P. Reuther Library, Wayne State University*

Below right: One of the rare photos of Henry Ford *(left)* while he was employed at the Willis Station of the Edison Illuminating Company in Detroit from 1891 to 1899. Ford was a fan of Thomas Alva Edison but did not meet the inventor until 1896, shortly after building his first car, the Quadricycle. Later, he forged a friendship with his idol. *Ford Photomedia*

Ford Motor Co.'s New Assembling Plant.

Quadricycle for about $200. But many other entrepreneurs were already at work in the fledgling automotive industry. In Lansing, Michigan, engine builder Ransom E. Olds launched Oldsmobile. In February 1897, the Winton Motor Carriage Company incorporated in Cleveland, and their chief engineer interviewed Ford. However, owner Alexander Winton wasn't impressed with the 34-year-old mechanic, and Henry returned to Detroit to build his second Quadricycle.

The following year, the United States and Spain plunged into war. King, by then an established engine builder with his own shop, left Detroit for the U.S. Naval Reserve and didn't return until 1900, when he joined Oldsmobile. Ford remained in Detroit.

Three years after his first ride, Ford finally attracted the financial backing of several investors, including Mayor Maybury, William H. Murray, U.S. Senator Thomas W. Palmer of Michigan, and other industrialists and brokers. They founded the Detroit Automobile Company on August 5, 1899, and made Ford chief engineer and partner. But Henry's new automotive career got off to a rocky start. As with many early car ventures, the company floundered. It dissolved in November 1900, after building about twenty automobiles.

As Detroit celebrated its bicentennial, Murray bought the company's assets in early 1901 and allowed Ford to build a race car. If Ford was successful, Murray reasoned, it would prove his mechanical abilities and ideas. Joining Henry was designer Barthel, draftsman Childe Harold Wills, Spider Huff, who still held his Edison job, and several others.

A series of steam-, electric-, and gasoline-powered car races was planned for October 10, 1901, at the Detroit Driving Club in Grosse Pointe, the exclusive community east of Detroit. No less a personage

than Alexander Winton, now a well-known car builder, participated. Ford entered the race, as did Murray, with his own car. Few of the 8,000 spectators thought that Ford's 26-horsepower, 2,200-pound car, called *Sweepstakes*, had a chance against Winton's more powerful and heavier machine.

Ford won the race and took home the cut-glass punch bowl trophy. But more important, the event renewed interest from investors to relaunch the Detroit Automobile Company as the Henry Ford Company. Ford, however, fell out with backers when they brought in machinist Henry Leland as a consultant in March 1902. Ford left with a $900 settlement and a copy of the car's blueprints. Leland renamed the company Cadillac, after Detroit's founder Antoine de la Mothe Cadillac, and turned it into a success.

Still, Ford gained the trust of a new financial backer, coal dealer Alexander Malcomson, whom he had met while working at Edison. They created the Malcomson & Ford Company, Ltd., in November 1902. Early suppliers included John and Horace Dodge. Natives of the tiny community of Niles in the southwest corner of Michigan, the carousing Dodge brothers had worked at a number of marine engine and bicycle machine shops until founding their own business. When the brothers insisted on payments Ford and Malcomson couldn't make, the partners created Ford Motor Company and gave shares to the Dodge brothers, with Malcomson and Ford each retaining 25½ percent of the stock.

Other shareholders included James Couzens, Malcomson's clerk, with 2½ percent; Couzens' sister, Rosetta, who bought one share for $100; and banker John S. Gray, who owned 10½ percent of the stock and became Ford's first president.

Above left: Henry Ford is at the wheel of this right-hand-drive race car *Sweepstakes*, with his riding mechanic, Edward "Spider" Huff, poised beside him. After the Detroit Automobile Company dissolved in November 1900, Ford built the car to prove the worth of his mechanical abilities and ideas to potential investors. *Ford Photomedia*

Above: The fledgling Malcomson & Ford Company Ltd. rented this one-story former wagon shop in April 1903 from carpenter Albert Strelow. The shop was in downtown Detroit, at the intersection of Mack Avenue and the Belt Line Railroad (tracks show at the far right corner). When Ford Motor Company was incorporated in June, with Strelow as a stockholder, Mack Avenue became its first factory. Within months, however, space became so cramped that the building was widened and a second story was added. The company's production needs outgrew even the enlarged factory. *Ford Photomedia*

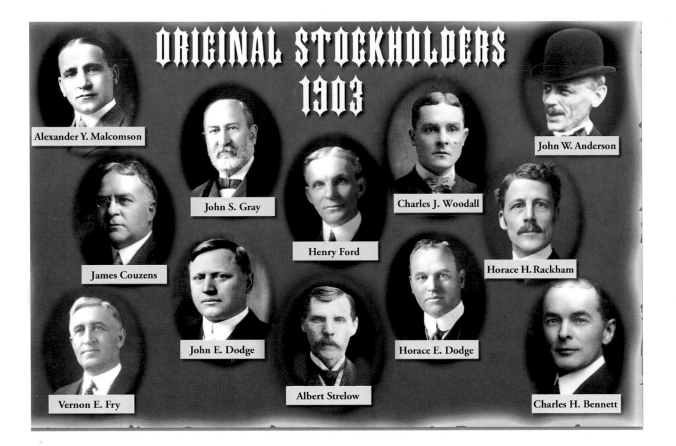

ORIGINAL STOCKHOLDERS 1903

Alexander Y. Malcomson

John W. Anderson

John S. Gray

Charles J. Woodall

James Couzens

Henry Ford

Horace H. Rackham

John E. Dodge

Horace E. Dodge

Vernon E. Fry

Albert Strelow

Charles H. Bennett

Above: This composite photo shows 11 of the 12 original Ford Motor Company stockholders in 1903, including Henry Ford and Alexander Y. Malcomson, who each held 25 ½ percent of the company's stock. Also pictured are the company's first president, John S. Gray, a banker and candy manufacturer; John E. and Horace E. Dodge, owners of the engine and transmission supplier for Model A; and James Couzens, Malcomson's bookkeeper. Not shown is the only woman stockholder, schoolteacher Rosetta V. Couzens, who bought one share of company stock for $100. In 1919, her investment netted her $335,000 in dividends and a $260,000 buyout payment from Ford. *Ford Photomedia*

Reproductions of Ford Motor Company's first two weekly payrolls show it had seven employees, who earned a total of $85.23 when week one ended on June 20, 1903. For the second week, total wages dropped to $63.75, as Henry Ford, Treasurer James Couzens, and engineer and car designer C. Harold Wills went without pay. *Ford Photomedia*

Henry and the other founders signed the incorporation papers on June 16, 1903, rented a wagon factory on Mack Avenue in Detroit, and began building cars. When the 1903 Model A proved a success, Ford built a factory in 1904 on Piquette Avenue, close to Woodward Avenue and near what was then the edge of Detroit.

Long and narrow, like a New England–style mill, Piquette had an abundance of windows, which allowed natural light and ventilation. A cargo elevator capable of carrying a car chassis linked the three floors. Unlike later Ford factories, Piquette was split into three sections by firewalls equipped with self-closing fire doors. It also had a sprinkler system. Ford insisted on the safety measures after seeing how a 1901 factory fire had crippled Oldsmobile.

The Dodge brothers built most of the components, the C. R. Wilson Carriage Company supplied the bodies, and Piquette workers assembled the Models B, C, and F, the $2,800 K roadster, and the $600 Models N, R, and S. Malcomson pushed for the company to build more expensive cars, such as the poor-selling six-cylinder Model K, because they yielded a higher profit per car. Henry, however, wanted to build cars for the masses and make up in quantity for lower per-unit profits. Henry won out.

With Couzens, Henry created the Ford Manufacturing Company in November 1905, to produce Ford Motor Company's engines, running gear, and other parts—items that had been made by the Dodge brothers. Significantly, Malcomson held no stock in the new company, and he realized that Ford Manufacturing could drain off the profits of Ford Motor. In early 1906, Malcomson sold his stock to Ford, giving Henry majority control, and Ford Manufacturing was folded into Ford Motor. That year, Henry also became the car company's president, following the death of John Gray.

An early "assembly line" experiment inspired by Walter Flanders, was started at Piquette before it succeeded later at Highland Park, Charles Sorensen claimed in his autobiography. Flanders was a machinist and sales agent who worked at Ford for about two years before leaving in 1908, but he taught the factory personnel how to rearrange the machinery for maximum efficiency and developed other timesaving techniques.

One weekend, Sorensen set up a crude assembly line on Piquette's third floor. Parts and tools were placed in a row as needed, and the car chassis were rolled from one end of the building to the other. Ford witnessed the experiment but told Sorensen to hold off making any changes to the production room. He was too busy with other concerns—namely, preparing to purchase 60 acres of land along Woodward Avenue in Highland Park, a community just north of the Detroit city limits, to build a larger factory. He had also set up a rocking chair in a walled-off corner of Piquette's third floor, where he and draftsman Joseph Galamb created the Model T.

When the Model T came out, it was about $200 more expensive than the Model N but more technologically advanced. It was the first

THE LEGEND IS BORN

Left: Built at the edge of Detroit, the factory at Piquette Avenue became Ford's new home at the end of 1904. As seen from the southeast, the main building copied the layout of a New England mill, measuring 56 x 402 feet. It had a brick façade, oak floors, abundant windows for natural light and ventilation, and a cargo elevator to link its three floors. The factory was divided into three sections by firewalls with self-closing fire doors, and it had a sprinkler system supplied with water from the rooftop tank at the far end of the building. A small powerhouse was also built at the same time as the factory, on the northwest corner of the 3.11-acre property, near the Michigan Central Railroad tracks. *Walter P. Reuther Library, Wayne State University*

Below left: Two rows of Model N Ford chassis nearly fill the narrow assembly room on the third floor of the Piquette Avenue plant in this photo taken November 1, 1906. The $600 Model N was a sales success compared to the $2,800 Model K roadster Alexander Malcomson wanted the company to build. It was also Henry Ford's inspiration to work on the Model T. In this pre-assembly-line era, each chassis was built in place by a team of men who worked on the car until it was almost ready to have the body attached. *Ford Photomedia*

Having outgrown Piquette, Ford Motor Company moved to its purpose-built and much larger Highland Park factory, which opened in 1910. This picture shows a new addition being built in 1918. However, the city had grown up around the building, leaving little space for expansion. Ford turned his attention to building a new factory in the marshy farmland along the Rouge River in Springwells Township. *Walter P. Reuther Library, Wayne State University*

car to use lightweight vanadium steel, a 20-horsepower, four-cylinder engine, a two-speed planetary transmission, transverse leaf-spring suspension, solid axles, and large, wagon-like wheels with pneumatic tires. It also shifted the steering wheel to the left side of the car, a design feature that would become standard in the industry. Simple to use and maintain, the Model T became a hot seller.

As the new design took shape, Ford succumbed to the temptation to sell his company to the owner of the Buick Motor Car Company, William Crapo Durant of Flint, Michigan. Ford wanted $3 million in cash, but the deal fell apart when Durant couldn't raise the money. Both went their separate ways and Durant would found General Motors.

Piquette reached its maximum production capacity, churning out some 12,000 Model Ts from 1908 to 1910. The car's success allowed Ford to move forward with his plan to build the largest auto factory of its time, Highland Park, and he turned to architect Albert Kahn to design it. Highland Park had two separate, four-story buildings with a vast, skylight-covered central assembly room.

Car parts were manufactured in the buildings' upper floors and fed down to the assembly room by gravity conveyors, while cranes moved materials across the factory and from one floor to another. On the assembly floor, Model Ts were built in place along two 600-foot-long

rows, with 50 workstations each. Some 500 assemblers worked these two rows, while another 100 workers fetched parts from the gravity conveyors. The factory also had a large power plant with steam generators, designed by self-taught engineer William B. Mayo.

Highland Park, nicknamed the "Crystal Palace" because of its glass walls and roof, became partially operational on January 1, 1910. The huge factory was a work in progress for the next five years, as Model T sales boomed, but a lawsuit called the Selden patent case looked like it was either going to put the automaker out of business or severely cripple it.

Lawyer George Selden had designed a nonworking gasoline-powered car in 1879 but didn't file a patent for his invention until 1895, just as the fledgling car industry took off. Selden sold his patent rights to investors who called themselves the Association of Licensed Automobile Manufacturers (ALAM). The association not only collected royalties from every auto sold, it limited the number of cars that manufacturers could make. In 1903, ALAM rejected Ford's application for a license, saying that Ford Motor merely assembled cars and was not an actual manufacturer.

ALAM sued Ford when the company refused to bend to its decisions. The wheels of justice turned slowly, though, and the case didn't go to trial until 1909. After weeks of testimony, the court ruled in

Albert Kahn, Architect of Highland Park and the Rouge

Henry Ford conceived of the River Rouge Plant, but it was a Jewish immigrant from Germany who turned his vision into reality.

The path that led Albert Kahn to a lifelong business relationship with Ford was uncommon and rocky. Born on March 21, 1869, the color-blind Kahn was the oldest of eight children of a financially struggling rabbi who moved his family to Detroit in 1880. When the land of opportunity turned sour for the Kahn family, Albert cut short his high school education to work a number of odd jobs.

Fortuitously, Mason & Rice hired him in 1884, and architect George Mason taught him the art of sketching and drafting. Kahn's architectural training continued when he won a scholarship to study in Europe. There he met Henry Bacon, the future designer of the Lincoln Memorial in Washington, D.C.

In 1895, Kahn and his brother Julius founded Albert Kahn Associates (AKA). Julius, who was AKA's chief engineer, created the "Kahn System" of reinforcing concrete with steel. Packard hired Albert to design Building No. 10 of its Detroit automobile plant in 1905, the first factory to use concrete floors and columns instead of fire-prone timber framing and wooden floors.

When Ford decided to build the Highland Park plant, he called Albert Kahn and asked if the architect could build factories. "Mr. Ford, I can build anything," Kahn responded, though, at the time, he thought it was a crazy idea to put all Model T operations under one roof.

That encounter cemented Kahn's relationship with Ford, which survived Ford's anti-Semitism. Ford called on Kahn to design the foundry for the River Rouge Plant and then the Eagle Boat factory, also known as "B" Building, or Dearborn Assembly. Like many of Kahn's factory designs, "B" Building featured a roof with sawtooth skylights, to maximize natural lighting and ventilation.

Kahn also left his mark on the Rouge with his designs for the Cement (1923), Motor Assembly (1924), Open-Hearth (1925), and Pressed-Steel (1925) buildings (these dates referring to when he accepted the contracts). While many of these structures have since been replaced, the Kahn-designed Glass Plant erected in 1922 was one of his most significant

Albert Kahn, president of the architectural firm Albert Kahn Associates, whose hand guided much of the Rouge River Plant's early development, examines blueprints in his office in this 1932 photo that ran in the *Detroit News*. Kahn's firm designed more than a thousand factories for Ford Motor Company, along with countless factories, hospitals, office buildings, clubs, and temples for other clients. *Walter P. Reuther Library, Wayne State University*

designs. A steel cage sheathed in glass supplied by Crittall of England, it was a simple, economical prismatic envelope and one of the most well-known steel-and-glass buildings in the world, carrying industrial architecture forward in the twentieth century.

Kahn also did work for the U.S. Army and Navy, General Motors, the University of Michigan, and Detroit's Henry Ford Hospital, in addition to designing public libraries, temples, mansions, 521 factories in the Soviet Union, Dodge's B-25 engine plant in Chicago, and Ford's Willow Run bomber plant. Following his death in 1942, Kahn's youngest brother, Louis, who joined AKA in 1918 and performed the accounting, personnel, and office duties, briefly became the firm's president.

AKA still survives today, with offices in the United States, Mexico, and Brazil.

---

favor of ALAM. Ford appealed, but not until January 1911 did the U.S. Court of Appeals decide that the Selden patent applied only to by-then obsolete designs.

As a vindicated Ford Motor searched for a new way to build cars more quickly and cheaply, a rift grew between Henry and the Dodge brothers. Ford was making more and more of its own parts, greatly lessening its dependence on the brothers, who had built an enormous factory in Hamtramck to supply Highland Park. Upset that they were losing business, the brothers informed Ford in July 1913 that they would stop making parts for the Model T within a year and would unveil their own car. John Dodge resigned from his Ford vice presidency

that August. When the Dodge car came out in 1915, it was priced above the Model T but offered more amenities.

The first major production improvement at Highland Park occurred in February 1913, when a conveyor system was installed in its foundry. Platforms moved around the foundry on a continuous basis, carrying the molds into which molten iron was poured from a "bull ladle." With this system, which Westinghouse pioneered thirty years earlier, Ford boosted production of Model T parts.

The foundry's conveyor and Sorensen's experiments at Piquette probably showed Henry and his engineers how an assembly line could increase productivity. Sorensen later wrote that the many rationales

On a crude assembly line in the summer of 1913, Highland Park workers build flywheel magnetos, part of the Model T's ignition system, producing each unit in only 5 minutes. Previously, working by hand, it took one worker 20 minutes to build a single magneto. Other departments at the factory soon adopted assembly line methods, greatly increasing production while cutting costs. *Lindsay Brooke Archives*

Then, on October 7, engineers constructed a crude, 150-foot-long final assembly line in an open space at the plant. After determining the optimum installation times, engineers placed parts at different intervals along the floor for the 140 assemblers. A winch then wound in a long rope, dragging each chassis across the floor. The man-hours required for final assembly dropped from 12 to less than 3.

By January 1914, the rope had been replaced with an endless chain that allowed managers to control the work pace to a degree never before possible, slowing down faster employees and forcing slower ones to pick up the pace. By April, Highland Park had three operating assembly lines, and it took just 93 worker minutes to build a car. Productivity jumped, cutting costs while increasing profits and output and maintaining quality. In 1912, Ford produced only 82,388 Model Ts, which sold for $600 each. By 1916, production had risen to 585,388 units, allowing Ford to drop the price to $360. (It's no coincidence that 1914 is the year it became standard to paint Model Ts black only—it was the color that dried fastest.)

Ford, however, was not the first to develop assembly lines. In Flint, Buick Works manager Walter P. Chrysler boosted production from 45 cars a day to 200 by having workers push car chassis along a line from station to station. Ford's use of the continuous moving line, though, was *the* major breakthrough that allowed mass production.

As Ford managers concentrated on speeding up the work, labor conditions at Highland Park reached a breaking point. Detroit was an "open shop" town, meaning that companies didn't have to give unionized workers special status and could easily replace them with strikebreakers. Ford's worker turnover in 1913 grew to almost 400 percent a month, as some 50,000 to 60,000 people passed through Highland Park's employment office, found they didn't like factory work, and quit.

At the same time, the radical International Workers of the World (IWW) labor union threatened to shut down Ford. The IWW leaders, or "Wobblies," believed in worker control of companies and the elimination of privately owned property. Henry Ford and his managers outmaneuvered the Wobblies by creating the "Five Dollar Day," which simultaneously lowered labor turnover.

Announced on January 5, 1914, the Five Dollar Day shook the business world by more than doubling pay, which was $2.34 a day, and by cutting the workday from nine hours to eight. While workers had to meet a number of conditions to earn this unheard-of wage—including stringent production quotas with little break time and a six-month probationary period—Henry Ford's name suddenly became well known worldwide as a hero to the workingman.

The business community and news media, however, roundly criticized the Five Dollar Day. *The New York Times* condemned it as a utopian experiment, while the *Wall Street Journal* opined that Ford had committed an economic blunder that would come back to plague all manufacturers. But Ford's workers were able to afford the cars they

given for Ford's instituting the assembly line—such as that he was familiar with the "disassembly lines" used by the meat-packing industry—were thought of much later. The company was simply continuing the timesaving process started by Flanders.

On or about April 1, 1913, a production engineer in Highland Park's flywheel/magneto assembly room began a radical experiment. Instead of building one magneto at a time, which took an average of 20 minutes, employees were instructed to place one part in the assembly or to start a few nuts before pushing the flywheel down the line to the next employee. By the end of summer, production time had been cut to 5 minutes per part. Other engineers at Highland Park started similar experiments. In the chassis room, teams of assemblers began moving from one chassis to another, installing the same part or subassembly on each. This was a "moving assembler line" instead of a moving assembly line.

By January 1914, Highland Park's assembly lines had continuous moving chains to pull the cars along, at a pace determined by the foremen. Instead of being built along extensive rows of nonmoving benches, the Model Ts moved along a line, their wheels guided by a track. The workers here are dropping the T's 20-horsepower, four-cylinder engine in place, while another chassis just down the line waits its turn. *Lindsay Brooke Archives*

built and accepted the tradeoff of higher wages in exchange for demanding labor.

A January 23, 1914, letter from the anonymous wife of a Highland Park worker to Henry Ford captured this paradox: "The chain system you have is a slave driver! My God!, Mr. Ford. My husband has come home and thrown himself down and won't eat his supper—so done out! Can't it be remedied? . . . That $5 a day is a blessing—a bigger one than you know but oh they earn it."

With the assembly line and the Five Dollar Day—high production and high wages—the term "Fordism" first came into being. Only years later did the term "mass production" replace it. Fordism took on other connotations.

High wages caused other challenges. Soon after news of the Five Dollar Day spread, thousands of men came to Highland Park in the

middle of winter, causing a riot. The mob dispersed only when fire hoses were turned on them.

Next, Henry Ford instituted a peculiar form of corporate paternalism by creating the "Sociological Department." Ford believed that given the high wages he was providing, he had the right and responsibility to make sure his workers used their newfound wealth responsibly. Sociological Department investigators checked unmarried employees' homes to see if they were cohabiting with women, renting rooms to boarders, or living in unsanitary conditions. The investigators also talked to neighbors. If a problem turned up, the company decided whether to discipline or fire the worker.

Heading the Sociological Department were John R. Lee and the Reverend Samuel S. Marquis, the minister of Ford's church. Marquis and Lee attempted to improve the welfare of Ford's workers, many of

The assembly line at Highland Park becomes even more mechanized. The chassis rides on rails as the continuously moving chain pulls it along. A worker at this station tightens the lug nut on a Model T's front left wheel, while another sits atop the gasoline tank, working on the wooden dashboard. The third man holds an air gauge and has probably checked the pneumatic white rubber tires. Note the cleanliness of the plant, in which the sunlight from the overhead skylights reflects off the office glass next to the line. *Ford Photomedia*

Lewis Ford, a nephew of Henry's, drives an experimental Ford tractor pulling a 12-inch, double-bottomed plow in Dearborn on July 12, 1917. Henry was a farmer at heart and wanted to make an affordable, mass-produced tractor. He kept tinkering with different designs, leading to the creation of the Fordson. *Ford Photomedia*

whom were foreign-born and poorly educated, by creating English classes and other programs at Highland Park.

As Highland Park boomed, Ford and his officers realized the plant had little room to expand, and they began looking for a new location. Instead of a smooth, planned expansion, like the move from Mack Avenue to Piquette and then to Highland Park, events at home and abroad tossed Ford's ideas into turmoil.

Before a new site was selected, the July 1914 assassination of Austrian archduke Franz Ferdinand in Bosnia by a Serbian nationalist set off a chain reaction in which governments invoked defense pacts and put dusty war plans into motion. The European continent was soon bogged down in trench warfare. America was a nation of immigrants, and President Woodrow Wilson's administration was reluctant to get involved in the conflict. At Ford, with its workforce composed of nationals on both sides of the war, Henry was even more unwilling to show favor to either the Allies—Britain, France, Russia, and Italy—or the Central Powers: Germany, Austria-Hungary, and the Ottoman Empire. As a pacifist, he was, however, aghast at the bloodshed.

Ford's pacifism rubbed James Couzens the wrong way, and he resigned as vice president and treasurer on October 13, 1915, but retained his stock and his seat on the board of directors. Couzens entered politics, becoming Detroit's mayor from 1919 to 1922 and then was appointed to a seat in the U.S. Senate. With Couzens gone, Ford embarked on a grandiose scheme to end the war.

While Ford's secretary, Ernest Liebold, a man of German descent, was away visiting Ford branch plants near Denver, a Jewish-Hungarian woman named Rosika Schwimmer met with Henry on November 17, 1915, and urged him to sponsor a neutral peace mission to Europe. In less than a week, Ford held several other meetings with Schwimmer and other activists.

The day before he was scheduled to meet President Wilson, a plan coalesced in Henry's head when someone suggested chartering a ship to carry a delegation to Europe. Almost immediately, over the objections of Wilson and others, Ford chartered the Scandinavian-American liner *Oscar II* to carry a delegation with the declared mission of getting "the boys home by Christmas."

Dubbed the "Peace Ship," the *Oscar II* set sail from New York City on December 4. Despite Henry's clout, the press savaged the affair, and numerous prominent figures, including Ford's friends Thomas Edison and naturalist John Burroughs, declined to participate. En route to Oslo, Ford fell ill, sparking reports that he was on his deathbed. Once the Peace Ship docked, the Reverend Marquis and Ray Dahlinger, Ford's driver, whisked him aboard a ship back to New York. The Peace Ship had failed, but Ford supported the delegates for the next year.

While the Peace Ship was a noble effort to try to end the bloodshed, Ford's crusade had failed and it left him bitter and resentful of his critics. The effort had also distracted him from building the Rouge.

When he returned home, he began pushing the project forward in earnest. "One thing the Peace Ship expedition did was to set off a chain reaction which culminated in the great River Rouge Plant," Sorensen noted in 1956. "Its immensity and completeness are now so much a matter of course as to cease being a wonderment."

Henry Ford personally bought the Rouge property. Because he had pushed for the passage of the Weeks-McLean Migratory Bird Act of 1913, some speculated that he was going to create a bird sanctuary. Ford had other intentions, which he revealed to John and Horace Dodge in early 1916. "The stockholders [have] already received a great deal more than they had put into the company," he told the brothers. It was his intention to take the company's earnings and expand the business.

At first the Dodge brothers didn't react publicly, taking a wait-and-see approach. As Ford mapped out his dream factory, which would be the first and only time a carmaker attempted to integrate its own steel mills, the Dodge brothers' Hamtramck Plant produced 100,000 cars by fall. In September, the brothers demanded that Ford Motor distribute 50 percent of its $58 million surplus as dividends. Ford refused, and the brothers countered, offering to sell their stock for $35 million. Again Ford refused. He had as much stock as he wanted.

As the fight between the Dodges and Ford simmered, Edsel Ford married Eleanor Clay on November 1. Eleanor was a relative of deceased department store magnate and financier of the Hudson Motor Car Company, Joseph L. Hudson, and a friend of John Dodge's daughter, Isabel.

The next step on the way to building the Rouge was set in motion the day after Edsel's marriage, when the automaker's board of directors decided to reinvest $23 million, half the company's profits, in the business. A little more than $11 million would be spent to build the Rouge steel plants; the rest was earmarked to expand Highland Park. The board's resolution for the Rouge called for two blast furnaces, docks, a turning basin for freighters, ore and coal storage bins, a coke oven plant, plus other foundries and office buildings. But the Dodge brothers had other ideas.

The day the board met, the Dodge brothers filed suit in Wayne County Circuit Court to force Ford Motor Company to distribute three-fourths of its cash surplus as dividends. The brothers also asked for an injunction against the Rouge project and for the court to appoint a receiver, if needed, to manage Ford Motor Company. The fight was in the open.

Within a month, the court gave the Dodges their injunction and, soon afterward, ordered that Ford couldn't smelt iron at the Rouge. On appeal, the court allowed Ford to develop the Rouge after posting a $10 million bond to safeguard the Dodge brothers' interests.

As the case was fought in the courts, the country and Ford Motor Company were confronted with far deeper problems. The sinking of the famed liner *Lusitania* by a German U-boat in May 1915 had killed

Nowlin Street in Dearborn Township has yet to be paved, but the first Ford homes are nearly complete on August 26, 1919. The Dearborn Realty and Construction Company, a Henry Ford–owned enterprise, built 156 houses (Models A through F) just south of Michigan Avenue, to help solve an employee housing crisis. Although plans called for 350 homes, Ford abandoned the effort during the recession of 1920. *Dearborn Historical Museum*

more than 1,201 people, including 120 Americans, and the sinking of the unarmed French ferry *Sussex* in 1916 had whipped up fury in the United States. Henry Ford still promoted peace, but suddenly shifted his attitude when President Wilson severed diplomatic ties with Germany on February 3, 1917.

When Wilson presented his case against German aggression on April 2 and Congress declared war four days later, Ford's transformation to a war supporter was complete. He remarked, "I am a pacifist if to believe that war is the worst thing in the world. . . . But if we can't have peace without fighting for it, by all means let us fight. And let us fight in a manner that we mean business—that we are in it to stay, with all our hearts and souls, until the finish."

As America sounded a call to arms, excavation for the Rouge's mile-long storage bins for coal, iron ore, and limestone began in April. Two months later, land was cleared for the blast furnaces. Because the site was marshy, it was necessary to drive 200,000 60-foot-long wooden pilings

into the ground, to create a secure foundation (the pilings are still there). The Edison Portland Cement Company of New Jersey supplied the nearly 50 railcar loads of cement needed each week for the construction.

Another Henry Ford venture, which would soon be linked with the Rouge and the Dodge brothers' lawsuit, was the creation of the Henry Ford & Son Company on July 27, 1917, to build Fordson tractors, farm implements, and appliances. It was a Ford family-owned operation, or as Henry said, it had "no shareholders . . . no parasites."

Sorensen set up the tractor plant in Dearborn, some 3 miles from the Rouge, at the site of an old brick factory. To solve a housing crisis for the tractor plant employees, Ford created the Dearborn Realty and Construction Company in 1919 and erected 156 homes—although 350 were originally planned—just west of the factory. Designed by Ford architect Albert Wood, the six styles of homes, called the Models A through F, sold for $6,750 to $7,250 apiece. The housing project was discontinued after the tractor plant moved to the Rouge.

Chapter Two

Creating the Vertical Factory, 1918–1927

"It was in order to eliminate lost motion—which is just as fatal in a factory as in a bearing—that we began, some years ago, the plant which we call Fordson and which has now become the heart of our industries. Four years ago, it had a blast furnace, several shops, and about three thousand men. We had taken over the ground and put up some buildings to manufacture Eagle boats for the Government during the war—fast little boats to go after submarines. Now the plant covers more than a thousand acres, has a mile of river frontage, and employs upward of seventy thousand men."
—Henry Ford, Today and Tomorrow, 1926

enry Ford's conversion into a "fighting pacifist" had taken years, but after America declared war against Germany, he determined to bring the manufacturing power of his enterprises, including the Highland Park Plant, his tractor factory, and even the incomplete Rouge, into the war effort as quickly as possible.

Highland Park, for instance, built a limited number of civilian Model Ts throughout the war, while making upward of 2,000 ambulance chassis, 820,000 steel helmets, and cylinders for the American-designed Liberty aircraft engine.

The Henry Ford & Son Company, on the other hand, built 7,000 Fordson tractors for the war—not for duty on the front lines but to help Great Britain's farmers overcome a severe food shortage. The 2,500-pound tractor had a four-cylinder, 20-horsepower motor that drove the 42-inch rear metal wheels, while its 28-inch front wheels were used for steering. Initially, Ford planned to build the tractors in the city of Cork, Ireland, but the British wanted the factory in England. Sorensen was dispatched to England, but German air raids forced production to be moved to Dearborn. (Once the tractor order was filled, the Dearborn tractor factory was converted to making tanks.)

Ford went in over its head, however, when it accepted a government contract to build submarine chasers called "Eagle Boats." (The term originated in a *Washington Post* editorial that called for "an eagle to scour the seas and pounce upon and destroy every German submarine.")

Germany's announcement in 1917 that it would resume sinking all ships it suspected of carrying war munitions to the Allies—even vessels

of neutral countries—elicited a great public outcry for a solution. By the beginning of January 1918, Henry Ford proposed that his car company could make 500 U-boat hunters on an assembly line. The boats would be designed to carry a secret device developed by General Electric to detect the underwater craft: sonar. Existing navy ships were too noisy to be retrofitted with sonar. On January 18, U.S. Secretary of the Navy Josephus Daniels telegraphed Ford, instructing him to "Proceed with one hundred submarine patrol vessels. Details of contract to be arranged as soon as possible."

Ford turned to Highland Park's architect, Albert Kahn, to design the Eagle Boat factory to be built near the Rouge blast furnaces, which were still under construction. William Knudsen, who had established 14 of the company's branch assembly plants, was placed in charge of the Eagle plant.

Ground was broken in the frozen soil on February 18 for the "A" Building, a 450 x 156–foot fabricating shop. Meanwhile, the Michigan Central Railroad built a spur off its mainline to the site in three days, opening the track on February 20. The western half of the Eagle plant's property was creek bed, which required 175 carloads of cinders to bring to the proper elevation. Additionally, the cement foundation was sunk 3½ feet into the marshy ground. "A" Building was finished in only 24 working days, while construction had started on "B" Building, the main Eagle factory, on February 20.

The official government contract, issued by Assistant Secretary of the Navy Franklin D. Roosevelt, arrived on March 1, by which time the

The "Henry" blast furnace *(center)* sits silent, cold, and incomplete in November 1919. In the foreground are the Hi Line railroad tracks—three standard gauge and one wide gauge. Once the furnace was operational, the transfer cranes brought raw materials from the 1½-mile storage bins to the Hi Line, where scale cars weighed them to ensure a proper mix of iron ore, limestone, and coke. The scale cars then dumped the materials into a skip car that was hoisted to the furnace's charging bell at the top. To the right of the 92-foot-tall blast furnace are its dust catcher and dry cleaner facilities and the four stove towers. Turbo blowers in the Rouge powerhouse supplied air to the stove towers, which heated the air before pumping it into the bottom of the furnace. Peeking up behind the "Henry" are the smokestack and stove towers of the "Benson" blast furnace, which wasn't completed until 1922.
Ford Photomedia

Steam-powered American Bridge Company crane No. 50 sets the last steel roof truss into place as workers continue construction of the massive "B" Building on May 11, 1918. The north end of the factory had been completed four days earlier, and the keel laid for the first Eagle Boat submarine destroyer. *Dossin Great Lakes Museum*

Navy had raised its order to 112 Eagle Boats. Legend has it that after Ford signed the contract and mailed it, the letter was returned because someone forgot to attach a stamp. The federal government paid the $3.5 million construction costs for the shipyard but gave Ford the option to buy the factories at a substantially reduced price after the war.

At first, Ford believed that the 200-foot-long, 500-ton, steel-plated boats could be sent down a continuously moving assembly line. He constructed a full-size prototype at Highland Park to see how the parts fit together. However, the craft's sheer size made it necessary to use a "step-by-step" movement down the "B" Building's three assembly lines, called "shipways." The hulls were moved aboard enormous, tractor-drawn flatcars on standard gauge tracks, while overhead cranes hoisted large assemblies into position.

Ford built the boat's turbines, reduction gears, and boilers, while Navy-approved suppliers made the pumps, condensers, and other equipment. Special machines cut each hull plate to exact measurements

The foundation of the Eagle Plant's "E" Building is laid on May 20, 1918. Due to the marshy ground of the site, Ford used hundreds of wooden pilings to stabilize the land under this structure. The Rouge blast furnaces, docks, and many other structures were similarly supported by thousands of pilings. In the background are stacks of wooden pilings, along with the steel skeleton of an unidentified building and a partially constructed smokestack with the letter "D" of the "FORD" name visible at the bottom. *Dossin Great Lakes Museum*

and bent them to shape, as great punch presses accurately made 50 rivet holes at a time.

The Eagle factory's payroll grew to 4,077 men in July 1918 before jumping to 7,194 by October. One of the shipyard workers was Harry Bennett. Small in stature yet muscular, Bennett was a former Navy deep-sea diver and professional boxer who fought under the name "Sailor Reese." One story has it that Knudsen hired him to keep an eye on the factory's watchmen, who were suspected of stealing construc-

tion materials. Bennett, though, maintained that Hearst columnist Arthur Brisbane introduced him to Henry Ford in New York following the failed Peace Ship initiative and that he impressed the auto magnate. Either way, Bennett joined Ford in 1918 and served in the art department, specializing in company films before becoming the Ford family's bodyguard soon after.

The Rouge's "B" Building, or "Ship Building," was 1,700 feet long and 350 feet wide, covering 13 acres under one roof. Its three assembly

Amid much fanfare, the stern of the 540-ton *Eagle 1* emerges from the "B" Building on July 11, 1918, just four and a half months after groundbreaking for the ship factory. Construction of this boat exposed many flaws in the assembly-line system, and production did not go well for the next several boats. *Dossin Great Lakes Museum*

lines could house 21 Eagle Boat hulls, 7 per line, in different stages of construction. This was the only time anyone ever attempted to mass-produce warships inside a building.

The factory had one main floor, plus offices on a mezzanine level at the north end, but was made so it could eventually house four floors. By March 25, the building's concrete foundation was complete. On April 9, the first steel columns were erected, and by May 11, a steam-powered railroad crane set the last steel truss into place. At the time, it was considered a world record in erecting a steel-framed building.

The north end of the factory was completed May 7, and the first Eagle boat keel was laid that day, even though half the building was still open to the sky. The entire "B" Building was finished on May 25. Its construction required 4,150 tons of steel, 350 carloads of roofing tile, more than 2 million feet of lumber for the floors, and 56,000 panes of glass.

That the construction of the boat factory went as well as it did is amazing, considering that spring floods turned the site into a mire and that the Spanish flu, which hit the United States in March 1918, caused high absenteeism. The influenza pandemic killed about 675,000 Americans and an estimated 20 million to 40 million people worldwide—more than those who had died on the battlefields of Europe. Additionally, because the disease struck down not only the very young and old but also healthy middle-aged adults, it caused a panic that shut down factories and businesses in Detroit and nationwide for days.

While "B" Building was under construction, the *Niagara* of the Duluth-Superior Dredging Company dug out the Rouge's boat slip and turning basin. The latter was essential for the future development of the factory complex: there was insufficient room for the freighters to turn around, and they could not simply back out of the Rouge River.

Next came the formidable task of launching of *Eagle 1* on July 5. Because "B" Building was not next to the boat slip, the 500-ton boats were placed onto a "transfer table" as they exited the factory. This apparatus rode on 11 rails and took the boats to a hydraulic elevator that lowered them into the murky waters of the boat slip. Once in the water, the Eagle Boats went from station to station down the boat slip to be outfitted with additional equipment, including depth-charge racks and deck guns.

The making of *Eagle 1* exposed many flaws in the assembly-line system, and production did not go well for the next several boats. As the company worked out its problems and costs ballooned from $275,000 per boat to $400,000, the war in Europe began grinding to a halt and the U-boat menace had lessened considerably.

Still, the Eagle Boats had boosted Henry Ford's reputation, and the Democratic Party convinced him to run for U.S. Senate, to help counter Republican opposition to President Woodrow Wilson. Ironically, in 1916, the Michigan Republican Party had nominated Ford for president, an effort that had not panned out. His senate race also turned sour. Ford refused to openly campaign for the seat, but the race against the Republican candidate, Truman Newberry, nevertheless grew nasty.

In October 1917, 23-year-old Edsel Ford received an exemption from the draft, because his son Henry II had just been born and because, as a Ford supervisor, he was considered "indispensable" to the war effort. Edsel's deferment became a campaign issue, with charges that the Fords had received special treatment. Newberry narrowly won the election but soon became embroiled in allegations that he had exceeded campaign-spending limits. He resigned in 1922.

Above: *Eagles 2* through *5* are docked on the east side of the Rouge boat slip, formerly a part of Roulo Creek, a tributary of the Rouge River. The boats are proceeding from station to station down the slip, to be outfitted with additional equipment. Behind the boats, two of the Rouge's huge transfer cranes are in various states of completion and will eventually be used to scoop raw materials from the huge storage bins. *Dossin Great Lakes Museum*

Left: Outfitted for battle, *Eagle 1* is ready to enter naval service but will not fire a shot against a German U-boat in World War I. By the time the armistice was signed, the Navy Department had accepted only three Eagle Boats. Twelve others had been launched, and the keels of 28 more were laid. The navy allowed Ford to finish 60 boats by the fall of 1919, most of which were transferred to the Coast Guard, sold, or scrapped before the next major war 20 years later. *Dossin Great Lakes Museum*

Workers fabricate hull plates for the last remaining Eagle Boats in the summer of 1919. The federal government canceled most wartime contracts when the armistice was signed in November 1918, but the navy asked Ford to finish the 32 vessels for which the company had parts. *Dossin Great Lakes Museum*

Peace came to Europe on November 11, 1918, just days after Ford's defeat in the election. Ford immediately halted production of armaments at Highland Park and of tanks at his tractor factory, converting them back to peacetime production. At the Rouge, 28 keels had been laid, 12 Eagles had been launched, 7 were commissioned, and the Navy had accepted 3 boats. None of the vessels had fired a shot in the war. Additionally, Ford had built and tested 66 turbines, 60 gears, and 26 boilers for the incomplete vessels. The question was, what would become of this equipment?

The government canceled most wartime contracts forthwith, but the Navy allowed Ford to make up to 60 Eagle Boats, minus the sonar devices, provided the order was completed by November 15, 1919. Ford, meanwhile, purchased the Eagle factory for $180,000, a fraction of the cost it took to build. This outcome raised a stink in Congress.

In December 1918, Senator Henry Cabot Lodge of Massachusetts accused Ford of war profiteering, and the Senate Naval Affairs Committee launched an immediate investigation. The Eagle Boats, the Rouge factory, and an incomplete Eagle factory on the East Coast had cost the U.S. government $50 million. The program was a complete failure, the senator claimed, because the vessels hadn't been delivered on time and were leaky, top-heavy, and general unseaworthy. "The Navy's refusal to cut short the construction looms up as the biggest industrial scandal of the war," Lodge stated.

The navy, though, came to Ford Motor Company's defense. Before the Senate committee, Admiral Taylor testified that the Eagles were "excellent seaboats." Further, the admiral said, the navy wanted 60 Eagles because they could perform missions larger destroyers could not. The Senate held Ford harmless for any war profiteering, and the

Workers at the "B" Building assemble Fordson tractors in 1923. The vast factory started producing tractors and Model T parts for Highland Park in August 1919. Note that African-Americans are working side by side with whites on the line. By 1917 Ford employed more blacks than any other domestic automaker and hired many to work on the higher-paying assembly line jobs. Some blacks were even supervisors, with the power to fire and lay off white workers. *Ford Photomedia*

navy transferred most of the Eagle Boats to the Coast Guard in 1919. Most of the ships were sold or scrapped in the 1930s and 1940s, but a few remained in service for World War II.

Employment at the Ford shipyards dipped to 5,385 in December, but workers did their jobs with gusto. For example, the hull of *Eagle 59* was completed between April 2 and 12, 1919, establishing a world record for building a 200-foot boat. The keel of *Eagle 60* was laid March 30.

If the Senate investigation weren't enough, Ford's battle with his stockholders also came to a head. In the midst of this swirling chaos, Henry Ford mysteriously removed himself from the legal wranglings and officially resigned as company president on December 31, 1918, handing the office to his son before jumping aboard a ship.

On February 7, 1919, the Michigan Supreme Court ruled that Ford Motor Company immediately had to pay a $19 million dividend

to its stockholders. As majority shareholder, Henry Ford received nearly $11 million, while the Dodge brothers were paid $1.9 million. Then the Wayne County circuit courts blocked further expansion of the Rouge River Plant. Henry Ford was incommunicado for nearly two months. After the court orders came down, Ford circulated rumors that his tractor company would build a better and cheaper car than the Model T.

At this point, John and Horace Dodge probably realized that Henry Ford was outmaneuvering them. If Henry succeeded with the rumored new car, the value of Ford Motor Company's stock would plummet and possibly become worthless. The minority stockholders made a deal with Henry to sell their shares for $105 million. It is said that Henry Ford was so happy, he "danced a jig" around his office at Highland Park.

Working on the Ford Rouge Railroad

"Back in the old days, Henry Ford used to like his steam engines polished up, bright as a penny, and outside trainmen would kid us about it. We'd just smile back and rub our fingers together, meaning 'They pay good money here.'"

—*Rouge Railroad engineer Bill Dengler, Ford World, 1966*

Henry Ford entered the railroad business in 1920, when he paid $5 million for the dilapidated Detroit, Toledo & Ironton Railroad Company (DT&I). Critics thought he was wasting his money, but the railroad was another piece of the vertical integration plan for the Rouge.

The DT&I had been founded in 1849 as the Iron Railroad, serving the Ohio city of Ironton, and had grown in a haphazard fashion, with a line extending from the Ohio River to Detroit and a spur to Toledo. Yet it was in a nearly perpetual financial crisis. When the Interstate Commerce Commission (ICC) ordered it to rebuild its bridge over the Rouge River as part of the river-widening project for Ford's plant, the DT&I could not raise the $400,000 it needed.

Henry heard of the DT&I's financial troubles and noted that while the north-south railway didn't service any major cities, it did cut across several major east-west trunk lines. If purchased and renovated, the DT&I could speed the delivery of raw materials into the Rouge and the flow of finished products out.

Since federal laws prevented the auto company from owning an interstate railroad, Henry Ford made a confidential bid for the DT&I and gained full control, with only two minority shareholders refusing to sell out. After the 1920–1921 recession ended, Ford upgraded the railroad's 456 miles of rails, overhauled or replaced its aging locomotives and cars, improved its freight and passenger services, and added radio dispatching. A 15-mile-long double-wide track for electric trains was built between the Rouge Plant and Flat Rock, Michigan, and numerous horseshoe-shaped concrete arches, called catenary towers, were built along the route to hold the overhead electric lines. Some of the arches still exist along parts of the old DT&I line.

As improvements were made, the railroad's workforce was slashed from 2,760 to 1,650 employees. Those who remained received Ford's $6-a-day wage, which was an increase for most of the remaining workers. Notably, too, the DT&I's employees were allowed to join unions, and it was the only railroad to avoid a nationwide railroad strike in 1921.

Despite the revitalization of the DT&I, the tedium of complying with ICC regulations grew on Ford, and he sold the railroad for $36 million to the Pennsylvania Railroad in 1928.

With the DT&I gone, Ford's involvement with the "iron horse" continued with the formation of the Ford Rouge Railroad, the FRDX. The FRDX operated the complex's 110 miles of track, switching all inbound and outbound cars, and acted as part of the Rouge's vast conveyor system. Its engines performed tasks as varied as moving glowing red-hot ingots from the Open-Hearth Building to the blooming mill and pulling empty cars out of the Pressed-Steel Building during lunchtime, to prevent production delays.

Ford added its first diesel engines to the FRDX in 1931, the same year then-25-year-old Windsor, Ontario, native Bill Dengler was hired as a train fireman. During the Great Depression, Dengler had wrestled in Michigan under the villainous pseudonym "Bill Dillinger." He earned $15 per match and got a cauliflower ear out of the deal. Before he retired in 1966, Dengler was one of the hundreds of men who worked on what was then the world's largest private railroad.

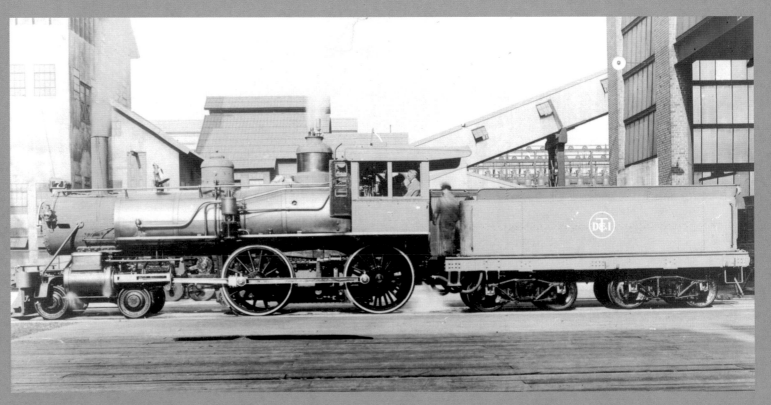

Henry Ford rides in the cab of DT&I locomotive No. 7 in the early 1920s. Ford bought the nearly bankrupt railroad for $5 million in 1920 and restructured it to serve as an integral part of the Rouge's supply chain, ferrying raw materials to the complex and taking out completed cars and components. *Walter P. Reuther Library, Wayne State University*

In 1937, when the country appeared to be coming out of the Great Depression, the Rouge railroad had 16 company-owned locomotives and handled more than 1,100 cars daily, carrying in coal, gasoline, limestone, lumber, oil, iron ore, and new machinery and hauling out auto parts and finished cars. Normally, it took the railroad three hours to deliver loads between the Rouge's factories, but the yard office could process rush orders.

By 1937, Ford owned two diesel-electric engines and 14 steam locomotives. One of the steam engines was No. 29, nicknamed the "Teakettle" because it was a fireless locomotive. Every four hours, "Teakettle" took on a charge of steam and water, up to 200 pounds of pressure, on which it could work up to eight hours. It was used inside the factories without fear of hot cinders igniting a fire or spewing smoke and fumes into enclosed spaces.

Ford locomotives were clean, with "shining bright work, fresh black paint, aluminum painted wheels and red-topped cabs. One could easily believe the locomotive was on display, but for the obviousness of work being done. Inside the cabs every part touched by the engineer's or fireman's hands in the operating engine is chrome-plated," the *Ford News* reported.

Near the Rouge's locomotive shop, the engines were washed every other day with soap, water, and fine oil. Before leaving the cleaning pit, a fresh coat of aluminum paint was applied to wheels, the windows cleaned, and the headlights checked.

Monthly, the steam engine's boilers were washed, and quarterly the gauges and valves were inspected. A yearly overhaul was done at the Rouge locomotive shop. Workers used gas torches to heat the steel tires of the driving wheels, so the metal would expand for easy removal and replacement.

The major railyards around the Rouge Plant were—and remain—the Fordson and Rougemere on the complex's southeast side and the Livernois Yard along Michigan Central's (now Norfolk & Southern's) mainline.

The interior of the Rouge Locomotive Shop is crowded in 1923, as the company rebuilds a number of engines from the decrepit DT&I. The older steam engine to the left, with a "balloon stack," did not belong to the DT&I but is probably an engine Henry Ford acquired as a working collector's piece. *Ernest B. Novak Collection*

No. 1003, one of the first two diesel-electric switching engines Ford bought in 1937, is painted in the Rouge Railroad's traditional red-over-blue colors. The engine looks clean because it was washed every other day with soap, water, and fine oil. Before it left the cleaning pit, its windows were cleaned and headlights checked. *Ford Photomedia*

The shareholders weren't badly off. Couzens, the second largest shareholder, received $29.3 million in 1919; he had paid only $2,000 for his shares in 1903 (and had bought some shares years later). His sister Rosetta, who had bought her one share of company stock 16 years before for $100, had received about $335,000 in dividends over the years and a $260,000 buyout payment.

The Dodge brothers received $25 million for their shares and turned their attention to building a car to rival Ford. They had little time left to savor their victory, though. While the brothers celebrated at the New York Auto Show in January 1920, both contracted a virulent strain of the flu that quickly turned into pneumonia. John Dodge died January 19; Horace lingered in ill health for much of the year before succumbing to cirrhosis of the liver on December 10.

As a result of the settlement, Henry Ford was the unquestioned leader of his automotive empire, even though Edsel Ford was officially president and had ambitious lieutenants, such as Charlie Sorensen, under him. (Henry had by now nicknamed Sorensen "Cast-Iron Charlie" because of his dedication to using cast metal instead of forgings).

Nineteen nineteen was a giddy time for the auto industry, as cars sold briskly in the face of soaring postwar inflation and material shortages. Because there were still an estimated two horses for every car on the road, the market seemed wide open. Henry Ford was not immune to the expansion fever that gripped the industry; he borrowed more money for the Rouge and bought a railroad and other properties.

Even as the last of the Eagle Boats was completed, the Rouge became a massive components plant for Highland Park. "B" Building was renovated, with a second floor added to either side of the central bay, to begin producing car and tractor parts. Auto bodies came out the door as soon as August 1919, and the former Ford shipyards became known as the "River Rouge Plant."

A battery of coke ovens went on line in October 1919. Coke was an essential ingredient for the blast furnaces. The early coke ovens used 4,800 tons of coal a day to produce 3,600 tons of coke and 33 million cubic feet of hydrogen and methane gas, plus byproducts such as benzol, ammonia, and coal tar, which the company recovered and used in other operations.

Running between the coke ovens and the storage bins was the "Hi Line," which had one wide gauge and three standard gauge railroad tracks. Once the blast furnaces were operation, the transfer cranes over the storage bins brought the raw materials and dumped them into the Hi Line's scale cars that weighed the material to ensure there is a proper mix of iron ore, limestone, and coke. The scale cars then dumped the materials into a skip car that was hoisted to the furnace's charging bell at the top.

The Dearborn tractor plant's operations were moved to the first floor of "B" Building, and the first Fordson rolled off the line at 9 a.m. on February 23, 1920. About 36,000 tractors were made by year's end. The River Rouge Plant became such a prominent tractor factory that its name was changed to the "Fordson Plant" in March 1926.

With the tractors came Sorensen and his assistant, Mead L. Bricker. One of Sorensen's first acts was to find office space for his people, who took over the "Wash and Locker Building" used by draftsmen and engineers. As Sorensen's people moved in, they pitched drawings out a second-story window and into a waiting truck below. The not-so-subtle Dane was consolidating his control of the growing factory complex.

The next major event at the Rouge was the lighting of the "A" blast furnace, nicknamed "Henry," on May 17, 1920. Workers stacked cordwood and coke into the blast furnace. Then Henry picked up his two-year-old grandson and, with everyone looking on, Henry II touched a match to pieces of oil-soaked excelsior in the furnace, igniting the fire.

With the Rouge taking shape but business hampered by parts shortages, Ford decided he needed to acquire the sources of raw materials to feed into the plant. In 1919, he hired real estate agent E. G. Kingsford of Iron Mountain, Michigan, to find properties with iron and lumber resources in the state's Upper Peninsula.

Wood was a major component of the Model T's body, and Kingsford, also a Ford car dealer whose wife was a relative of Clara Ford, found 313,447 wooded acres that Ford bought in March 1920 for $2.5 million from the Michigan Iron and Lumber Company. Ford constructed a sawmill nearby and later that year purchased the Imperial mine at Michigamme, north of Iron Mountain, the first of several such purchases. To the south, Ford bought two coal mines in Kentucky and a coal mine in West Virginia.

At the Rouge, the 595 x 1,188–foot Dearborn Iron Foundry was completed. Smoke rose from its 24 cupolas as the first Model T cylinder block was cast on December 23. Henry Ford's vision of vertical integration was taking shape, but 1920 ended on a sour note.

Ford had massive bills due that year, including $37 million of the $70 million the company had borrowed to buy out the minority shareholders, $18 million for the new federal income tax, and $7 million in bonuses for its officers. This spending might not have been a problem if Model T sales had remained hot, but the nation's economy took a decided turn for the worse. Sales plunged, and by the end of the year, Ford had $58 million flowing out of its coffers but only $20 million in hand.

Other automakers also suffered from overenthusiastic spending. Willys-Overland, then second in overall car sales, slipped into bankruptcy, and Walter P. Chrysler was brought in to rescue it. General Motors founder William Durant had overspent so much that his financial backers, the House of Morgan and the Du Pont family, kicked him out. The Lincoln Motor Car Company, founded by Henry Leland, the man who had created Cadillac, was also in financial crisis.

Artist Charles Sheeler took this photo at the base of one of the blast furnaces. The two motionless workers standing near the crane *(center)* almost blend into the machinery as they watch a fiery river of molten steel flow out of the blast furnaces to ladle railcars waiting outside. The blast furnace is a large steel shell lined with heat-resistant bricks. It "cooks" iron, coke, and limestone at up to 2,700 degrees Fahrenheit while air is forced in at the bottom to make raw iron. *From the Collections of The Henry Ford*

Henry Ford holds his two-year-old grandson, Henry II, after the toddler lit the new River Rouge "A" blast furnace on May 17, 1920. Henry helped the boy touch a match to oil-soaked excelsior in the furnace, igniting its fire and finishing the "blowing in" process. *Ford Photomedia*

This photo, which appears to have been taken from an ore ship docked in the boat slip, shows the twin rail lines next to the storage bins, which could hold 1.5 million tons of limestone, iron ore, and coal. The tail end of one of the Rouge's two Hulett ship unloaders can be seen at the right. The Huletts moved up and down the dockside on their own tracks and, working together, could unload 1,000 tons of ore an hour. Crossing over the storage bins is one of the 519-foot-long transfer cranes. *Walter P. Reuther Library, Wayne State University*

On September 21, 1920, Ford announced sizable price cuts on Model Ts—the price of the popular Touring model dropped from $575 to $440—while increasing production. The company sold its cars below production costs but shipped unordered cars to dealers, who bore the brunt of financing them. Ford pressured parts suppliers for price cuts to make up the difference.

As Christmas approached, Ford was headed for bankruptcy. Bankers expected the embattled company to turn to them for loans, but Henry Ford was hostile to financiers, especially given his prior experiences. Highland Park shut down on December 23 for an announced two-week period for "inventory reduction," but six days later came word that it would remain closed until February 1, 1921.

Work on the Rouge slowed, and Ford slashed white-collar employees and sold all surplus equipment, such as lamps, tables, typewriters, telephones, and all pencil sharpeners. With no federal unemployment compensation, the 55,000 Highland Park and Rouge workers made do with their savings or any other work they could find.

With the downturn came the dismissals or resignations of several of Ford's longtime associates, including sales manager Norval Hawkins, engineer C. Harold Wills, and Vice President and Treasurer Frank Klingensmith. John R. Lee and Samuel Marquis also left, bringing an end to the Sociological Department, and Knudsen was let go.

Wills unsuccessfully launched his own car company, the Wills Sainte Claire. Knudsen joined General Motors and built Chevrolet into a brand that would surpass Ford within a decade. After Knudsen's departure, the tattoo-armed Harry Bennett fell under Sorensen's supervision, but that would change as his power grew.

The postwar recession ended in 1921, and by autumn, Highland Park was making a record number of Model Ts. Ford even had enough money to buy Leland's bankrupt Lincoln luxury car company, with its large factory about 4 miles from the Rouge, for $8 million in February 1922. Although Henry Leland and his son Wilfred assumed they would retain operating control, within six months Edsel Ford was in charge of Lincoln, and the Lelands were out.

That year, the Rouge's second blast furnace, the "Benson," was lit. In 1923, the first steel was tapped from the newly completed electric furnace, and the Glass Plant's furnaces fired up. Other factories followed, including the Open-Hearth Furnace, on which construction began in 1925, and other steelmaking facilities, such as blooming, billet, and merchant mills. The Rouge's factories also included the massive Powerhouse No. 1, which was the heart of the complex; a sawmill, which cut 140,000 board feet of lumber a day for car bodies and frames; a paper mill that turned waste paper into binder board for boxes and car-seat backing; and a plant that used blast-furnace slag to make Portland cement. In addition, the Motor Building opened in 1924, and the Stamping Plant, or Pressed-Steel Building, began operating in June 1925.

In keeping with Ford's abhorrence of waste, other facilities refined the byproducts of the coke ovens to make light oil, naphthalene, diammonium phosphate, and tar. Ford's recycling efforts led to the creation of

Ford employees play an outdoor hockey game on an improvised rink at the River Rouge Plant on January 29, 1922. Workers were involved in many after-hours sporting events, including baseball and bowling. The steel mill in the background is unidentified, although its shape is similar to the steel skeleton of a structure in the background of the photo on page 31. If this is actually the Rouge, the mill was probably demolished, like a host of other buildings, as the vast plant grew.
Ford Photomedia

Sailing Aboard the Ford Fleet

"As the Rouge Plant began to need huge volumes of raw materials to feed the completed blast furnaces, coke ovens, power house, open hearth furnaces and glass plant, Mr. Ford made plans for his own fleet of ships."

—*Clare J. Snider*, The Ford Fleet, 1994

Another element of Henry Ford's plan was to use nature's highway, the water, to bring raw materials and finished products in and out of the Rouge Plant and its satellite factories.

The Rouge River, which flowed into the Detroit River, was a shallow, winding stream that varied from 75 to 100 feet wide before the Eagle Boat factory was built. Cargos had to be transferred from Great Lakes steamers to small barges at the mouth of the river, which tugs then towed up the 5 miles of winding stream.

The U.S. Army Corps of Engineers changed that forever when they dug the 3,000-foot-long, 400-foot-wide "short cut channel" at the mouth of the river, creating Zug Island while lopping 2 miles off the trip to the plant. The corps also widened the rest of the river to the complex to 200 feet and dredged it to a depth of 21 feet. The bridges for Dix, Fort Street, and Jefferson Avenue had to be torn down and rebuilt, as did the railway bridges for the Detroit, Toledo & Ironton; Pere Marquette; and Wabash railroads.

The 5,500-gross-ton *Cletus Schneider* was the first large ore ship to visit the Rouge River Plant on July 11, 1923, starting continual shipments that have been interrupted only by the wintertime shutdown of ship traffic on the Great Lakes. Also in 1923, Ford ordered two 612-foot-long ore freighters, the *Henry Ford II* and the *Benson Ford*—named after Henry's two oldest grandsons, just like the original two Rouge blast furnaces. The freighters were the first large diesel-powered ships on the Great Lakes, with engines that produced 3,000 to 3,500 horsepower, helping the vessels attain speeds of 10 to 12 knots.

The *Henry* was built in Lorain, Ohio, by the American Ship Building Company and launched on March 1, 1924, by seven-year-old Henry Ford II, who operated a remote control in Detroit. The *Benson* was launched April 16 at the Great Lakes Engineering Works in Ecorse, Michigan, near the mouth of the Rouge River. The *Benson* entered operation on August 2, sailing to Michigan's Upper Peninsula to pick up a load of iron ore for the Rouge. The *Henry*

The *Barlow,* originally built with coal-fired steam engines at Elizabeth, New Jersey, in 1919, sits in the ice-covered boat slip at the Rouge on December 9, 1927. The boat is one of seven steel-hulled tugs Ford bought from the federal government in 1925, to supplement the factory complex's growing shipping needs. Ford converted the *Barlow* and its other tugs to run on oil and equipped them with radios and direction finders. These tugs were first used to tow the surplus freighters Ford bought for scrap metal; they later pulled barges around the Great Lakes. *Ford Photomedia*

set sail on its first voyage August 24, delivering 12,000 tons of coal that had originated in Ford's Kentucky mines to steel mills in Duluth, Minnesota.

Each ore ship, the longest on the Great Lakes in the early 1920s, could carry up to 13,000 tons of coal or iron. The *Henry* had two master staterooms and two smaller staterooms on a lower deck for guests, while the *Benson* had only two master staterooms. In keeping with Ford's desire for cleanliness, the engine rooms were finished in gray and white enamel paint with nickel-plated trimmings. The officers' and crew's quarters had hardwood finishings, and shower-baths were available for everyone.

The *Henry* and the *Benson* weren't the first operational ships in the Ford fleet. In May 1924, Ford purchased the *Oneida* and *Onodaga*. Both vessels were four-year-old, 261-foot-long, 2,300-gross-ton "Laker" freighters. They were the first Ford vessels used to haul coal to the company's facilities in the Upper Peninsula and also brought lumber back to the Rouge.

The Lakers were built between 1917 and 1919 to ferry cargos directly from the Great Lakes ports to England and France during the war. Only about one-fourth the size of typical oceangoing freighters of the time, Lakers measured 247 to 261 feet long and were no wider than 43½ feet, with 3,200- to 4,300-ton cargo capacities. These ships were the only ones that could fit through the existing Canadian locks and channels to get to the Atlantic Ocean.

Ford greatly expanded his fleet in 1925, when the U.S. Merchant Marine decided to sell many of its mothballed World War I freighters and tugboats. Ford purchased the *East Indian*, an 8,200-ton ship built for the U.S. at Japanese shipyards. At 461 feet long, *East Indian* was too large to fit through the St. Lawrence River lock and channel system, so it never visited the Rouge, but it carried knockdown Model Ts and auto parts to foreign plants.

Ford also bought seven surplus tugs, including the *Barlow*, *Barrallton*, *Buttercup*, and *Humrick*. These 20-man, 142-foot-long vessels could be used on the Great Lakes and canals and on the seas. Ford later supplemented them with the *Dearborn*, an 85-foot-long harbor tug built in 1932 at Great Lakes Engineering in the city of River Rouge, Michigan.

While buying the tugs, Ford purchased 199 surplus World War I freighters for $1.6 million on August 18, 1925. About 150 of these ships were Lakers, and the rest were larger "subs"—324-foot-long freighters built by the Submarine Boat Company of Newark, New Jersey. The great majority of these boats were scrapped to feed the Rouge's open-hearth furnaces. The subs were too large to travel the canals, so they were chopped up and their parts put into Lakers that were towed to the Rouge between 1925 and 1927. Boilers, winches, and other usable equipment were at first removed from the scrapped ships and stored for future use but were later melted down as well.

Four of the Lakers were reconditioned in 1925 and 1930 to become part of Ford's oceangoing fleet, while 13 of the ships were turned into barges (their engines were removed, along with the center superstructure) to be towed by the tugs around the Great Lakes.

In the 1930s, Ford ordered four special canal vessels to transport auto parts from the Rouge to Ford plants and ports on East Coast. The 300-foot-long *Chester* and *Edgewater,* built in 1931 by Great Lakes Engineering Works, had retractable pilothouses and funnels. They also had folding masts, so they could go under the bridges of the New York State Barge Canal. These two ships were joined in 1937 by the *Green Island* and the *Norfolk*.

By 1941, the Ford fleet had grown to 31 vessels: the large *Henry* and *Benson* ore ships, 5 other tugs, the 4 canal vessels, 13 barges, and 5 oceangoing ships. A small lighter—a flat-bottomed barge—was used at the Ford Edgewater plant in New York, and a tiny tug in Brazil served Ford's rubber plantations, which fed the Rouge's Tire Plant. World War II radically altered the Ford fleet as the federal government requisitioned most of its ships for wartime service.

The propeller and rudder of the 612-foot-long, 14,000-ton *Henry Ford II* are seen here, just prior to the ship's launching at the American Ship Building Company in Lorain, Ohio, on March 1, 1924. The three electronically operated guillotines shown in the picture cut the ship's hawsers during the launch. Along with the *Benson Ford*, the *Henry* was one of the largest ore freighters on the Great Lakes at the time. *Dossin Great Lakes Museum*

The *Chester*, one of two specially built Ford canal boats made by Great Lakes Engineering Works in Ecorse, Micigan, is pictured in the early 1930s loaded with Ford V-8 coupes and sedans as it departs the Rouge boat slip and enters the turning basin. *Walter P. Reuther Library, Wayne State Univeristy*

Above: Only three smokestacks rise from Powerhouse No. 1, which is still under construction on December 17, 1920. Designed by William B. Mayo, who also created Highland Park's powerhouse, Powerhouse No. 1 will be equipped with about 27,000 direct-current electric motors, because Henry Ford, like his friend Thomas Edison, believed DC was better than alternating current. *The Henry Ford Collection*

Right: The giant ladle hook of the 175-ton overhead crane hangs a few feet off the floor of the Open-Hearth Building as a worker uses a flathead shovel to pick up debris in this Charles Sheeler photograph. A portion of the 75-ton ladle can be seen to the far right. The ladles are used either to either pour molten iron into the open-hearth furnaces or to pour molten steel from the 10 furnaces into ingot molds. Several 10-ton ingot molds are sitting upright on the flatcar *(center)*.

charcoal—originally called "Ford Charcoal" and later "Kingsford," after E. G. Kingsford—by turning scrap wood into charcoal briquettes.

Besides its factories, the Rouge had a railroad, fire department, police department, hospital, and company newspaper, the *Ford Rouge News*. But a dark chapter in the company's history began when Ford moved the *Dearborn Independent*, his hometown newspaper, in 1918. The paper was to be Henry's "chronicler of neglected truth," to spread folksy wisdom around the country. He installed *Detroit News* editor Edwin G. Pipp to run it, and Pipp recruited *News* columnist William J. Cameron. Ford's personal secretary, Ernest G. Liebold, was made the paper's general manager. The *Independent* was initially moved to the old Fordson tractor factory, and was possibly housed for a short time in the Rouge's "B" Building.

After two years of publishing sedate stories, the paper began a 91-issue series of anti-Semitic stories on May 22, 1920, that began with the article "The International Jew: The World's Problem." The stories were based on a polemic booklet left over from czarist Russia called the *Protocols of the Learned Elders of Zion*, which had been written to shove that country's Jewish community to the fringe. Ford's paper popularized the dead czar's propaganda that a Zionist conspiracy, led by Jewish bankers, was out to take over the world.

Pipp resigned from the paper in disgust, but Cameron ran the series through 1922 and another series in 1924 and 1925. He also reprinted the stories as pamphlets. After several lawsuits, Ford closed the *Independent* in 1927 and issued an apology. By then, his reputation was greatly damaged in the Jewish community and in Hollywood. The "Protocols," however, influenced Adolph Hitler in demoralized postwar Germany, and Hitler mentioned Ford in his book *Mein Kampf* as the "single great man" who was resisting the Jews. Some have blamed Liebold and/or Edison for planting anti-Semitic ideas in Ford's head, while other historians point the finger at the auto pioneer's own prejudices.

As the uproar caused by the paper played out through the 1920s, the Rouge continued to grow. But, even as Ford's vertically integrated factory hit its stride, the Model T was slowly dying. The Tin Lizzie's production had jumped from 200,000 units in 1913 to a peak of 1.8 million in 1923, and manufacturing efficiencies had allowed Ford to cut prices from $600 to $295 for the basic car. However, Ford was facing increased competition from GM, Dodge, and the newly formed Chrysler Corporation, all of which were making stylish, six-cylinder cars priced comparably to the Model T.

By the mid-1920s, half the cars registered in America were Model Ts, but sales of the newer models were competing with older, used Lizzies among buyers who wanted basic transportation. Despite design freshening by Edsel Ford, the new Model T was basically the same car—durable and easy to repair but cranky. With its large wheels meant to navigate muddy dirt tracks, the "T" looked ungainly on paved city streets. Ford stubbornly resisted the suggestions of his son and other

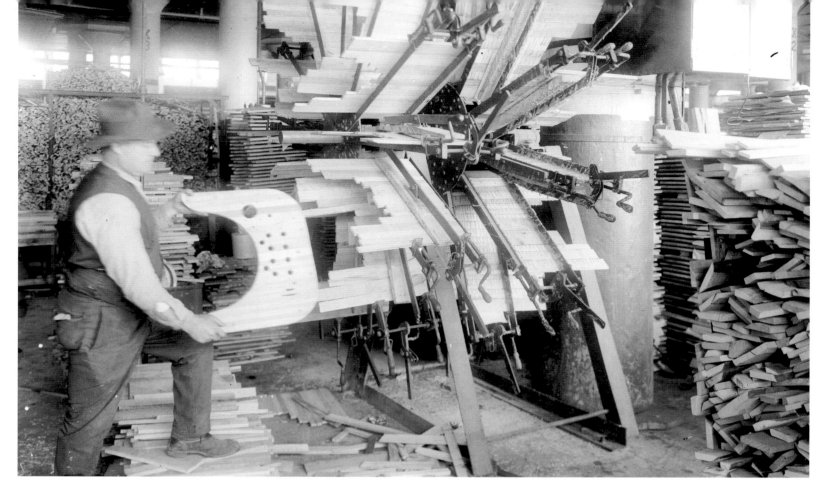

officers to develop a new car or even offer a second model. When Ernest Kanzler, Edsel's brother-in-law, strongly urged Henry Ford to replace the Model T with a six-cylinder car in 1926, he was fired.

Henry Ford was experimenting with a new motor called the "X engine," in reference to the arrangement of the pistons. Ford tried four- and eight-cylinder versions, but he could never overcome the X engine's high temperature and friction problems.

On Thursday, May 26, 1927, the fifteen millionth Ford car was made. Its engine was produced at the Fordson (Rouge) Plant at 10 a.m. before being transported to Highland Park. When the car was finished, Edsel hopped in the driver's seat, Henry climbed in beside him, and they drove it off the line for a simple ceremony.

By this time, Henry Ford realized that his favorite sales technique of cutting prices was no longer working and that the Model T had to be discontinued. A total of 15,458,781 had been made, about 11 million of which were still on the roads. To keep sales of the last new "Ts" from falling off, Ford pledged to make parts for the cars for the next five years.

Then Ford ordered massive layoffs. Highland Park, Fordson, and the company's 30 branch assembly plants were closed for months. Ford didn't have a new model ready for production, and the company scrambled to design a worthy successor to the Tin Lizzie.

One hundred thousand people—60,000 in Detroit alone—were thrown out of work for nearly six months as Ford Motor Company's engineers scrambled to finish the Model T's replacement. While many people would be rehired when the company geared up for its new car, Charles Sorensen purged some employees as he tightened his grip as Ford's de facto manufacturing chief.

With Ford's plants shut down, General Motors' Chevrolet and Hudson Motor Car Company's Essex surpassed Ford's sales, and the upstart Chrysler Corporation was nipping at Ford's heels. Many car buyers, however, waited to see the new Ford, causing a mini-recession. As the months dragged by, a group of investors offered Henry $1 billion to sell out, but he refused.

Henry had actually given his blessing for the new car in August 1926. It was Ford's first all-new car in nearly two decades, so Henry thought it was fitting to go back to the beginning of the alphabet for its name. Working on the Model A were veteran engineer Joseph Galamb, who helped create the "T"; Eugene J. Farkas, an engineer on the failed X engine project; and an up-and-coming manager, Laurence S. Sheldrick. Edsel Ford designed the body, using elements from the Lincoln.

With its body set closer to the ground than the "T," the Model A was 113$\frac{7}{16}$ inches long, with a 103$\frac{1}{2}$-inch wheelbase. It had a four-cylinder engine and was able to reach a top speed of 65 miles per hour, up significantly from the Model T's 43-mile-per-hour limit. The car also featured aluminum pistons, a sliding-gear transmission, hydraulic shock absorbers, a 10-gallon gas tank, standard battery ignition, and came in a choice of seven body colors, plus special colors for the Fordor (four door) model. The "A" was also the first car to have laminated safety glass, made at the Fordson (Rouge) Glass Plant,

as standard equipment. However, it still featured mechanical brakes (Henry didn't trust hydraulic brakes) and the obsolete transverse leaf springs.

The first blueprints were finished in January 1927, and the first rolling prototype was running in March. Getting the car ready for production was a massive undertaking. Because most of its 5,580 parts were new, it required new production machines, including 30-foot-tall, 240-ton presses (twice the size of those used for the Model T) that were installed at Fordson's Pressed-Steel Building. On top of that, car production and other operations were permanently moved out of Highland Park into Fordson's "B" Building. Ford would lease parts of Highland Park out to supplier companies, such as Briggs Manufacturing to make car bodies, and the plant would be used to make Ford tractors and trucks until it was sold in 1981.

Sorensen, who had gained a reputation for taking sledgehammers to the desks of supervisors who got too big for their britches (a charge he denied), worked tirelessly to root out Edsel Ford's supporters and anyone he viewed as wedded to old-fashioned thinking. "We want to fire every Model T son of a bitch," Sorensen purportedly said as the company rehired workers.

In May, thousands of diemakers, millwrights, and other skilled tradesmen were rehired for the Fordson Plant. By July, some 17,000 workers were busy retooling both factories, and by September, the assembly line had been moved from Highland Park to the "B" Building. Other workers were recalled beginning in June, and by late November, about 100,000 were working primarily at Fordson.

By this time, Ford had erected two large pedestrian bridges over Miller Road to handle the flow of workers at Gates 2 and 4. Eagle Avenue, which plunged under the Pere Marquette trunk line and was made using

Production of the 1928 Ford Model A, the company's first new car in nearly two decades, had been underway for about five months when this picture was taken on March 8, 1928. The Rouge's "B" Building is finally being used to assemble automobiles, and the scores of workers seen here on the final assembly line are attaching spoked wheels to the car. *Ford Photomedia*

51079-3-8-28

Above: Henry Ford hand-stamps the serial number on the first engine for the 1928 Model A on Thursday, October 20, 1927. This four-cylinder engine attained 40 horsepower, about twice that of the Model T's engine, and could power the Model A to a top speed of 65 miles per hour. It used aluminum pistons and started with a battery ignition. *Walter P. Reuther Library, Wayne State University*

Right: Charles "Cast-Iron Charlie" Sorensen became Henry Ford's de facto head of manufacturing by the late 1920s, although technically he was junior to Vice President P. E. "Pete" Martin, another stern taskmaster known for speeding up assembly lines. *Walter P. Reuther Library, Wayne State University*

31,500 barrels of Portland cement from the plant's cement factory, was opened to link Miller with nearby Wyoming Road.

There were some 70,000 parking spaces for Fordson employees, but many rode the buses and streetcars that came in on Miller and Schaefer roads. At quitting time, workers rushed through the gates to catch their rides. Some were harried, too, remembers Robert Lindsay of Brownstown Township, Michigan. Lindsay once drove to the plant with his brother-in-law Charles Sisenstein to pick up his father-in-law as a surprise. "We saw him running out, and Charles went to tug on his arm, and he yelled, 'Not now! I'm going to miss my streetcar.' He was in too much of a hurry to recognize his own son."

During the spring of 1927, a redheaded 19-year-old man making 60 cents an hour at Briggs in Detroit saw a want ad in the *Detroit Free Press* that said Ford was hiring veteran tool-and-die makers. Called the "slaughterhouse" by its workers, Briggs was known for low pay, long hours, and frequent accidents. Having worked for three years at the Wheeling Steel Company in West Virginia before being drawn to Detroit by the promise of what was then the "Six Dollar Day," Walter P. Reuther figured he might as well apply for the job.

After talking his way past a guard at the Fordson Plant, Reuther convinced a supervisor that he had enough experience for his age. The supervisor gave Reuther a two-day trial. He passed, becoming the youngest man to be hired as an elite skilled tradesman, earning $1.10 an hour. Reuther, however, was looking for more than just a job. He was on a mission to become a future union leader.

Reuther's father, Valentine, had been a labor activist and member of the American Socialist Party. He had also campaigned for Eugene V. Debs, the radical labor leader who helped found the Wobblies before leaving that union. The second of five children in the Reuther family, Walter followed in his father's footsteps, as did his brothers Victor and Roy and his sister, Christine. Only Walter's older brother, Theodore, was the "white sheep" of the family, becoming a manager at Wheeling Steel.

Reuther remained at the Rouge for the next five years, growing in confidence and boldness at the same time the 5-foot, 6-inch Harry Bennett was expanding his power. During the early 1920s, Bennett turned the guards and network of worker-spies, who "ratted" on unionists and other troublemakers, into a coherent force called the Service Department. This organization, which also included the Rouge firemen, was infamous as Ford's private army. Bennett populated the department with boxers, wrestlers, former policemen, ex-convicts, and University of Michigan football players.

By the mid-1920s, Bennett was director of personnel, remaining under Cast-Iron Charlie's command . . . for a time. During the Model A launch, Bennett increased his contact with Henry Ford, visiting him nearly every day. Affable to those he wanted to impress, and a storyteller, Bennett became Henry's close confidant. But he massaged

Two workers remove a body panel from one of the 4,000 stamping presses at the Pressed-Steel Building, which began operation at the Rouge in 1925. At peak times, the plant used about 2,500 tons of milled steel each day to manufacture more than 2,000 different parts. It took a series of presses to stamp sheet metal into the final form; some of the dies weighed 30 tons. The largest presses were 450 tons and could exert 800 tons of pressure on the metal. To support the weight and pounding of these presses, their foundations were sunk 120 feet into the bedrock. *Walter P. Reuther Library, Wayne State University*

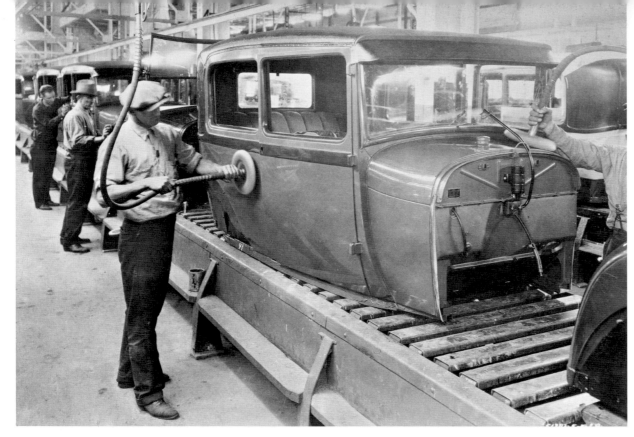

Henry's ego and fed the auto magnate's fears that his grandchildren would be kidnapped for ransom—a possibility that would prove not farfetched after the 1932 kidnapping and murder of aviator Charles Lindbergh's baby son. As the forces that shaped the company and the Rouge in the next decade coalesced behind the scenes, production on the Model A was off to a fitful start.

The public finally heard a few details of the new car on August 10, 1927, when Edsel Ford said it would be faster, smoother, and more rugged than the Model T. But it wasn't until October 20 that Henry Ford hand-stamped the serial numbers on the first Model A engine off the line at the Motor Building. By November 1, final changes were made to the tooling, and the vast plant began producing about 20 cars a day, a far cry from Highland Park's rate.

The company began advertising the car on December 1, with a price range of $385 to $570. Within a short time, 400,000 orders came in, but production of the all-new car at an entirely new location still crawled at a few hundred units per day. Not until February 1928 did each dealer have at least one sample car.

Above: The body of a Ford Model A Tudor Sedan is polished during its journey down the assembly line. *Ford Photomedia*

Right: Rouge workers head for the streetcars and the adjacent parking lot at the end of their shift in the late 1920s. Streetcar lines had been installed to shuttle war workers to the Eagle Boat plant in late 1918. They remained a popular way for workers to get to and from the Rouge until Detroit discontinued them in 1955. *Walter P. Reuther Library, Wayne State University*

Ford's delays initially hurt sales, but in 1929 and 1930, the Model A outsold all General Motors cars combined. About 3.25 million units were built in three years, but the car would soon be rendered obsolete as competitors brought out less expensive six-cylinder models.

Still, in 1928, Ford expanded the Rouge's role as a center of vertical integration by creating rubber plantations in Brazil. Ford's venture into rubber resulted from British restrictions on the production of crude rubber. The British said the limits were to protect planters from ruinously low prices, but costs jumped dramatically, impacting the tire industry. Harvey Firestone and Ford financed Thomas Edison's attempts to develop alternatives to rubber, while both looked for a location to grow their own rubber plants. While Firestone selected land in Liberia, Ford turned to Brazil.

The automaker bought 2.5 million acres along the Tapajos River, a tributary of the Amazon, and named the 3,906-square-mile plantation "Fordlandia" in 1928. The *Lake Ormoc*, one of Ford's Laker freighters, served as the headquarters ship for the venture and was refitted with a hospital, laboratory, machine shop, and refrigeration equipment. The

Above: A 5-ton charger pushes scrap metal through the middle of the five small doors to Open-Hearth Furnace No. 3 in the early 1930s. This is one of 10 furnaces at the Open-Hearth Building; each one had the capacity to make 180 tons of steel at a time. These furnaces consumed 5 million cubic feet of coke oven gas and 70,000 gallons of oil a day. *Walter P. Reuther Library, Wayne State University*

Left: Another piece of Henry Ford's vertical integration plan for the Rouge was this Brazilian rubber plantation. Between 1929 and 1934, about 8,300 acres of rubber tree seedlings were planted along the Tapajos River, south of the Amazon. These trees took 8 to 10 years to mature before they could begin producing rubber for Ford's Tire Plant, which opened at the Rouge in 1939. The venture, however, was a severe financial drain on the company and was sold before it came to fruition. *Walter P. Reuther Library, Wayne State University*

Visions of Steel and Blood

Artists, photographers, novelists, and others have tried to capture the immensity of the Rouge Plant and the full scope of the human and industrial endeavor played out there.

In 1927, the N. W. Ayer & Son advertising agency commissioned photographer and painter Charles Sheeler of Doylestown, Pennsylvania, to photograph the Rouge Plant, which then had the world's largest foundry. Over the course of six weeks, he carefully staged 32 shots, taking hours for each one. Only 12 of the negatives survive.

"The subject matter is incomparably the most thrilling I have had to work with," Sheeler wrote about working at the Rouge. One of his most famous prints, *Criss-Crossed Conveyors*, showing the coal conveyors near the Rouge Power House, originally appeared in the February 1928 issue of *Vanity Fair*. His photos emphasized the plant's massive machinery, which dwarfs any of the people who appear in his work.

Mexican painter Diego Rivera's interpretation of the Rouge was far different from Sheeler's. An avowed communist, Rivera's talent won him several commissions in the United States, including a project to paint two murals in the Detroit Institute of Art's neoclassical Garden Court.

Arriving in Detroit with his wife Frida Kahlo shortly after the bloody 1932 Hunger March, Rivera toured the city's factories, foundries, and chemical plants, sketching and taking photographs of the frenzied mechanical conditions in which man and machine worked. But the Rouge Plant captured his attention most. Rivera petitioned DIA curator Dr. William R. Valentiner for permission to paint all four walls of the courtyard, 27 panels in all.

Despite facing his own financial crisis in the dark days of the Depression, Edsel Ford, who was a DIA director and patron, was so impressed by Rivera's work that he agreed to fund the project to the tune of $25,000. With the DIA in dire financial straights, Valentiner had to take a yearlong leave of absence, and the museum laid off staff to help pay for Rivera's work.

Working from May 1932 to March 1933, Rivera's controversial and renowned frescos captured the stern faces of men who worked on the Rouge assembly lines. Larger than life, the men are still not in control of their environment. Entitled *Detroit Industry*, the frescos also feature other symbols that blend technology, people, the earth, war, and peace in a way that follows the vertical integration aspects of the Rouge.

Diego Rivera works on a portion of his famed murals at the Detroit Institute of Arts, while two women work on a clay bust of the painter. Rivera's frescoes, called *Detroit Industry*, captured much of the essence of the Rouge Plant during the middle of the Great Depression. Rivera was surprised that Edsel Ford was not a typical "exploiting capitalist" and included his image, along with drafting tools and a table, in a corner of the *Detroit Industry* frescoes. *The Henry Ford*

Above the assembly-line murals, large hands thrust from the ground, holding rocks to indicate the mineral wealth of the earth. Huge nudes represent different elements: the Asian male, the sand used in the factory; a black female, the coal; the red American Indian male, iron ore; and the white female, lime.

Rivera was surprised that Edsel was not an "exploiting capitalist" and included his image in a corner of the mural with drafting tools on a table in front of him. Also appearing is a small likeness of Henry Ford, lecturing apprentices on the V-8 engine, and a glowering Cast-Iron Charlie Sorensen. Rivera also incorporated double-edged meanings in the frescos, including a red star painted on a worker's glove and a hat of a worker with the words "We Want," which could stand for the anti-Prohibition slogan "We Want Beer" or a labor message.

When the Rivera frescos were unveiled, there were calls from some museum patrons to destroy them. The *Detroit News* said the walls should be whitewashed, but Edsel prevailed to save them.

Three years later, in 1936, comedian Charlie Chaplin, who had taken a tour of the Rouge in the 1920s and met Henry and Edsel Ford, satirized the plant in his silent film *Modern Times*. The motion picture shows humans' inability to keep up with the pace of machinery and includes a commentary on red-baiting.

The following year, novelist Upton Sinclair, known for his left-leaning social commentary, skewered Ford in his book *Flivver King: A Story of Ford-America*. Taking elements of fact and fiction, Sinclair wove a tale about a naïve Henry Ford's anti-Semitism, linking it to Nazism, the Ku Klux Klan, the Black Legion, and other hate groups.

White-hot slag from the "Henry" blast furnace pours into a slag pot waiting on the track siding in February 1931, while Ford steam locomotives work in the background. A byproduct of the iron-making process, slag is lighter than molten iron and contains a number of impurities, such as sulfur, that would make the finished steel brittle. Since it floats on top of the iron, it is skimmed off. The slag will be dumped into a pit to cool and will then be recovered to make cement. *Walter P. Reuther Library, Wayne State University*

Fordlandia project, however, collapsed by the mid-1930s, when the rubber plants, which required the shelter of jungles, succumbed to root and leaf blight in the open fields and forced a change of plans.

As the rubber plantation failed to take root, Ford officials moved from Highland Park into the Rouge's Kahn-designed four-story Administration Building, fully occupying it by January 26, 1928. Kahn said the building was made to last a thousand years. Its exterior featured several materials, notably marble, bronze, and brass, and it had a roof of Spanish tile, much like the Engineering Building. Above the bronze doors of the entryway, the company's name was etched into marble.

The main lobby, used as a gathering space for visitors on the factory tours until the Rotunda was built, had travertine (Italian) marble walls and dark furniture. Three bronze elevator doors were adorned with figures symbolizing the automobile, railroad, motorships, and the airplane.

The southern wing that housed the executive offices, including Henry and Edsel Ford's, was finished in walnut, while the other offices were finished in oak and had rubber tile floors. The cafeteria was on the fourth floor, along with recreation rooms for men and women employees, the kitchen, and executive and private dining rooms. In the basement was the photographic department, with Bennett's office nearby, and a stairway to the executive garage. Notably, the men's restrooms had signs with the admonition "Please Adjust Your Apparel Before Leaving," but there were no such signs in the women's facilities.

As the Rouge/Fordson plant grew, it left its mark on the surrounding region, drawing people from all over the world.

The village of Springwells changed its name to Fordson in 1925, while Dearborn absorbed Dearborn Township to form a city. Within two years, residents proposed the consolidation of Fordson and Dearborn, to fend off annexation by Detroit. At first Sorensen, the master of the Fordson Plant, opposed the idea, but Dearborn's Mayor Clyde Ford, a Ford dealer and a distant cousin of Henry's, supported it.

Henry finally endorsed the merger plan, and voters approved it. On January 14, 1929, the new city of Dearborn was created out of the two communities, with the rotund Clyde Ford as its first mayor. In 1920, the villages of Springwells and Dearborn had only a few thousand residents. In 1930, the new city of Dearborn boasted 50,000 citizens.

To the south and southeast of the Rouge Plant—it was renamed again in February 1929—Detroit's Downriver communities took form, and the cities of River Rouge and Lincoln Park were created. In 1932, the 4-square-mile city of Melvindale was incorporated, directly across the river from the factory complex. Melvindale was cut into four sections by the railroads feeding into the Rouge.

Nineteen twenty-nine was also notable because it marked the Golden Jubilee for Thomas Edison's invention of the light bulb, for which Henry Ford planned an enormous celebration at his new museum. Just upstream from the Rouge Plant, ground had been broken in 1928 for a museum to preserve the history of places and things Henry Ford gave "a tinker's damn about," including old wagons, locomotives, cars, kitchen appliances, watches, and tools. Originally called the Edison Institute and later the Henry Ford Museum & Greenfield Village, the museum has a reproduction of Independence Hall, while Greenfield Village features historic structures transported there from around the country, including Edison's Menlo Park Laboratory.

The dedication of the Edison Institute occurred October 21, 1929, with a reenactment of Edison's invention as power was turned on to the

museum, which had been illuminated by candles. Newsman Graham McNamee broadcast the event to the world, and President Herbert Hoover was even on hand for the spectacle. It would be the last joyous day for many—eight days later the stock market crashed, and some $30 billion vanished. The Great Depression was officially underway.

The Great Depression had a plethora of causes, and the crash was just one symptom of great economic problems around the world. In the United States, for example, consumers had built up $2.9 billion in debt—nearly half of which financed the record 5.6 million car and

After all-steel bodies replaced wood, Ford used these large "balloon" welding machines on the second floor of the "B" Building to join the right and left rear quarter panels to the back of the of the body in a shower of sparks. The man in the middle of the sparkling scene is wearing glasses and gloves but no other protective clothing. *Walter P. Reuther Library, Wayne State University*

The Rotunda Is Born

During the bleakest days of the Great Depression, one of the bright spots was the 1933–1934 Chicago World's Fair, dubbed "A Century of Progress" to mark the city's centennial. Ford Motor Company joined the celebration by constructing an elaborate exhibition building called the Rotunda along the shore of Lake Michigan.

Designed by Albert Kahn, the 212-foot-diameter building looked like a series of nested gears from above, while its steel skeleton was sheathed in a special waterproof papier-mâché. It also had a 110 x 80–foot museum wing and a much larger industrial exhibit hall. The central hall had an inner ring of steel and glass, with chromium-plated copper columns. A central courtyard was open to the sky and featured a 20-foot-diameter globe showing the locations of Ford plants around the world.

Industrial designer Walter Dorwin Teague created the interior exhibits, including the attendants' uniforms, the floor tiles, and the selection and arrangement of the 110 large photomurals of the Rouge Plant that lined its inner walls.

The Rotunda was such a success that Henry Ford decided to move it to Dearborn instead of scrapping it. By that time, tours of the Rouge Plant were very popular, but visitors crammed into the Administration Building to wait for buses. It was so bad that Henry Ford stopped going to his office at the building, preferring the Engineering Building on the site of the old Fordson tractor factory.

Fred Black, a Ford executive and former board member of the *Dearborn Independent*, inherited the task of moving the Rotunda. Sorensen, thinking the job was impossible, called it "Black's Folly," but Kahn knew the project was doable. The building's steel skeleton was taken down and reassembled across Schaefer Road from the Administration Building.

Pilings were sunk into the earth to support the weight of the Rotunda (it didn't have a foundation), and its original walls were replaced with white buff Indiana limestone. Forgoing the large exhibit hall, the relocated Rotunda had two small wings, one that housed a theater and the other a display of Bagley Avenue, with a total of 25,150 square feet of floor space. The total cost for rebuilding the Rotunda was $2.5 million, including $176,000 for landscaping.

Before the outbreak of World War II, more than 1 million people toured the Rouge Plant and the Rotunda, representing the 48 states and U.S. possessions plus 75 countries. The tours continued into early 1942 before the Rotunda was turned into office space for Ford and the army air force, which had set up a training center at the Rouge Plant by that time. The Rotunda remained closed to the public until June 1953, when it reopened for the automaker's fiftieth anniversary.

Henry Ford and son Edsel pose next to the globe in the circular atrium of the Ford Rotunda on May 11, 1936, during the opening ceremony in Dearborn. The globe is inscribed "Ford Industries Cover the World" and shows the location of the company's factories, mines, and other properties. *Walter P. Reuther Library, Wayne State University*

Blind workers are taught how to assemble engine valve-guide split bushings by feel. Despite having abandoned much of his earlier idealism, Henry Ford remained committed to offering employment to men and women with physical disabilities at the Rouge and his Village Industries factories. *Walter P. Reuther Library, Wayne State University*

truck sales that year. As the nation's economy slowed down and slumped by the summer, banks tightened down on credit, causing a snowballing effect of personal bankruptcies and foreclosures. Also, speculators had driven the stock market to an unsustainable level. It was only a matter of time before the bubble burst. Deflation reigned as wages and prices dropped.

Initially, Ford, several other industrialists, and the Hoover administration believed the Depression would be short-lived, like the "panics" and recessions of the 1890s, 1910, and 1920. Exacerbating matters, however, was a trade war that started when European countries raised tariffs on imports and America reciprocated.

In an attempt to help restore consumer confidence, Ford used two formerly tried-and-true tactics: he raised minimum wages to $7 a day and cut prices. They didn't work. Worse still, on the eve of the New York Auto Show in January, Ford advertised nationally in newspapers for 30,000 additional workers at his Detroit plants. As unemployment soared across the country, a virtual army of 20,000 to 30,000 jobless

men camped out at the Rouge in freezing conditions, waiting for jobs that were never offered. Their desperation turned to a riot that was quelled only when fire hoses were turned on them.

Ford's failure to provide the promised jobs drew the wrath of Father Charles E. Coughlin, who broadcast a national radio program from WJR in Detroit. Ford's actions were driving people into the arms of the Communist Party, warned Coughlin, testifying before the U.S. House of Representatives Committee to Investigate Communist Activities, chaired by Hamilton Fish. Coughlin, the pastor of the Shrine of the Little Flower Catholic Church in Detroit's suburb of Royal Oak, had portrayed himself as an expert on the growth of communism in the United States.

After 1930 drew to a close, Ford had recorded a $40 million profit as Model A sales continued to roar ahead. The company had even started a vast car assembly plant at Dagenham, England, based on the Rouge, and looked to expand to the Soviet Union. But then the economy slid further into the abyss. Some six million people were thrown out of

Above: Hundreds of unemployed men line up outside the employment office at the Rouge's Gate 2 on November 8, 1931, hoping to find work during the depths of the Great Depression. The company is in the midst of preparing the V-8 for production and had announced it would be hiring soon. While some may have found work at the Rouge, many did not. *Walter P. Reuther Library, Wayne State University*

Right: A Ford flathead V-8 engine is dropped onto a waiting chassis on the assembly line as Ford launches a new car to replace the Model A. It was the first time in decades Ford had offered an engine with more than four cylinders. Just visible are the transverse leaf spring running from one side of the car to the other (near the front and below the chassis) and the mechanical braking system. *Walter P. Reuther Library, Wayne State University*

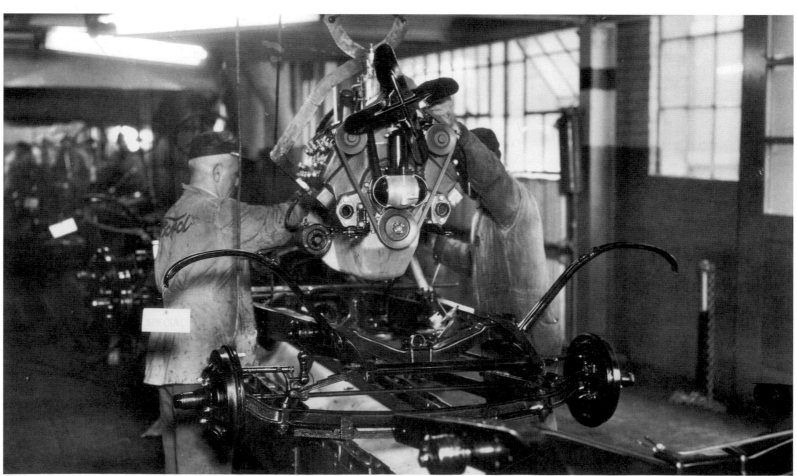

Above: A "shakeout man" removes the remains of the sand used to make the glowing-hot engine core mold, revealing the cast-iron V-8 cylinder block hidden inside. The engine block rests on vibrating steel platform with a grate. The sand falling through the grate will be recovered and used to make another mold. *The Henry Ford*

Right: Workers in the Rouge's iron foundry pour molten metal into a ladle. At this time, Ford employed half of all African-Americans who worked in the car industry. While many worked on the assembly line and other departments, a great many were employed in the company's hot, dangerous foundries. *The Henry Ford*

work as thousands of businesses and banks failed and factories shut down. Car sales became a mere shell of their 1929 level.

In this dim sales environment, Chevrolet and Plymouth released successful new six-cylinder cars that lured away Model A customers. Walter Chrysler was so pleased with the new Plymouth that he met Henry and Edsel Ford in June at Ford's Engineering Laboratory and gave them a demonstration ride. As a parting gift, Chrysler left them the car.

GM held 43 percent of the car market, while Ford sales plunged to 28 percent, or 619,757 units, and the company lost $37 million. Unable to stop the collapse, Ford cut its payroll. Skilled tradesmen like Reuther saw their hourly rate dip to 75 cents an hour ($6 per day) while the minimum wage dropped to $4 a day by 1932 and some 50,000 men were laid off.

Soup kitchens and bread lines became common sights in Detroit and other cities. Ford, perhaps remembering the economic panic in the

RIVER ROUGE

Members of Detroit's Unemployed Councils rally the Hunger Marchers on a frigid March 7, 1932, morning in southwest Detroit, before leading the throng of some 3,000 into Dearborn for a demonstration against Ford Motor Company. *Walter P. Reuther Library, Wayne State University*

Shortly after crossing the Fort Street Bridge and moving up Miller Road next to the Rouge Plant, Hunger Marchers clash with police officers firing tear gas into the crowd. Fierce winds dispersed most of the gas, and the demonstrators threw the canisters back at police, along with whatever else was lying around. The marchers had attacked Harry Bennett, head of the Ford Service Department, when he tried to confront the leaders. Police responded with gunfire, killing four marchers and wounding 50 to 60 others. *Walter P. Reuther Library, Wayne State University*

This is the break-in room of the Motor Assembly Building in 1934, where each assembled engine and transmission was tested for defects and initial lubrication. The engine is hooked up to oil and water lines, and an electric motor powers the engine's components until mechanical friction has been reduced. *Walter P. Reuther Library, Wayne State University*

1890s, allowed out-of-work people to tend garden plots on his farms in Dearborn. He also saved his hometown from disaster by providing funds to keep local banks solvent. When Inkster, a predominantly black city west of Dearborn, fell behind on its payments and the power was shut off, Henry also stepped in to help, but he deducted the cost of restoring the electricity from the wages of his workers from Inkster.

In August 1931, Ford halted production of the Model A, and again the company went into crisis mode to develop a replacement. In fact,

the company briefly offered two models: a more advanced version of the Model A, renamed the Model B, and a car equipped with a V-8 engine, aptly named the Ford V-8. Henry's rationale for creating a low-priced car with an eight-cylinder engine was to give the public more of what it wanted: horsepower.

The V-8's engine produced 65 horsepower. It had larger tires, hubcaps to conceal the lug nuts, 14 body styles, softer seats, and (in response to Plymouth) more rubber mountings to cut down on vibration. Outside, the car had a distinctive V-shaped grille. The major technological challenge Ford gave his engineers was to produce the engine block as a single casting, to reduce parts and costs. This required new tools, machines, and methods, but despite the doubts of Sorensen and others, the design became a reality. The Rouge's Dearborn Iron Foundry was the first in the industry to mass-produce single-cast V-8 blocks in early 1932. The first V-8s came off the line in "B" Building in late February and were priced from $460 to $650. The company also announced it would begin rehiring workers soon.

Ten days after the V-8's triumphal launch, any celebratory mood at the Rouge ended with the bloody "Hunger March" of March 7 and the subsequent clampdown by Bennett's Service Department.

The Hunger March was one of several protests by the jobless in cities across the United States to demand relief from the hardships of the Depression. The protest against Ford was organized by Detroit's Unemployed Councils, which operated soup kitchens in the city. The councils were heavily influenced by communists, socialists, and other radicals who turned their attention toward Henry Ford and his mostly idled Rouge works as symbols of the failing capitalist system. The stated purpose of the march was to present the carmaker with a list of their demands.

The march began peaceably on a frigid winter day, as some 3,000 to 5,000 crowded into streetcars and rode to the edge of Dearborn. Some refused to pay the fare, telling the conductors to charge Ford. When the marchers reached Dearborn city limits, they were met by 40 policemen, who told them to turn around because they didn't have a parade permit.

The leaders of the march, however, urged their followers on, crossing the Fort Street Bridge and proceeding up Miller Road. The situation devolved into a melée when police fired tear gas into the crowd and the wind blew the gas back at the officers. The marchers responded by throwing stones, bricks, and coal from nearby piles. Responding to a police call for assistance, Dearborn firemen arrived on the scene and were attacked by the mob. Despite the freezing temperatures, the firemen turned their hoses on the marchers, while Dearborn officers called Detroit police for backup.

Bennett later recounted that he was reviewing films at the Administration Building on Schaefer Road—Henry and Edsel were away at lunch—when he heard of the riot. He drove out to Miller Road, carrying a white flag, to tell the marchers that the automaker would begin rehiring people soon. When he identified himself to those at the front of the mob, they immediately began pelting him with slag.

The ex-boxer responded by grabbing nearby 19-year-old Joe York, who was a member of the Young Communist League, as a human shield, but Bennett fell and was knocked unconscious with a fractured skull. Dearborn Police at Gate 3 and Detroit officers on the pedestrian

Next page: Two workers take a lunch break near Open-Hearth Furnace No. 3, probably the only time they had to sit down during the workday. *Walter P. Reuther Library, Wayne State University*

overpass fired into the crowd, killing four men, including York, and wounding about 50 to 60 more. Many of the wounded were initially treated at the Rouge's hospital, though one wounded demonstrator later died of his injuries.

Inside the plant, word of the battle outside quickly spread. Walter Reuther recounted that other workers on his shift asked him to give the signal for "revolution," but he didn't want to join the violence.

Several hundred technicians from the Soviet Union were also being trained at the Rouge at the time of the Hunger March as part of the automaker's effort to expand into that country. "It must have puzzled those Soviet technicians to observe, from the windows of that citadel of capitalism, the American proletariat throwing stones and epithets at Henry Ford, the hero of the technologically starved Russian people," Victor Reuther later observed.

In the aftermath, police raided the Detroit Communist Party headquarters, homes, and ethnic halls, arresting 60 suspected agitators but finding no weapons. No charges were brought against the marchers or the policemen. However, a Wayne County grand jury ruled that the conduct of the marchers was reckless and that the police showed poor judgment. The Unemployed Councils lost members due to the stain of being associated with communists.

Ford Motor Company was criticized from all sides for the bloodshed, and Henry Ford lost much of his reputation as a "friend of the working man." Five days after the march, an estimated 15,000 people (some placed the number at 60,000) turned out for the funeral of one of the marchers in Detroit. One Ford employee was fired after a company spy reported that he was collecting money to help pay for the funerals.

In an effort to silence radicals and the unionists, Ford workers were forbidden to speak to one another before work and during their lunch breaks about the labor movement. Security was tightened at the Rouge as guards searched toolboxes and lunch pails. Undeterred, Walter Reuther modified the rumble seat of his Model A into a small platform from which he spoke about unionism. Once, while he was parked in a vacant lot, Dearborn police arrived to arrest him for not having a public speaking permit. Reuther pulled out the deed to the land.

Reuther continued to work at the Rouge until Franklin D. Roosevelt defeated Hoover in the 1932 presidential election, at which time Reuther was pink-slipped. Walter and Victor Reuther pooled their money and took a trip to the Soviet Union, where they became foreign workers at Ford's Albert Kahn–designed Gorky plant, southwest of Moscow and at the "gateway to Siberia." The two brothers didn't return to the United States until mid-October 1935, by which time other changes were afoot with Ford and the Rouge.

Chapter Four

Battling for the Soul, 1933-1941

"To no one is given
Right of delay
Noted in heaven
Passeth each day
Be not thou fruitless
Work while you may
Trifling were bootless
Watch thou and pray."

—A saying on the window of Fair Lane's entrance hall

The story of the Rouge through the Great Depression is less about vertical integration and cars than about Ford's clashes with the Roosevelt administration and the United Auto Workers union.

The composite of old English sayings in the center of Fair Lane's 15 x 18–foot entrance hall window probably best describes Ford's view of labor unions, noted Donn Werling, retired director of the Henry Ford Estate–Fair Lane. To Henry, no one but God had the right to stop the sun and to delay time—in other words, to strike.

Henry Ford retained the luster of being the "friend of the working man" even after the 1932 Hunger March. The company was far more liberal in the treatment of its employees than most large employers. Furthermore, in 1920, Ford started an investment fund that guaranteed workers a 6 percent interest rate. There were "safety drives" to reduce accidents, and the National Safety Council recognized the company as the best in the country. Also, Henry was obsessed with cleanliness. The Rouge had 5,000 workers dedicated to scrubbing, painting—even disinfecting coat racks. Water fountains abounded, and lunch wagons, operated by outside vendors, offered a variety of food.

"The floors of factory are actually clean enough to eat off of, although none ever does," *Life* magazine reported in 1940, while noting the workers' harried pace. "The men eat lunch in some cranny near the spot they work. Few leave the plant for lunch, because the nearest entrance is too far away."

The company was also concerned for the health of its workers. The September 1935 issue of the *Ford News* said, "For first time in the history of automobile manufacturing, temperature regulation and air-conditioning are being installed in machine shops and foundries at the Rouge Plant. . . . The purpose is threefold . . . to control the accuracy of fine machining operations, such as cylinder lapping; to increase the comfort of workmen; and to protect the processes from dust and dirt." The foundry also had an air-washing apparatus that collected 42 cubic yards of dirt a week, roughly 42 tons.

Despite Ford's efforts, the Rouge was no paradise. The foundries were the most dangerous and dirty areas of the plant, and the conditions there took a toll on the men, many of whom were black. It was said that Ford foundry workers were easy to spot, because they were the dirtiest and most exhausted ones on the streetcars.

The Dearborn Iron Foundry "was very hot and nasty and dusty," said Albert Stevenson, the UAW Local 600 Retirees first vice president, when interviewed in 2003. "The soot would get into your clothes. You had to throw them away afterward, so they issued you new coveralls. Ninety-nine percent of the workers in the foundry were black," added Stevenson, who actually worked at the plant after World War II. "It was the roughest job at the Rouge, and the plant foremen treated you like dogs. When they brought in the food wagons, you had to eat dirt along with your food."

With a moment's inattention, an assembly line worker could get maimed by the parts flowing past on the conveyors or dragged into a running machine and killed. The speed of the assembly lines was often cranked higher. For instance open-hearth workers were sometimes urged to scrap 225 used cars a day, up from their quota of 130. Many workers in the 1930s reported suffering from the "shakes" and nervousness, a syndrome nicknamed "Forditis."

Yet Rouge workers were proud of being at Ford—so much so that they wore their metal ID badges on their Sunday suits, recalled Joe Toth, second vice president of the UAW Local 600 Retirees. Toth grew up in Delray, a Hungarian and Polish neighborhood in Detroit about 2 miles from the Rouge.

Given the conditions at the Rouge, one would think that Ford workers would readily join unions en masse. However, before the Great Depression, few of the well-paid autoworkers gave labor a second thought. Labor leaders such as Samuel Gompers, the long-time president of the American Federation of Labor, even said Henry Ford's reforms were good for labor and management. As the nation's largest

Technology and production march on despite labor unrest. What appears to be the body of a 1937 or 1938 Ford V-8 is in the "B" Building's infrared drying oven. The lamps generated temperatures in the range of 300 to 325 degrees Fahrenheit, drying the soybean-based paint from the inside out in a few minutes. The man may be inspecting the quality of the paint finish. The car body appears to be on a sled. *Lindsay Brooke Archives*

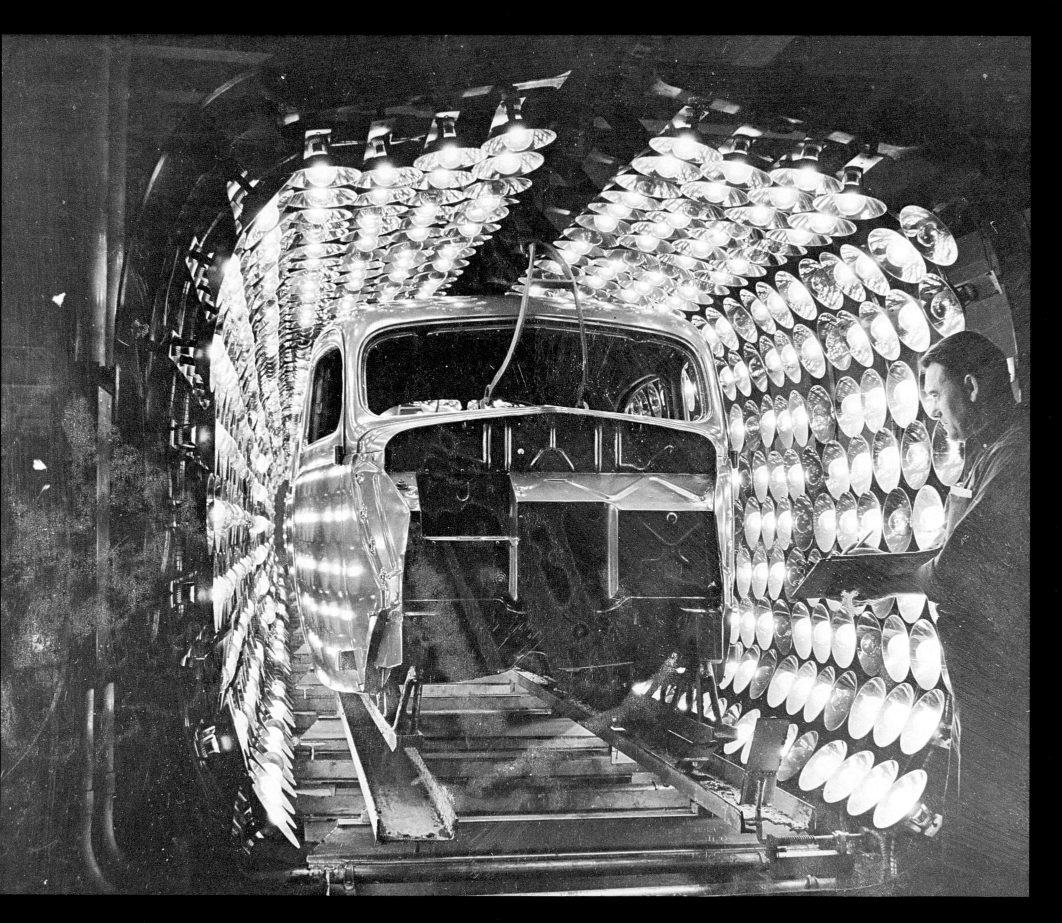

Two employees operate the Snyder crankshaft oil-hole-drilling machine, which was able to drill the entire oil system in one continuous operation.
Dearborn Historical Museum

labor organization, the AFL was a conglomeration of 100 "craft unions" that represented elite skilled tradesmen and made little effort to recruit autoworkers. Each affiliated union had its own officers, rules, and locals, but they banded together for greater strength.

The AFL had a few oddball affiliates called "industrial unions," including the United Mine Workers under John L. Lewis, which accepted all skilled and unskilled workers in an industry as members. But for the most part the AFL didn't tolerate industrial unions, and it expelled one of its few car-industry affiliates, the Carriage, Wagon and Automobile Workers Union, in 1918 for ignoring craft distinctions.

The CWAWU collapsed by 1921, after losing a number of mini-strikes. The AFL itself shrank from 4 million members in 1920 to 2.12 million by 1933.

The International Workers of the World still existed in the 1930s but had fallen into disrepute for its alleged connections to the "Reds" after the communist takeover of Russia. The American Socialist and Communist parties and a few independent unions tried, with little success, to make inroads into the car industry.

Labor saw a glimmer of hope with President Franklin Roosevelt's New Deal reforms that moved America from laissez faire to a planned

This food stand under the Gate 4 overpass was one of several lunch wagons scattered around the Rouge during lunchtime. Workers had only 20 minutes to leave their workstations, buy food, eat, and return to their jobs. Purportedly, Harry Bennett allowed known mobsters to operate the Rouge's food service. *Dearborn Historical Museum*

economy. Section 7(a) of the National Industrial Recovery Act (NIRA), which FDR signed on June 6, 1933, recognized the rights of unions to organize workers and engage in collective bargaining. The auto companies, though, easily circumvented the provision, creating "company unions" that officially represented the workers but did management's bidding. The NIRA also allowed industries to create production codes and quotas and to set wages and prices.

Most automakers accepted the New Deal as a way to survive, but Henry Ford refused to sign the codes created by the National Automotive Chamber of Commerce (NACC), the successor to the

Association of Licensed Automobile Manufacturers (ALAM). Henry distrusted NIRA, the NACC, and Section 7(a) but decided his company would observe or exceed the codes. Ford's intransigence led to a bitter feud with Hugh S. Johnson, the retired Army brigadier general who ran the National Recovery Administration. If Ford would not sign the codes, then the automaker would not be eligible for government business, which was fine with Henry.

Nineteen-thirty-two marked the bottom of the Depression for Ford Motor Company. In spite of the new V-8, sales sank to 262,106 cars, and only 30,000 employees were working at the Rouge. Less than

Growing Pains in Hard Times

Even as the company's sales fell behind those of Chevrolet and Chrysler, Henry Ford spent millions of dollars renovating the Rouge Plant. He also poured money into related ventures, including the rubber plantation, soybean research, and schools.

One expansion project was a 2.2-mile-long, 15-foot-diameter tunnel to bring water from the Detroit River to the Rouge. The $2.5 million tunnel, started in 1929 and completed in 1931, could draw a maximum of 930 million gallons of water a day to supply Powerhouse No. 1's steam turbogenerators and to cool the steel mills.

As the tunnel was completed, the powerhouse received a $5.5 million upgrade, with the addition of three 30,000-kilowatt turbogenerators to provide alternating current. Prior to this, the power plant generated only direct current. The building was also expanded to include eight smokestacks, even though it had only seven boilers. Henry Ford knew that one day a boiler would have to be replaced, and he wanted to add the space beforehand.

While still in the doldrums of the Depression, Ford announced a major expansion of the Rouge in November 1934. The following year, the Glass Plant was enlarged, a new cold-sheet finishing mill was added, the powerhouse received three 110,000-kilowatt General Electric generators, and the Hot Strip Mill was completed, the first of its kind in the United States. When it was decommissioned in the 1970s, the mill was one of the oldest still running.

Down in Brazil, undeterred by the failure of Fordlandia, Ford traded 703,750 acres of the plantation for land at the mouth of the Tapajos River in 1934 and planted native rubber tree stock, bud-grafted to Malayan rubber plants. As the rubber plants matured, Ford broke ground on the 250,000-square-foot, Albert Kahn-designed Tire Plant in 1937. Firestone personnel helped create the $7 million factory to have the most advanced equipment of the day. It opened in 1939, with the capacity to make 16,000 tires a day, and employed 2,000 workers.

Other developments at the Rouge included installing more efficient coke ovens in 1937 that reused blast furnace gas for fuel. A 2.5-million-cubic-foot gas tower, 269 feet high and 128 feet in

The Soy Bean Plant on April 14, 1941, about two years after its completion. Built south of Powerhouse No. 1, it had large windows, so people going by could see its inner workings. Ford extracted soybean oil to create paints, brake fluid, and lubricants, while the crushed and flaked beans became ingredients in a variety of plastic parts. Henry Ford even had a trunk lid made out of soy-based plastic. In the inset photo, he attempts to demonstrate its strength. *Walter P. Reuther Library, Wayne State University and Ford Photomedia*

diameter, was built near the entrance of the boat slip, to supply the coke ovens. In addition, the open-hearth furnaces were modified to reuse coke oven gas, so a huge, 10-million-cubic-foot gas holder, 390 feet high and 219 feet in diameter, was constructed on the opposite side of the slip. A service tunnel dug under the boat slip held conduits for coke gas, water, steam, oil, tar, and electricity for the huge storage tower,.

A box factory opened at the Rouge in 1938. Employing 300 men, the facility made 7,000 boxes a day and used 3 million board feet of lumber a month. A huge new Dearborn Tool and Die Plant opened the following year. Measuring 300 x 1,225 feet, it sat on 8.4 acres and contained $3 million worth of equipment.

As new buildings were erected, the company added lunchrooms with tables and chairs, and by 1940 there were cafeterias for the workers, who had only 20 to 30 minutes to eat their meals.

Another expansion of the Rouge resulted from Henry's fascination with turning soybeans into a cash crop. A wood-framed soybean processing facility was built next to the Glass Plant in late 1935. The soybeans were grown on the Ford Farms' 8,000 acres, and the plant processed them for oil to make paint, shock-absorber fluid, and foundry core oil. Soybean meal was used to create small plastic parts, such as molded horn buttons.

Four years later, a larger, showcase soybean factory was built south of the powerhouse, next to Miller Road. It had large windows, through which passersby could see its crisscrossing white pipes, and it made even more soybean-based products, such as brake fluid and additional plastic parts. When Ford started using its soy-based enamels, it installed infrared lights to bake the wet paint at 300 to 325 degrees Fahrenheit, cutting the drying time to minutes instead of hours.

The company even experimented by making a trunk lid out of soybean plastic, but when Henry swung at the lid with an ax to demonstrate its strength, he cleaved it in two. Ford's soybean experiments, however, led to the creation of the first commercially acceptable soymilk, which was used to make Presto Whip, an all-vegetable whipping cream.

The Rouge also housed the Henry Ford Trade School, on the third and fourth floors of "B" Building, from 1930 until it was discontinued in 1952. Founded in 1916 at Highland Park with only six pupils, the school was for boys 12 to 16 years old. The school taught critical skills needed to be competent factory employees, such as running lathes and grinders. The curriculum also included courses in mathematics, chemistry, economics, metallurgy, physics, and drafting.

The school received thousands of applicants each year (each boy had to apply in person), but only 700 to 1,000 boys were enrolled at any one time in the three-year program. Each student started with a $7.20 scholarship (stipend) per week, which was increased depending upon his ability and progress. After graduating, the young man often became an apprentice at Ford but could go on to a different company.

Some 9,000 boys graduated from the trade school, but eventually it closed, primarily because many of its graduates weren't staying to work at the car company. Its assets were donated to Fordson Junior College, which became Dearborn's Henry Ford Community College.

Another related education program at the Rouge was Camp Legion, which Henry Ford established in 1938 in a grove on his estate, Fair Lane. Camp Legion was for boys ages 17 to 19 who were sons of disabled World War I veterans. The teens lived in army squad tents, were paid $2 a day, plus room and board, and shared profits from raising and selling farm produce. During the winter, the boys could enroll at the Henry Ford Trade School or work at the Rouge Plant.

Henry Ford examines the work of Ralph Lill on January 17, 1939, at the Henry Ford Trade School, which had classrooms on the third and fourth floors of "B" Building. Lill was the 2,500th boy to enroll in the school, where teachers instructed him on the "useful skills" needed for factory work. *Walter P. Reuther Library, Wayne State University*

It's the harvest season, October 5, 1938, as two young men, one driving a Fordson tractor, work the field at the Camp Legion located near the Edison Institute in Dearborn. The farms in Dearborn and at Willow Run Creek near Ypsilanti gave unemployed youths, many of them the sons of disabled or dead World War I veterans, an opportunity to learn how to farm and make money selling their produce. *Walter P. Reuther Library, Wayne State University*

one-third of the company's 35 other assembly plants were active. The company spread the work around, sometimes having one employee work three days and another worker the remaining two days of the workweek.

While the economy and Ford's sales improved slightly in 1933, Chrysler shot past to become the number-two automaker. The Roosevelt administration declared a "bank holiday," and many teetering financial institutions, such as Detroit's Guardian Bank Group, in which Edsel Ford was heavily invested, were either greatly restructured or closed their doors. More than 11 million people remained out of work, and many a desperate applicant turned up at the Rouge's employment office at Gate 2.

As the economy improved in the mid-1930s, wages remained low, and foremen called for more production. Autoworkers looked to unions for a solution, but strikes by skilled tradesmen were ineffective. Many jobs had been so simplified by mass production that unskilled workers were used to replace the elite "craftsmen."

As smaller unions made inroads into the auto industry, the stodgy AFL was prompted to charter the United Automobile Workers and chose the union's first leaders in August 1935. The UAW was established as an industrial union, but once it became successful, the AFL wanted to break it up into traditional craft unions. Events soon altered the AFL's plans.

John L. Lewis and a number of dissatisfied labor leaders created the Committee for Industrial Organization (CIO) in November 1935, believing it was time for more severe action. Socialists, communists, and other militants rallied around the CIO banner. Nearly a year later, the AFL expelled the CIO, which became a rival national union, changing its name to the Congress of Industrial Organizations.

The UAW, which had merged with a several small, militant autoworker unions, also joined the CIO. Its members elected as their president the young, bespectacled Homer Martin, an autoworker and the former pastor of the Baptist Church in Leeds, Missouri, until his congregation dismissed him for his labor sympathies. Walter Reuther, back from Russia and newly married, was elected to the union's executive board.

Rejuvenated, the UAW was ready to take on the auto industry. Ford and other automakers, however, were employing spies to keep track of "Bolshevik" tendencies. (The use of spies dated to World War I, when the federal government hired detectives to uncover potential saboteurs. After the war, Ford and the other companies kept the system alive.) Since the 1932 Hunger March, Harry Bennett had strengthened the Service Department, whose personnel were also called "star men" because of the stars on their badges. Bennett also created an organization called the Knights of Dearborn, headed by ex-boxer and Ford foreman Sam Taylor, to keep track of things outside the plant.

Henry Ford gave Bennett wide latitude not only to keep unionists out of his plants but to protect his grandchildren. Bennett reveled in the role, developing relationships with numerous gangsters, including Joe Tocco, a rumrunner in Detroit's Downriver communities who was gunned down near his Wyandotte home; Hamtramck mob boss Chester LaMare, who was rubbed out in 1931; and the so-called Purple Gang, which collaborated with Al Capone and Lucky Luciano before most of its members were killed or arrested. Bennett purportedly gave LaMare and others lucrative concessionaire's licenses inside the Rouge.

Bennett simultaneously cooperated with the Federal Bureau of Investigation, ingratiating himself with J. Edgar Hoover by the late 1930s. John Bugas, head of the FBI's Detroit office, said that Bennett was a valuable source of information, especially on union troublemakers. Orville Hubbard, Dearborn's mayor from 1941 to 1977, later noted in interviews with *Detroit News* editor David L. Good that Ford's "little man" also had contacts in Michigan's capital, Lansing, and beyond.

In his basement office in the Administration Building, Bennett had an electronic board that flashed alerts from his operatives in the Rouge. Access to the executive garage also allowed him to secretly meet with any number of individuals.

The inevitable clash between Ford and the UAW started after the U.S. Supreme Court declared NIRA unconstitutional in May 1935, and Congress responded by passing the Wagner Labor Relations Act, making union-management collective bargaining mandatory. Businesses

Robert Kantor, Richard Frankensteen, and Walter Reuther *(from left)* commiserate after the May 26, 1937, "Battle of the Overpass." The hefty Frankensteen was better known and received a harsher beating, though J. J. Kennedy *(not pictured)* died four months later due to complications from his injuries. *Walter P. Reuther Library, Wayne State University*

immediately challenged the new law, but it took the Supreme Court a year to hear their case.

As the economy perked up in 1936, UAW strikes forced Midland Steel and the Kelsey-Hayes Wheel Company, both Ford suppliers, to sign union contracts. In both cases, instead of walking out and picketing, workers used the older tactic of sitting down at their machines and occupying the factories, making it difficult for the companies to bring in strikebreakers or for police to pull the strikers out.

Next came the famed sit-down strike against General Motors in Flint, which began December 30 and ended February 11, 1937, when GM became the first of the Big Three to sign a union contract. Sit-down strikes spread like wildfire in Detroit, and Chrysler, Hudson, and Studebaker capitulated to the UAW. Many of these strikes were the result of individual workers taking action and the union stepping in to orchestrate the outcomes.

In April, after the Supreme Court ruled the Wagner Act constitutional, Henry Ford called his son and Sorensen into his office. "I've picked someone to talk to the unions," said Henry. "I want a strong, aggressive man who can take care of himself in an argument, and I've got him. He has my full confidence and I want to be sure that you, Edsel, and you, Charlie, will support him." The man was none other than Harry Bennett.

Ford gave Bennett sweeping authority to hire, fire, and transfer nearly anyone on the payroll. Bennett also assumed the power to approve or deny expense accounts. Managers had to curry his favor or face dismissal or other humiliations. Bennett swelled the ranks of the Service Department to 800 "star men." An estimated 8,000 to 9,000 of the Rouge's 90,000 workers were paid stool pigeons.

On the heels of its victories over General Motors and Chrysler, the UAW set its sights on Ford. In January 1937, a strike at the Briggs Body Shop inside Ford's Highland Park complex threatened to shut down the automaker. Although the work stoppage was settled in a few days, Henry Ford ordered Sorensen to pull the car bodywork out of Briggs as soon as possible, leading to a major expansion of the Rouge's pressed-steel operations. About 10,000 people worked in the new Press Shop, which was built next to the sheet metal mills. The factory would have 4,000 presses making more than 2,000 different parts a day.

Some of the UAW's initial attempts to reach out to Ford workers were almost comical. For example, Walter Reuther and his brother Victor hired an airplane, which they modified with external speakers, and buzzed the Rouge, shouting out union slogans. But their messages were drowned out by the aircraft's noise and the wind. A more effective tactic was having organizers join the Rouge public tours and then flash buttons and hats to the workers that said: "Get Wise, Organize."

The next clash between the union and Ford was the so-called "Battle of the Overpass" at the gates of the Rouge Plant. The UAW asked for and received permission from the Dearborn city council to distribute leaflets outside the Rouge, despite a warning from Taylor of the Knights of Dearborn that this would cause trouble. On May 26, 1937, a group of 60 union organizers—many of them women, because the UAW thought that Ford wouldn't "rough up" the ladies—set off on streetcars to cover the Miller and Schaefer Road entrances to the vast complex. Detroit's newspapers sent reporters and photographers to record the event; they were not disappointed.

Ford servicemen harassed members of the UAW Women's Auxiliary near the Gate 4 overpass at the same time the union officers were beaten. *Walter P. Reuther Library, Wayne State University*

The Pressed-Steel Building at the Rouge was expanded in 1937, so the Rouge could start stamping its own car bodies instead of relying on outside suppliers. Pictured here are three rows of the more than 4,000 stamping presses in operation at the two-story factory. *Ford Photomedia*

When the UAW women gathered on the Schaefer side of the Rouge, Ford servicemen set upon them, forcing them back into the streetcars and beating several of the men. Dearborn police arrested several union members en route to the plant.

On the Miller Road side, Reuther joined Robert Kantor, Richard Frankensteen, and J. J. Kennedy as they climbed the Gate 4 pedestrian bridge to observe the leafleting campaign. Moments after posing for news photographers, Taylor and 34 servicemen approached Reuther's group, and one yelled, "You're on Ford property. Get the hell off here!"

The union men headed to the stairs, but more servicemen stopped them. The thugs attacked. Reuther reported being kicked, punched, and picked up and thrown down several times before being tossed down the stairs and pushed and slugged for about a block.

Frankensteen, who had greater notoriety, received a worse beating, but one union man, Richard Merriweather, received a broken back. Kennedy was hospitalized and died four months later, due to complications from his injuries. Nearby Dearborn police officers stood pat during the assault. Servicemen even attacked the photographers, trying

The Ford V-8 underwent various cosmetic changes in 1937. Because the two-piece windshield could no longer be opened for ventilation, for example, the wipers were relocated just below it, on the cowl. *Ford Photomedia*

Workers prepare the 60-horsepower V-8s for testing at the Motor Building as the engines are pulled down the line.
Lindsay Brooke Archives

unsuccessfully to destroy their film. Stories condemning Ford ran in papers nationwide. Bennett countered that the company had not been involved in the attack—that it was Ford workers who had taken offense at the union's activities. The National Labor Relations Board (NLRB) investigated the incident, but Ford stonewalled the government for several years.

The August following the Battle of the Overpass, Reuther returned to Gate 4 with hundreds of UAW toughs to pass out literature. This time, the servicemen and Dearborn police watched without interfering.

Despite the public show of unity outside the Rouge, UAW leaders were quarreling. At the union's convention that year, Reuther called Martin the "pimp of the madams of industry," setting off a fistfight.

With the union torn, the industry saw its second best sales year, producing 4,975,000 cars and trucks in the United States and Canada,

second to 1929's all-time high of 5,621,715 units. Car prices and profits, however, were much lower than in 1929. Still, Ford hired more men, including Joe Toth, as the Rouge expansion gained steam. Except for a stint as an army medic during World War II, Toth remained employed at the Rouge for 43 years. He became involved with the union after secretly meeting organizers under the blast furnaces.

Toth had another interesting encounter early one morning when he felt a tap on his back. Without turning around, he told his visitor that he was too busy to talk. Finally, he turned around to see Henry Ford standing there. "He used to wander around the Rouge plants every day," Toth recalled. "He saw that I was busy and didn't talk to me."

Ford offered an improved version of the V-8 in 1937, with a choice of 60- or 85-horsepower engines, 22 to 27 miles per gallon, and a top speed of 75 miles per hour. The car also had better steering and numerous minor improvements but still lacked hydraulic brakes and used the obsolete transverse leaf springs. At the end of 1937, Henry turned his attention back to tractors, striking a deal with Harry Ferguson of Ireland. In June 1939, the first Ford-Ferguson tractors rolled off an assembly line at "B" Building. By year's end, 10,233 had been built.

However, dark clouds were on the horizon as 1938 started. Excessive inventories of unsold cars built up, forcing automakers to cut production by 20 percent and prompting massive layoffs. By the end of January, some 200,000 autoworkers were on shortened hours, and more than 300,000 were laid off, many of them union members. Enrollment in the UAW fell off. With Martin's union presidency teetering, he tried to discredit rivals by calling them "communists."

Then, bizarrely, Martin allied himself with Jay Lovestone, the former secretary of the American Communist Party, who had started an anti-Stalinist communist party. Initially, Frankensteen supported the embattled labor president, while Reuther aligned with a coalition of leftist groups called the Unity Caucus. By spring, Reuther was talking to the New Deal Democrats when the Unity Caucus wooed Frankensteen to its side. The communists in the caucus also earned Walter's enmity by withdrawing their support for Victor Reuther's bid to become secretary-treasurer.

With the UAW weakening, Ford resisted the Wagner Act's dictates by creating company unions with the help of the radio priest Father Coughlin. Coughlin had criticized Ford in 1930, but the two became friends, despite Henry's membership in the Freemasons. Coughlin said he often kept in contact with Ford, using parishioner Louis Ward, founder of the trade journal *Ward's Automotive Reports*, as a go-between.

Irish by descent and Canadian by birth, Coughlin had been picked by Detroit Catholic Bishop Thomas Gallagher to create a parish in the Ku Klux Klan stronghold of Royal Oak, along Woodward Avenue just north of Eight Mile Road. Despite once having a cross burned on the lawn of his church, Coughlin made peace with the Klan, perhaps portending his fascination with fascist organizations as bulwarks against godless communists.

To support the financial needs of his tiny congregation, Coughlin turned to radio to reach a larger audience. He started by giving children's sermons on Detroit's WJR. By the time of the Depression, the priest's program, then called the *Hour of Power*, had grown in national popularity as he expressed concerns for "social justice" and living wages for workers' "sacred commodity": their labor. Coughlin had supported Roosevelt but grew disenchanted with the New Deal and launched a failed third political party.

Coughlin had even helped form the Automotive Industrial Workers Association, which joined the UAW, and Frankensteen had been one of his protégés. By the late 1930s, however, the vitriolic radio priest turned toward fascism as a way to remain influential, even

From his studio at the Shrine of the Little Flower Catholic Church in Royal Oak, Michigan, Father Charles E. Coughlin delivers one of his famed discourses on events of the day, broadcast on Detroit's WJR radio station. Coughlin was a controversial demagogue who defied other church officials until they were able to silence his broadcasts in the late 1930s. The NUSJ—the third-party movement Coughlin started—backed Louis Ward's unsuccessful run for Michigan's U.S. Senate seat in the 1936 election. Ward was the founder of *Ward's Automotive Reports* and a go-between for Coughlin and Henry Ford. *Walter P. Reuther Library, Wayne State University*

The unlikely pair of UAW President Homer Martin *(left)* and Ford personnel director Harry Bennett is pictured during a meeting in October 1938. While committed to labor's cause, Martin was perceived by many UAW members to be a weak and ineffectual leader and came under political attack by rivals within the union. Without the knowledge of most of the UAW's leadership, he started secret negotiations with Bennett. Instead of strengthening his position, talks with Ford's much-loathed "little man" led to Martin's downfall. *Walter P. Reuther Library, Wayne State University*

reprinting the *Protocols of the Learned Elders of Zion* booklet. He marginalized himself in the process and was rebuked by Catholic bishops outside Detroit.

Henry Ford also seemed to drift toward fascism when, on his seventy-fifth birthday, on July 30, 1938, he accepted the Grand Cross of the Supreme Order of the German Eagle. Ford had the dubious honor of being the first American to receive Hitler's highest award for a non-German. Cleveland's German consul, Karl Kapp, and Detroit's German consul, Fritz Hailer, presented Ford with the decoration in his office,

Help Americanize *Ford*

Why did Ford receive the highest Nazi decoration?

Why did Ford employ Fritz Kuhn, <u>Convicted</u> Bund Leader?

Why did Ford refuse to build plane motors for England?

Why has Ford refused to abide by the laws of the U. S. A.?

BE AMERICAN: BUY UNION-MADE CARS

Ford, Only Non-union Car Made in America

**FORD COMMITTEE
UNITED AUTOMOBILE WORKERS**

Above: This sign indicates that selling and distributing goods or leaflets at the gates of the Rouge are prohibited, although food carts and a newspaper stand were found around the pedestrian bridges over Miller Road. Following the 1932 Hunger March, the city of Dearborn passed an ordinance prohibiting union organizers from distributing literature within the city. Judge Lila Neuenfelt of Dearborn declared the law unconstitutional in October 1940. *Walter P. Reuther Library, Wayne State University*

Above right: This union-organizing leaflet distributed in 1940 criticized Henry Ford for accepting the Grand Cross of the German Eagle from the Nazi government, for scorning President Franklin Roosevelt's pro-labor policies, and for refusing to build military aircraft engines for England. *Walter P. Reuther Library, Wayne State University*

and Kapp read the Führer's citation at Henry's party of 1,500 guests later that evening. Hitler congratulated Ford for his pioneering efforts in making the automobile available for the masses, a concept he would re-create with Volkswagen.

To placate critics, Henry Ford had his friend, Rabbi Leo Franklin, announce that in accepting the medal Ford was not a Nazi sympathizer. Coughlin attacked Franklin's announcement as untrue, and Bennett further confused the matter by offering a third version of what Ford supposedly told the rabbi.

"The upshot was that Ford products were shunned by Jews in the most complete boycott of automotive vehicles by any group in American history," noted historian David L. Lewis. "Jews virtually stopped buying Ford products, and some of their Gentile sympathizers did the same. This boycott was to cost the Ford Company tens of millions of dollars in lost sales."

Ford was unmoved, but shortly after his birthday, he suffered his first stroke. It was hushed up, and the feisty Henry pursued an aggressive treatment regimen that allowed him to return to his activities within a month.

A Reuther family birthday party in the summer 1938 was also memorable. Two gunmen confronted Walter at his apartment door, and one ordered, "Okay, Red, you're coming with us." Instead, Reuther and his guests fought back, and the gunmen left without firing a shot. Two men were later arrested for the incident, one of them a former Ford "star man." During the trial, however, the defense claimed that

Reuther had hired them to fake a kidnapping to make him a hero to his fellow union members. The prosecutor didn't challenge the defense's story, and the men were acquitted.

At the Rouge, the automaker prepared to launch the Mercury brand as a 1939 model. The brainchild of Edsel Ford, Mercury was created to fill the gap between the low-priced Fords and the luxury Lincoln and Lincoln Zephyr.

With the Mercury about to début, Father Coughlin arranged for secret negotiations between Homer Martin and Harry Bennett. When word of the talks leaked out in January 1939, the UAW Executive

Left: UAW organizers drive around the Rouge Plant in an old Model T, in this 1940s photo. The union tried numerous tactics to recruit Ford workers in the face of oppression by Harry Bennett's Service Department. *Walter P. Reuther Library, Wayne State University*

Below: Even as tensions mounted between labor activists and Ford, headlines on the papers sold near the Gate 4 overpass in 1940 suggest that many people probably had the war in Europe on their minds. *Dearborn Historical Museum*

Committee called on their president to explain his actions, which they viewed as treasonous. Martin responded by suspending 15 of the committee's 24 members and stating that he wanted the UAW to rejoin the AFL. The two factions held rival conventions. Martin's UAW-AFL meeting was sparsely attended, while a greater number of delegates went to the UAW-CIO meeting and elected "R. J." Thomas, a former Chrysler worker, as its president.

Overshadowing the union's internal struggles and Bennett's conniving was news of the invasion of Poland by Germany and the Soviet Union in September 1939. War had again broken out in Europe, as the Roosevelt administration argued with Imperial Japan over their occupation of China. War jitters tainted the Ford-UAW conflict as union literature sought to tie Fordism to fascism.

Between 1937 and 1941, Bennett fired more than 4,000 workers for suspected union activities. Many who weren't fired were beaten or threatened by servicemen. Harry also organized the "black" Service Department, a corps of African-American workers to foil the union's efforts to make inroads into the black community. Despite the intimidation, the UAW-CIO began recruiting more and more Ford workers.

RIVER ROUGE

Right: A spontaneous walkout of 50,000 workers on April 1, 1941, started the first massive strike against Ford Motor Company. A few Ford workers, many of them African-Americans, didn't join the walkout and instead armed themselves with makeshift clubs, preparing to clash with the strikers. These Dearborn police officers may be telling one strikebreaker to back down. *Dearborn Historical Museum*

Below: Union members escort a bloodied strikebreaker who, moments before, had been beaten by picketers and tossed over the fence onto the train tracks during the 1941 strike. *Walter P. Reuther Library, Wayne State University*

The union received a boost in October 1940 when Dearborn Judge Lila Neuenfelt ruled that the city's anti-leafleting ordinance was unconstitutional. Hundreds of UAW-CIO members went to the Rouge's gates to pass out handbills. The union flexed its muscles, launching lawsuits against Ford and protesting to the NLRB. In February 1941, the Supreme Court upheld an NLRB decision to force the automaker to rehire a number of workers. The returning workers openly promoted the UAW by wearing buttons and posting signs. The servicemen stepped up their beatings of troublemakers, leading to a series of mini-strikes at the Rouge.

The final break came on the night of April 1, when Bennett fired the eight men on the Rolling Mill's grievance committee, sparking a spontaneous walkout by 50,000 workers. Hundreds of Ford workers, many of them black, remained in the plant. They armed themselves with iron bars, wrenches, and other homemade weapons and twice tried to break the picket lines, but the strikers drove them back. About 20 people were hurt.

Left: Sightseers thronged to Miller Road outside the Dearborn Iron Foundry after hearing about the April 2 riot between pro-union and pro-company forces. Motorists slowly drove two and three abreast down the road in a steady stream, some pausing briefly at the gates. The only fatality on the first day of the strike was a 68-year-old Highland Park man, who died of a heart attack in one of the plant's parking lots. *Walter P. Reuther Library, Wayne State University*

Right: Members of the UAW "Flying Squadron" attack a man attempting to cross the picket lines outside the Rouge Plant during the 1941 strike. This photograph, taken by *Detroit News* photographer Milton Brooks, won the first Pulitzer Prize for photography in 1942. *Walter P. Reuther Library, Wayne State University*

RIVER ROUGE

Right: Strikers waving American flags parade down Miller Road. The turnout stretches from the Soy Bean Processing Plant at the south end of the complex to somewhere past the Gate 2 pedestrian bridge, nearly a half mile away. The signs compare Ford's labor practices with Hitlerism. *Walter P. Reuther Library, Wayne State University*

Below: Harry Bennett *(with bow tie)* signs the first-ever labor contract for Ford Motor Company on June 29, 1941. He is flanked by Philip Murray *(left)* of the Congress for Industrial Relations and R. J. Lewis *(right)*, president of the UAW-CIO.

Strikers also overturned a car carrying black workers who tried to enter the plant, and beat them. Club-wielding members of the UAW's "Flying Squadron," the union's "toughs," similarly attacked other workers who tried to cross the line.

Detroit patrolman John Lasanen also encountered the strikers' fury while driving down Miller Road en route to the nearby Veterans Hospital. Although union leaders gave him a pass, a mob stopped Lasanen, stripped him of his gun and badge, beat him, and damaged his patrol car. The only fatality on the first day of the strike was worker Thomas H. King, 68, of Highland Park, who died of a heart attack in the Rouge's parking lot.

The *Detroit News* reported the melées the next day, and hundreds of sightseers thronged to Miller Road, driving cars two and three abreast, pausing at the gates to watch the strike. The Navy Training School at the Rouge (see Chapter Five) closed when instructors couldn't get through the picket lines.

Bennett and Dearborn police chief Carl Brooks, a former Ford serviceman, petitioned Michigan governor Murray Van Waggoner to intervene, but the governor sent in only the state police to keep the two sides apart. With the governor's promise not to interfere, the UAW reduced its picket lines to some 400 to 500 people, mostly marching in circles around Gates 3 and 4.

Hoping to avoid a race riot, the Detroit chapter of the National Association for the Advancement of Colored People and many black clergy came out in support of the UAW-CIO and pleaded with the black foundry workers to come out.

On April 11, the company finally agreed to discuss a contract with the UAW and hold an NLRB-supervised election. A jubilant Henry Ford called Sorensen, saying that the strike was over and that the CIO had lost. Apparently Henry thought his workers would never vote to unionize. He was wrong.

It took Ford 10 days to get the Rouge back into full production, partially because some equipment, such as the open-hearth furnaces, had been damaged when the strikers didn't shut them down properly.

The union vote was scheduled for May 21, when Homer Martin unexpectedly stepped in with a resurrected UAW-AFL, trying to woo Ford workers to his side. When the election was held and the votes tabulated, the UAW-CIO won with 70 percent of the vote, compared to 28 percent for Martin's faction. Only 2 percent voted for no union at all.

Henry Ford was incensed, feeling that he had done more for his workers than any other industrialist. When Bennett showed Ford the proposed contract on June 28, he refused to sign. He told Sorensen he'd rather close the company down. That night, Clara Ford threatened to leave Henry if he didn't make peace with the union.

Sorensen later said he was surprised when he awoke the next day and heard on the radio that Ford had agreed to become a union shop, complete with a dues checkoff system. The settlement was more than what the UAW had asked for and, consequently, made moot several union complaints before the NLRB. Two days after the signing of the contract, UAW Local 600 was created. It was by far the largest local in the UAW, with more than 100,000 members, including 10,000 African-Americans, the largest segment of black workers in the union at the time. Ford, in fact, employed half of all black workers in the industry.

UAW leaders had little time for backslapping. The automaker had little time to lick its wounds. Six months later, the country was completely drawn into World War II, and the Rouge plant with it.

Rouge, was producing armaments and had been bombed in the blitz. The Nazis had taken over Ford's German and French factories, and just 800,000 square feet of manufacturing floor space. A 270 x 952–foot, four-story wing held engine testing and dynamometer rooms.

engines for Martin B-26 Marauder medium bombers. *Ford Photomedia*

RIVER ROUGE

As World War II rages in Europe, the Albert Kahn–designed aircraft engine factory takes shape at the Rouge in late 1940 before the onset of winter. Ground was broken in September 1940, and by the time the factory was completed, the $39-million, two-story building had grown to 360 x 1,408 feet. During the winter it was placed under a "box" of tarpaper and wooden framing. This, along with coal-filled pots burning underneath, kept temperatures above freezing while construction continued. *Walter P. Reuther Library, Wayne State University*

Even though Nazi aircraft couldn't reach the United States, the factory was the first "blackout" plant at the Rouge, made almost entirely without windows, so it would be nearly invisible at night. The interior was lit artificially and air-conditioned throughout. The design became the industry standard after the war, when Ford and other manufacturers tarred or painted over the skylights and windows of their other factories. Construction of the Aircraft Building, as it was also called, was done during the winter by enclosing it under a wood-and-tarpaper "box" equipped with coal-filled pots, to keep the temperatures inside above freezing. It was completed by February 2, 1941, and employed about 10,000 skilled mechanics.

The engine blocks were cast at the Rouge foundries, and the first Double Wasp was completed that August. Another 322 would be finished by year's end. The engines were assembled on the first floor of the building, with a machine shop on the second floor. The factory also housed lunchrooms, washrooms, and the training school for apprentice aircraft engineers, who learned skills such as machine tooling and assembly.

As part of the aircraft engine project, the automaker also constructed a magnesium smelter, to create 110,000 castings of lightweight engine parts per month, and an aluminum foundry, both at the Rouge. Barracks for the army air forces personnel were constructed behind the Rotunda. By war's end, the workers at the Aircraft Building had completed 57,851 engines, though the work was spread out to several other Ford plants, including Highland Park, Kansas City, and St. Paul.

After the groundbreaking for the Aircraft Building, Edsel Ford told Sorensen that his two older sons, Henry II, who had married Anne McDonnell that July, and Benson, wanted to learn how the business worked. Despite their conflicts, Edsel and Cast-Iron Charlie began working together more, as Harry Bennett undercut their authority. "Bennett always carried a gun and had [an air] pistol range in his office. Here he and Henry Ford used to have target practice," Sorensen wrote in his autobiography. "I mentioned this one day to Mrs. [Clara] Ford, who demanded indignantly, 'Who is this man Bennett who has so much control over my husband and is ruining my son's health?'"

While officially president of the automaker, Edsel suffered a number of humiliations from his aging father. For example, when Edsel had authorized the construction of a battery of new coke ovens at the Rouge, Henry ordered Bennett to knock them down after they were

Left: Workers inspect an air-cooled Pratt & Whitney R-2800 Double Wasp after its initial test run at the Aircraft Engine Building in 1941. The radial engine had 18 cylinders arranged in two rows. With a displacement of 2,804-ci (46 liters), it produced nearly 2,000 horsepower and was destined for a twin-engine B-26 Marauder medium bomber. *Walter P. Reuther Library, Wayne State University*

Right: Chief Petty Officer Charles Crich leads a group of sailor-students onto the grounds of the Navy Training School at the south end of the Rouge Plant on February 3, 1941. Behind them is the Open-Hearth Building, with its ten smokestacks and silver water tower. *Walter P. Reuther Library, Wayne State University*

RIVER ROUGE

Sailor L. G. Miller of Albion, Oklahoma, learns how to use a Landis grinding machine from apprentice toolmaker Fred Ball of Highland Park in January 1941. . The Rouge's Navy Training School was open to some 990 sailors at a time for three-month courses on machine operation and repair, fire control, electricity, metalsmithing, carpentry, boilermaking, and other shipboard skills. The skylights of the factory have yet to be covered over to conform to blackout conditions. *Walter P. Reuther Library, Wayne State University*

A sailor works on an electric motor during one of the trade courses at the Rouge Plant in early 1941. *Walter P. Reuther Library, Wayne State University*

completed. The elder Ford had lost confidence in his son, often believing that Edsel was too much under the influence of his brother-in-law, Ernest Kanzler.

Edsel is often portrayed as acquiescing to his father's decisions, but Sorensen offers a different view of the father-son conflict. He claimed that Edsel was just as headstrong as his father and wanted to live his own life but that he knew who had built the company and who had ultimate power. Relations between father and son had reached a breaking point by 1940, and Edsel's health was in decline as he suffered from stomach ulcers.

In late 1940, probably because Harry Bennett was still considered part of the Naval Reserve and could have been called up for active duty, Henry Ford agreed to build the Rouge Navy Training School to accommodate nearly 1,000 enlisted men at a time for a three-month instruction program on machine operation, repair, fire control, electricity, metalsmithing, carpentry, boilermaking, and other shipboard skills.

The groundbreaking for the school was held December 6, 1940, at the south end of the factory complex, between the Open-Hearth Building and the bank of the Rouge River. By January 15, 1941, the first school buildings were completed, some 150 sailors had unpacked in their quarters, and Ford officially turned over the facility to Rear Admiral Chester W. Nimitz.

Edsel Ford rides in back of the first Ford-built Jeep, then called a "Blitz Buggy," on February 28, 1941, along the banks of the Rouge River. Joining Edsel are the driver and U.S. Army Brigadier General Charles Hartwell Bonesteel II in the front passenger seat. *Walter P. Reuther Library, Wayne State University*

The school initially had a mess hall, sleeping quarters for 1,200 or more men in its eight barracks, a steam plant, reading and recreation rooms, showers, kitchens, and an athletic field. The facility also had an administration building and a 60-bed hospital. A recreation hall was added and opened on December 4, 1941, with an auditorium for movies and plays. Later an Olympic-size swimming pool was built, to train navy frogmen. The pool was also open at select times for civilian use.

Sailors came to the Rouge from the naval training stations at Great Lakes, Illinois; Newport, Rhode Island; and San Diego, California. Ford Trade School instructors gave them about 8 hours of lectures and 32 hours of shop work in the Rouge's factories each week. By war's end, thousands of sailors had been taught at the plant.

The Rouge became involved with the history of the Jeep when the army put out a call for a lightweight reconnaissance vehicle in 1939.

Only Willys-Overland, a struggling carmaker called American Bantam Company, and Ford (despite its long-running feud with the Roosevelt administration over labor issues) bid on the contract. The army wanted a vehicle with four-wheel drive, a 600-pound payload, a 75-inch wheelbase, and a fold-down windshield, plus an impossible gross vehicle weight of 1,200 pounds. Bantam delivered the "Blitz Buggy," the first running prototype, in 1940, which was followed by the Willys Quad and the Ford Pygmy, also called the "GP" (the "G" stood for "government" and the "P" for the vehicle class, although many people thought it was an abbreviation of "general purpose").

Bantam's Blitz Buggy was superior to both the Willys and Ford entries, though Willys had a better engine, the 60 horsepower "Go Devil." Yet the army doubted that the tiny Pennsylvania-based company could meet its production demands and ordered it to turn its design

On March 12, 1943, Ford tested about 11 Seeps in the Rouge boat slip. Reports are that these craft were slow in the water and would flood and sink in waves greater than a slight chop. On land, the Seeps' extra weight made them ungainly. Still, Ford built 12,778 units before the end of the war, and they are now rare and highly collectable. *Ford Photomedia*

over to Willys-Overland. When it became apparent that both Willys and Bantam couldn't manufacture enough vehicles, half the production was given to Ford, which designated the quarter-ton trucks the "GP" model. The name "Jeep" evolved either as military slang for "GP" or from the name of a character in the Popeye cartoons. Ford engineer Laurence Sheldrick later claimed that Ford originated the name, but Willys obtained the trademark after the war.

Although Ford was supposed to follow the Bantam/Willys design down to the last bolt, Ford Jeeps had a nine-slot grille rather than the familiar seven-slot of today's Jeeps, plus a different rear storage

compartment and the script letter "F" stamped onto its bolts. Very early Ford Jeeps are known as "script" models, because Ford stamped its name on the rear panels until it was ordered to stop. The army wanted Jeeps to look interchangeable, without blatant manufacturer emblems.

The first Ford Jeep, still called the Blitz Buggy, came off the line on February 28, 1941, and Edsel joined an army driver and Brigadier General Charles Hartwell Bonesteel II for a jaunt along the banks of the Rouge River.

After Pearl Harbor, the army asked Ford to develop an amphibious Jeep, called the "Swamp Buggy," or "Seep." The hybrid car-boats were

Right: Sailors set up chairs in the Navy Training School's new recreation hall on December 4, 1941. The school initially had a mess hall and sleeping quarters for 1,200 or more men, a steam plant, reading and recreation rooms, showers, kitchens, and an athletic field. The auditorium could show movies and provided a stage for plays. *Walter P. Reuther Library, Wayne State University*

developed by Marmon-Herrington and the yacht designers at Sparkman and Stevens, who dropped the Jeep into a modified hull with wheel cutouts. Although the first prototype nearly sank, on March 12, 1943, 11 Seeps were ready for testing on a road course and in the waters of the Rouge boat slip. Although the Seeps were ungainly on land and inoperative in waters with more than a slight chop, the army ordered about 12,700 units before the end of the war.

The army turned toward Ford again in 1940, to see if it could develop a powerplant for the army's new M-4 tank. Fortuitously, the automaker had an engine design on hand. With a bit of bravado, as he had in World War I when he said he could make antisubmarine ships, Henry had announced in early 1940 that the company could make 1,000 aircraft a day and had his engineers design a 12-cylinder, liquid-cooled engine. Ford invested $2 million in the project, even without a contract.

The engine was heavily modified into an eight-cylinder design, and Ford won the contract to make the tank, engine, and armor at the Rouge. But when production delays cropped up and only 1,683 tanks had been made by May 1942, the army gave the contract to GM's Fisher Body and Chrysler Corporation. Ford was plagued by a shortage of workers because of the draft and its aircraft programs but continued making M-4 engines and armor plates.

Civilian automobile production was curtailed by August 1941, as America, the "arsenal of democracy," geared up for war, and Henry Ford suffered his second stroke prior to December 7. By most accounts it greatly slowed down him down, both physically and mentally. Sorensen asserted that Henry started suffering from hallucinations.

Life changed for Rouge workers on a blustery, overcast Sunday, when around 3 p.m., the first radio reports were broadcast of the Japanese attack on Pearl Harbor. America had been fully drawn into World War II.

On Monday, December 8, army guards were posted at the Detroit-Windsor Tunnel and the Ambassador Bridge. Soon afterward, anti-aircraft guns were set up in Detroit parks and other strategic locations. A civil defense organization was created, air-raid warning sirens

Below right: Four days after the Japanese surprise attack on Pearl Harbor, armed guards patrol the Schaefer Road entrance to the naval barracks at the Rouge, checking the identity of the navy commander seated in the driver's seat of the car. *Walter P. Reuther Library, Wayne State University*

RIVER ROUGE

A 1942 Ford, the company's last peacetime car, rolls off the assembly line at the "B" Building on February 10, 1942. After the Japanese attack on Pearl Harbor, the U.S. government gave automakers two months to finish civilian vehicle production. Except for the chrome bumpers, the War Production Board ordered the "bright work" on the last cars covered up. The workers hold a sign that reads, "Watch out Japs here comes the little jeeps next. V for Victory." *Ford Photomedia*

The first Ford-produced Jeep followed the last civilian car down the line. Although based on the Willys-Overland Jeep, it has a nine-slot front grille, a different rear storage compartment, and the letter "F" stamped on most of the bolts. This Jeep is probably also a rare 1942 "Script" model, meaning the Ford name is embossed on the rear panel. The army, wanting its Willys and Ford Jeeps to look interchangeable, ordered Ford to stop putting its name on the vehicles. *Ford Photomedia*

were mounted on public buildings, a military police battalion set up camp in the city of River Rouge, and thousands were trained as air-raid wardens to patrol city streets and enforce blackout regulations. It was highly unlikely that Japanese or German aircraft would ever reach the American Midwest, but the Roosevelt administration played the war propaganda to the hilt.

The government imposed price controls and rationing of gasoline, tires, meat, canned food, clothing, liquor, and cigarettes. Only essential house and building construction was permitted, and people were encouraged to carpool. All nonessential car sales were banned, and civilian car production stopped by the end of February. The last peace-time 1942 Ford rolled out of "B" Building on February 10. Workers held up a sign saying, "Watch out Japs here comes the little jeeps next. V for Victory," and a line of Jeeps followed the V-8. Ford made 277,896 Jeeps, also manufacturing the vehicles at its Dallas and Louisville plants.

During the war, scrap-metal drives spelled the end for millions of older vehicles. In one event at the Rouge Open-Hearth Building, plowshares were beaten into swords as old Fordson tractors were crushed and their metal melted down to make weapons.

To the consternation of some members, the labor unions made a no-strike pledge for the duration of the war. The UAW, however, lobbied Knudsen, who had been elevated to the rank of U.S. Army lieutenant, to protect the rights of autoworkers who went to fight the Axis. The federal government agreed that anyone who volunteered or was inducted into the military would have his job when he mustered out. The War Labor Board was created, with representatives from management, labor, and government, to resolve disputes.

Factories went into 24-hour operation, with workers on 10-hour or longer shifts, seven days a week. Most workers were "frozen" at their jobs, unable to quit or transfer without the War Labor Board's consent. Yet thousands of young men were called up for duty or enlisted, causing a shortage of workers at the Rouge, Willow Run, and other factories.

Women were urged to join the workforce, and they did, in unprecedented numbers. The need for additional workers created a massive influx of Southern whites and blacks to Detroit. In 1930, only about 120,000 African-Americans lived in Detroit, a little more than 10 percent of the population. By 1940, that segment had grown to 200,000 and would keep rising, along with anti-black discrimination.

On February 28, 1942, a white mob beat several blacks moving into a Detroit federal housing project. Racial tensions boiled over on June 20, 1943, as thousands flocked to Detroit's Belle Isle, when fistfights broke out between whites and blacks in a park there. The violence quickly spread into the city proper, and Governor Harry F. Kelly sent in 2,500 troops with Jeeps, armored personnel carriers, and a tank to quell the city's worst race riot since the Civil War.

Detroit operated under martial law for 10 days. Thirty-four people had been killed—23 were African-Americans—hundreds injured, and

Above: The Ford tug *Barlow* and the barge *Lake Folcroft* approach the Rouge Plant's docks for one of the last times before being requisitioned by the U.S. government for the war effort. The *Folcroft* would be reconverted into an oceangoing vessel and was lost in a hurricane in 1944, while the *Barlow* and most of the surviving Ford vessels were sold after the war's end. *Walter P. Reuther Library, Wayne State University*

Left: Henry and Clara Ford pose with their grandson, Navy Lieutenant Henry Ford II, at Gaukler Point, home of Edsel and Eleanor Ford, in Grosse Pointe, April 1943. Within a month, Edsel Ford would be dead after suffering from the effects of stomach cancer and undulant fever. *Ford Photomedia*

Bomber Plant Captivates America

During World War II, the fate of the Rouge Plant became intertwined with, if not overshadowed by, the drama of the Willow Run B-24 Liberator bomber plant, located near the cities of Ypsilanti and Ann Arbor. Willow Run's development, however, is an eerie parallel to the Rouge. Both came about during wartime; both were placed in locales that seemed odd for major factories; and both built military craft that stretched the automaker to its technical limits.

The genesis of Willow Run began on May 28, 1940, when an increasingly erratic Henry Ford, echoing claims he made regarding antisubmarine boats two decades earlier, boasted that his company could build 1,000 fighter planes a day. The claim seemed preposterous, though Walter Reuther proposed a similar scheme.

Having worked at the Ford plant in Gorky, Russia, Reuther knew that the Soviets had equipped the factory to be converted to make aircraft components. He suggested that American manufacturers do the same but proposed putting the factories under the control of representatives from government, industry, and labor. William Knudsen, director of the Office of Production Management, dismissed the "Reuther Plan." Instead, the Roosevelt administration supported industry's idea of building specialized war plants run, for the most part, by the corporations.

When Ford accepted the $200 million bomber plant contract, it could have been argued that the car company knew how to make aircraft. In the 1920s, Ford had teamed with the Stout Metal Airplane Company to build the Tri-motor passenger plane at Ford Airport in Dearborn. But the venture had folded in 1932, and those who had participated had either left the company or were dead.

Henry Ford wasn't concerned, telling Charles Sorensen that the war would be over before the bomber plant was completed. Cast-Iron Charlie oversaw the construction of the plant and its airport, 1,878 acres in all, which he con-

sidered his greatest challenge. Control of the Rouge, meanwhile, fell to Ray S. Rauch, an ally of Harry Bennett.

Although the Michigan Central's trunk line passed nearby, as did Michigan Avenue, Willow Run was remote, built on land where Henry Ford had established a boys' camp for the sons of World War I veterans. Like the Rouge, Willow Run was named after a creek, a tributary of the Huron River that meandered through the site. But the land had good drainage and offered room to expand the airfield's 7,000-foot-long concrete runways up to 2 miles for an airport of the future, Edsel Ford explained in a March 1943 *Washington Post* story.

Before construction began on Willow Run, Sorensen visited the designer of the B-24, the Consolidated Vultee Aircraft Corporation. At Consolidated's factory in San Diego, where the manufactuirer was building just one aircraft a day, Sorenson found a number of disturbing problems. For instance, the company was doing the final assembly on a steel fixture that was outdoors in the bright California sun. The heat and temperature changes so warped the fixture that no two planes could be assembled the same way.

Workers wire the right inboard engine on a B-24 as it proceeds down one of the Willow Run assembly lines. Each medium-heavy bomber had four Pratt & Whitney R-1830 Twin Wasp 14-cylinder, air-cooled radial engines. While specifications on the planes were tweaked throughout the war, these engines generally produced 1,200 horsepower. *Walter P. Reuther Library, Wayne State University*

A war worker emerges from the entrance of his trailer home, stepping on a cinder block to avoid the frozen, marshy ground in March 1943. This was one of the unofficial trailer communities that sprang up around the Willow Run bomber plant to cope with a severe housing shortage in the area. While this trailer is hardly bigger than one of today's SUVs, the head of a small child, held by someone in the trailer, can be seen in the shadows behind the man. *Walter P. Reuther Library, Wayne State University*

The four-engine B-24, also called the "Box Car," was a complex machine, with 488,000 components. From nose to tail, a completed Liberator was 66 feet, 4 inches long and could carry a crew of ten. It weighed 60,000 pounds when fully loaded with 8,000 pounds of bombs and 2,750 gallons of fuel. The plane was capable of speeds up to 300 miles per hour at 30,000 feet and had an operational range of approximately 2,290 miles. It would become, in large part due to Willow Run, the most extensively produced American bomber of the war.

Sorensen decided that the B-24 should be built in sections, with each section coming to the proper point on the assembly line as needed. But when he asked Consolidated for detailed blueprints, Cast-Iron Charlie discovered that there were no such documents. Military aircraft designs were fudged, because the models were constantly modified—nearly every B-24 was customized to make the parts fit. It was pre-Highland Park thinking. Sorenson roughly sketched Willow Run's layout on a piece of paper to try to determine how planes could be built on an assembly line.

As had become a tradition for three decades, Ford called upon the 71-year-old Albert Kahn to design the massive 3,121 x 1,275–foot factory. Just like the Rouge's Aircraft Engine Building, Willow Run was a "blackout" plant, lit entirely by electrical fixtures, air-conditioned, and with few windows. Under its roof were 67 acres of manufacturing space, able to accommodate two assembly lines for bombers with 110-foot wingspans. The factory was tall enough for overhead cranes to lift engines, tails, and wings into place.

The pieces of aircraft fuselages started at one end of the plant, and components were added as the planes went down the assembly lines. The twin lines merged at the far end of the plant, where the building took a 90-degree turn to the right. From there, the planes entered the final assembly area. Ideally, the factory would have been laid out in a straight line, as in Sorensen's sketches, but that would have meant extending from Washtenaw County into Wayne County, and Ford didn't want to deal with two rival county governments. The New Deal Democrat–dominated Wayne County levied much higher taxes then Republican-leaning Washtenaw County.

Another quirk of the plant's construction was that Henry Ford insisted the course of the Willow Run creek not be altered, so the waterway was encased in a culvert that ran under the plant and emerged where it had naturally flowed on the other side. Henry's attitude seems a far cry from his efforts in the 1910s to alter the course of the Rouge River.

The bomber plant had its own hospital, equipped with men's and women's wards of 20 beds each and auto and scooter-car ambulances. The hospital employed 100, including a head doctor, six assistant physicians, and 40 registered nurses. Willow Run also had an Airplane Apprentice School, similar to the one established at the Rouge.

Construction didn't start until August 15, 1941, and even with crews working under floodlights after the attack on Pearl Harbor, it wasn't finished until May 15, 1942. Originally, Ford's monthly quota was about 50 B-24 Liberator "knockdowns"—parts that would be assembled at the Curtis Wright factory in Fort Worth and the Bell Aircraft plant in Tulsa—plus 50 completed bombers. But in May 1941, the army raised its order to 65 knockdowns and 75 "flyaways" a month and later hiked production targets to 400 aircraft a month. This required a major expansion of the final assembly room and caused production delays, as Edsel Ford noted.

Two major problems with Willow Run became painfully obvious before the first B-24, *The Spirit of Ypsilanti*, came off the line on October 1, 1942: a shortage of worker housing and inadequate roads to handle traffic to and from the plant.

In 1940, the village of Willow Run had a population of 331 and just 94 homes, but as the factory was built, more than 10,000 people moved into the area. Because initial provisions for federal housing fell through, most workers had to find shelter in a squalid jumble of trailer first federal dormitories for single men and women didn't open until February 1943, and they had no indoor toilets. By June, another 15 dormitories opened, but they could house only 3,000 of the plant's 42,331 workers. It wasn't until six months later that temporary family housing units for 2,500 were opened.

The company had anticipated that many workers would drive to the bomber plant, but that was before the federal government ended civilian automobile production and imposed gasoline and rubber restrictions. The transportation difficulties led to huge employee turnover and absenteeism. Initially, Sorensen estimated that Willow Run would need 110,000 workers, but it had fewer than half that. Many were reluctant to commute from Detroit, even after Cast-Iron Charlie offered to retread their tires at the Rouge.

To make the plant accessible, the federal government funded the expansion of the east-west thoroughfares of Michigan Avenue and Ecorse Road. Then, on September 12, 1942, Undersecretary of War Robert S. Patterson dedicated one of the nation's first highways, which linked Willow Run to Ford's Rouge and Lincoln plants. The highway, commonly called the "Bomber Expressway" and later a part of I-94, was not fully completed until near the close of the war.

With production crawling—only 56 Liberators were built by the end of 1942—the media nicknamed the plant "Willit Run?" The press, however, didn't count the fact that the plant was producing a great many more knockdown components for other factories and that the military was constantly changing its specifications, causing chaos on the assembly line.

"The War Department made the mistake of raising false hopes," Edsel stated in the March 1943 *Washington Post* story. "It announced in the middle of last year that Willow Run was in production when we had made only one bomber. The inevitable time lag between that date and the actual beginning of production was bound to create an unfavorable reaction."

After the first year, production at Willow Run started clicking, especially when Sorensen transferred some of the subassembly work to the Rouge. By February 1944, the plant was making 455 planes in 450 hours, exceeding the goal of one plane an hour.

Although the Dodge war plant in Chicago was larger, the ability to produce a bomber an hour captured the public's imagination and catapulted Sorensen into the national spotlight. Another figure who helped make Willow Run a success was Charles Lindbergh. The aviator had been pilloried because he had opposed Roosevelt's preparedness plans and, like Ford, had accepted Hitler's German Eagle medal in 1938. But Lindbergh was a valuable advisor and a sometime test pilot, Sorensen recalled.

Willow Run also became linked to another war icon: "Rosie the Riveter," the government's fictional red-haired woman who encouraged women to work in the war factories. By 1943, the bomber plant employed about 15,000 women, more than a third of its workforce of 42,000. Three out of four of the women workers were more than 35 years old, and more than half were married and had children.

In June 1945, the last of the B-24s, *Henry Ford*, rolled off the Willow Run assembly line in a ceremony that brought out Henry Ford and his grandson, Henry Ford II. When the elder Ford said he wanted the aircraft to be named after the workers who built it, his name was erased and workers autographed it.

In the end, Ford had made about 8,500 of the bombers, nearly half the 19,256 Liberators produced. The company surrendered the plant to the federal government, which sold it to the upstart Kaiser Frazier Corporation in September 1945. Eventually, the factory passed into the hands of General Motors, while the airport survives as metropolitan Detroit's cargo airdrome. One of the World War II-era wooden hangers remains and houses the Yankee Air Museum, dedicated to preserving Willow Run's history.

Two "Rosie the Riveters," Rhoda Hale *(left)* and Rose Kovrine, have lunch while sitting in the bomb bay section of an incomplete B-24 Liberator on February 8, 1943. People like Hale and Kovrine were the inspiration for the fictional Rosie of propaganda posters. *Walter P. Reuther Library, Wayne State University*

communities with inadequate (if any) septic systems that contaminated the shallow water supply. Fortunately, no outbreaks of typhoid fever occurred, but there were no playgrounds for the workers' children, no places to shop, no place to put a pair of muddy boots, and schools were overcrowded.

The housing and production problems at Willow Run became such national concerns that a U.S. Senate committee under Harry S Truman visited Willow Run in 1942. Finally, Henry Ford sold a portion of Ford Farm land in October 1942 for a housing project, but the

1,800 arrested. The property damage from the riot was estimated in the millions of dollars. While the Rouge Plant was not directly impacted, it was a prelude to future challenges that Ford and the Motor City would face.

Edsel Ford had faced his own fateful moment in January 1943, when doctors at Henry Ford Hospital in Detroit discovered the cause of his ailments—stomach cancer—and removed nearly half his stomach. The cancer, however, spread to his liver, and Edsel's failing health kept him from fighting off Bennett's machinations. In the meantime, knowing how their father had been viciously attacked for receiving a deferment in World War I, Henry II and Benson signed on. Henry II joined the navy, became a lieutenant, and was posted to the Great Lakes Training Station. Benson joined the army air forces, despite being nearly blind in one eye, and was posted to Selfridge Field, northeast of Detroit.

Following the attack on Pearl Harbor, the federal government requisitioned all available vessels to support the war effort. Ford seamen were enlisted into the U.S. Merchant Marine, and Ford officers were given naval uniforms. The government also bought or compulsorily chartered Ford ships, either for convoy duty to Great Britain and the Soviet Union or to replace other merchant ships that had been called away for such duties.

The *Norfolk* was the first Ford vessel pressed into service for coastal duty, even though it was designed for use on the Great Lakes and along the New York Barge Canal. Next, the government pulled the MS *Lake Osweya*, one of the World War I-era ships Ford had refurbished in 1930, to be rebuilt as an oceangoing vessel. In November, *Green Island*, a canal ship, was chartered to work in the Caribbean.

The ships of the Ford fleet were called to duty just as the German navy began "Operation Drumbeat"—unrestricted submarine warfare against American coastal shipping in January 1942. In the first six months of the year, Nazi subs sunk about 500 ships in the Atlantic, most of them off the American coastline.

By late July, U-boats had claimed four Ford vessels, and in August, the government requisitioned six of Ford's large barges to convert into oceangoing cargo vessels. The canal ships *Chester* and *Edgewater* were taken later that fall, followed by the *Lake Ormoc*. A fifth Ford vessel, the *East Indian*, was lost to hostile fire in November, and a winter storm on December 3 claimed the barge *Lake Allen*. The barges *Lake Crystal* and *Lake Hemlock* were separated from the tug *Buttercup* during the same storm the next day and drifted to the tiny island of Miquelon, a French possession off Newfoundland, where the crews were rescued three and a half days later.

By the end of 1942, Ford's fleet of 30 vessels had shrunk to the *Henry Ford II* and the *Benson Ford*, both of which were too large to fit through the Canadian canals, plus the small barge *Lake Kyttle* and the harbor tug *Dearborn*. The *Kyttle* would be pressed into wartime duty in 1943. The last Ford vessel lost during the war was the *Lake Folcroft*,

which went down in a hurricane on November 21, 1944, off the coast of Cuba. At the end of the war, facing a financial crisis, Ford sold off most of the surviving ships, reducing its "fleet" to the *Henry* and the *Benson*. The Marine Office needed a complete overhaul, too, because Bennett had infiltrated his people into that department.

Other "casualties" of the war were the Rouge Cement Plant and the Tire Plant. The Cement Plant, located between the boat slip and the Hi Line, made its last batch in 1942. In its 18 years of operation, according to employee Lloyd Lockhart in a *Ford Rouge News* story, the plant had made 8.5 million barrels of cement, "enough to pave a two-lane highway from Detroit to San Francisco," using blast furnace slag mixed with raw limestone. Ford later sold its slag to outside companies. Demolition of the cement plant began in 1948, to make way for expanded ore bins.

A long line of women, with a few men interspersed, hand-assemble aircraft turbochargers in the Pressed-Steel Building on October 19, 1944. Some 52,281 turbochargers were made at the Rouge between September 2, 1942 and October 31, 1944. *Ford Photomedia*

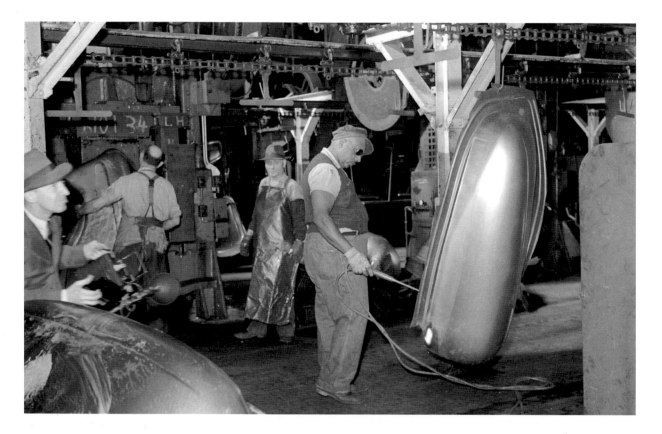

The demise of the Tire Plant, which had made 8 million Ford-brand tires by 1942, was the result of a federal government scheme. The Soviet Union had abundant synthetic rubber but inadequate tire-making equipment. The United States, meanwhile, had a rubber shortage, so the Roosevelt administration bought Ford's tire equipment and shipped it to Russia, where, according to stories, it was never reassembled properly. The automaker never reentered the tire business.

As the war continued, Henry Ford remained as distrustful as ever of Roosevelt. When the president and Eleanor Roosevelt toured Willow Run on September 18, 1942, Henry remained aloof and glared at Edsel and Sorensen as they explained the functions of the bomber plant.

Edsel's health continued to decline. In November 1942, he came down with undulant fever after drinking, at his father's insistence—for health reasons—unpasteurized milk from Ford Farms. This, along with Sorensen's occupation with Willow Run, created an administrative vacuum. Harry Bennett used his power to appoint his people to key positions at the automaker.

A. M. Wibel, a Ford employee since 1912 who had started as a machinist and worked his way up to manage the purchasing division, got into a heated dispute with Bennett concerning a disreputable supplier Bennett wanted to use. Edsel sided with Wibel, but Henry fired him anyway. Sales manager John R. "Jack" Davis was sent into virtual exile in California, and engineer Laurence Sheldrick was forced out after running afoul of Bennett.

The weakened Edsel broke down and told Sorensen he wanted to quit, but Cast-Iron Charlie encouraged him to stay on. The young Ford's health finally gave way in April, and at 1:10 a.m. on May 26, 1943, Edsel died, age 49. The next day, before Edsel's funeral, the frail Henry Ford, nearly 80 years old, resumed presidency of the company, much to the amazement of Sorensen and others.

Bennett urged Henry to make a secret amendment to his will to set up a board of trustees that would run the car company for 10 years after Henry Ford's death. None of Edsel's children were listed as board members—Bennett continued to play on Henry's fears that Kanzler had too much influence over Henry II and Benson.

With control of Ford Motor Company teetering, the Roosevelt administration released Henry Ford II from his duties at the Navy Great Lakes Training Center in August. Although he was officially elected a company vice president, young Henry wasn't given any official duties and faced extreme pressure from Bennett and hostility from his grandfather.

Sorensen, who also became a company vice president after Edsel's death, decided he'd had enough of the internecine battles and informed the elder Henry that he was stepping down from his duties at Willow Run on January 1, 1944. Ford didn't officially recognize Sorensen's resignation for two months. The Roosevelt administration then wanted to take over the automaker and asked Sorensen to become its president,

Above: Fenders for the first postwar vehicles arrive at the "B" Building. Most likely the fenders were brought from the Pressed-Steel Building a short distance away. *Walter P. Reuther Library, Wayne State University*

Right: Henry Ford II and Ford Production Vice President Mead Bricker inspect the first postwar cars about to be shipped to dealers on October 17, 1945. *Walter P. Reuther Library, Wayne State University*

but Cast-Iron Charlie told the government to put its faith in Henry II. Soon afterward, Sorensen joined Willys-Overland as its president.

Behind the scenes, Henry II found allies in Jack Davis in California, Mead Bricker, who had succeeded Sorensen at Willow Run, and John S. Bugas. As the FBI's former chief agent in Detroit, Bugas had uncovered thefts at the Rouge and Willow Run plants. Bennett had Bugas to help deal with labor after Henry II returned to the company, but the former agent refused to fall under Bennett's control. When Henry II discovered that his grandfather's will had been altered, Bugas confronted Bennett, who agreed to destroy the codicil. With pressure from Clara Ford and Edsel's widow, Eleanor, Henry Ford allowed his grandson to be elected executive vice president of the company in April 1944.

While Henry Ford II fought to gain control of the tattered company, World War II was grinding to a halt, first with the surrender of Germany on May 8, 1945. Although the war was still raging in the Pacific, the Truman administration (Roosevelt had died on April 12) allowed Ford to resume planning and production of civilian vehicles in June 1945. On August 6, the U.S. Army Air Force dropped the first atomic bomb on the Japanese city of Hiroshima. Eight days later, the second A-bomb fell on Nagasaki, causing Emperor Hirohito to surrender unconditionally.

The company's war production statistics are impressive. In addition to the figures cited earlier, it should be noted that the Rouge and Lincoln plants made a total of 25,741 tank engines and reconditioned another 1,648. The Rouge's Pressed-Steel Building made 52,281 turbochargers for aircraft engines and built 42,381 aircraft jettison fuel tanks. The Rouge Aluminum Foundry began making jet engines and parts in 1945, and a 300-mile-per-hour wind tunnel was erected behind the plant.

The end of the war meant many imminent changes at the Rouge Plant and Ford's surrounding properties. Dearborn's Ford Airport became a full-time test track for the company. The navy and air force training schools were dissolved, and Ford purchased the Rouge Aircraft Building from the federal government in 1947, temporarily using the vast structure as a warehouse. Public tours of the Rouge resumed on August 21, but the Rotunda remained closed to the public until 1953.

As the Rouge was converted to peacetime production, the last act of the power struggle between Henry Ford II and Bennett played out on September 20, 1945, when Henry Ford stepped down and allowed his grandson to assume presidency of the company. Bennett was fired, but he spent about a day burning personnel files in his office. There are several versions of how the "little man" left. One is that Henry II personally went to Bennett's basement office and delivered the news. Another holds that Bugas delivered the message and disarmed Bennett. Bennett's version is that Bugas fired him but never took his gun away.

Ford's first postwar 1946 cars and trucks received their final inspection in the Rouge's garage on October 17, 1945, before being

shipped out. The 1946 models were the same as Ford's 1942 vehicles, except for a few cosmetic changes to the grille. Ford would launch the all-new F-1 pickup truck in 1948, but buyers would have to wait until the 1949 model year for the company to roll out its first all-new postwar cars.

Despite the pent-up demand for cars after the war, the assembly lines at the Rouge fell silent several times in 1945 and 1946, due to parts shortages caused by nationwide strikes. Federal government wage and price controls and the continued rationing of resources further exacerbated the company's efforts to return to peacetime production.

The workers on the final line at the "B" Building in 1946 are still showing their pride from the end of the war, as evidenced by the American flag hanging overhead. The return to peace, however, was turbulent, with production interrupted by material shortages, strikes, government-imposed production controls, and rising inflation. *Ford Photomedia*

Chapter Six

Charting a New Direction, 1946–1960

"The Rouge was the last place in the world that I wanted to work. Before the war, I brought my cousin out here to get a job, and they had a big platform in the parking lot, and a black fellow was doing the hiring. They picked me, but I didn't want a job there. I don't know what I was thinking."

—Samuel Cain, Ford Rouge retiree, interviewed 2003

At the end of World War II, millions of young men, mustered out of the military, returned to their old jobs, if they still existed, at the Rouge Plant and other factories. America's postwar economy was rough, with rising inflation, despite federal wage and price controls, and numerous strikes. Veterans displaced many of the war workers, but blacks and women would come to comprise a larger percentage of Detroit's workforce than ever before.

One such veteran was Samuel Cain of Ecorse, Michigan, a former army sergeant who had gotten a job at Briggs. He often napped on the streetcar ride home from the factory, but one day in 1946 was particularly rough: he had been through three strikes in the previous 48 hours. Cain had dozed off, only to awaken around 10 a.m. and find that the streetcar had been diverted to the Rouge's Gate 4, to pick up Ford workers.

Cain, who at that time still wore his old army uniform as work clothes, got out to walk down Miller Road, intending to go to Fort Street and then home, when a man came out of the employment office and called out, "Come get your job at Ford. All ex-soldiers are welcome."

"I told him that I was a truck driver and they didn't have any black truck drivers at Ford," Cain said in 2003, recounting the event.

Although he continued walking, the Ford man called out for Cain to stop and walked out to talk to him. "Look at it this way, soldier," the man said. "Some things are not open to you yet, but they're changing." Cain was hired into the Rouge machine shop, but it would be a few years before he was able to drive trucks.

Ford Motor Company was in a financial mess after the war, losing about $1 million a month. It hadn't made a profit in more than a decade, according to the official company history. Supposedly, accountants in some departments estimated bills by weighing the receipts.

Yet some historians, such as David Lewis, discount stories that Ford was so badly off, arguing that new cars hadn't been made in three years, and consumer demand was so pent up that manufacturers couldn't build them fast enough. If the extent of Ford's losses was exaggerated, its recovery would have looked spectacular.

Ford was still a family-controlled enterprise, with Henry Ford II as its president. Initially, it looked like his brothers Benson and William Clay would play significant roles in the company as they became members of the board of directors. Benson was named executive of Lincoln-Mercury in 1948, and William Clay, or "Bill," studied under other Ford managers. But Henry II realized that he himself was inexperienced and that the company needed experienced managers.

On October 19, 1945, a Western Union telegram arrived from a stranger promising help. Army Air Forces Colonel Charles "Tex" Thornton's message merely said, "I would like to see you regarding a subject which I believe would be of immediate interest. This concerns a system that has been developed and applied successfully in the management of the Army Air Forces for the past three years. Reference if desired is Robert A Lovett Asst Secy of War for Air."

Thornton had created the Statistical Control office, which allowed the air forces to keep track of men, planes, equipment, and munitions. The Haskell, Texas, native had assembled a team of nine other young officers with the intention of finding a hard-luck company, helping turn it around, and then taking it over. Thornton's team included Robert Strange McNamara, a former junior faculty member at the Harvard Business School; Francis C. "Jack" Reith, a lieutenant colonel who had saved the air forces nearly $1 billion during the war; J. Edward Lundy, a former Princeton University economics instructor; and Arjay R. Miller, who had been a planner at the Federal Reserve Bank of San Francisco.

The eerie glow of welders' torches lights the slab-sided body of a two-door 1949 Ford. This was Ford's first new car since the end of World War II and is credited with saving the automaker from financial ruin. *Ford Photomedia*

executive vice president on May 6, 1946. Breech, whose office was next door to young Henry's in the Administration Building, brought several GM executives with him, including Lewis Crusoe and Del Harder, who later coined the term "automation." Thornton's ambitious group was placed under the GM men.

Growing tired of the intense rivalries that resulted, Whiz Kid Wilbur Andreson left Ford in August 1946. That same month, the company recruited another young ambitious man who had started his training at the Rouge—Lido "Lee" Iacocca of Allentown, Pennsylvania.

Iacocca was one of 51 male engineering graduates recruited that year. Ford gave its student trainees hands-on experience in the different departments at the vast plant. Iacocca wrote in his 1984 autobiography, for example, that he even worked on the final assembly line for four weeks, attaching a cap to a wiring harness inside a truck frame, a job he called "tedious as hell." Iacocca had gone through nine months of training when he realized he might spend years engineering small car parts before he could do anything else, so he jumped over to sales.

Coincidentally, the same month Andreson left and Iacocca hired in, Breech pulled his prewar Lincoln over to the side of the road near the Rotunda and looked across the street at the Administration Building, deep in thought. Ford's early postwar cars were really just dolled-up 1942 models, with inadequate engine lubrication and cooling systems. Many of its manufacturing plants were obsolete, despite Ford's renovations in the late 1930s. The company had only 2,300 engineering employees—including draftsmen, clerks, and sweepers—who were outnumbered by the Rouge's 5,000 maintenance people. And the UAW was pressing the car companies for wage increases, to keep up with spiraling inflation.

Ford's new heavy-duty pickup truck, the F-1, was scheduled to arrive in January 1948, but trucks were utilitarian work vehicles. What Ford needed was new cars, and soon, if it were to remain competitive. Breech went into the office that August day and put the wheels in motion to create the slab-sided 1949 Ford. In addition, the company's operations were reorganized into six divisions: the "Rouge," which included the company's heavy industrial operations, such as steel, glass, and tool-making; "Parts and Equipment," with 10 specialized plants; "General," a catchall division that included Highland Park's spare parts and tractor line operations, plus other self-standing factories; "Foreign Operations"; "Ford"; and "Lincoln-Mercury."

By scrapping the current car design, Breech had unwittingly started yet another "crash" program to get a new model on the road, which would be called the "Model B-A" or, more simply, the "1949 Ford."

The car offered buyers a choice between a carryover 100 horsepower, 239-ci V-8 or a 90-horsepower, six-cylinder engine. The rest of the 1949 Ford was all new, with improved steering, the new "Hotchkiss Drive" transmission, individual front spring suspension, rear leaf springs (no more transverse leaf springs), and four-wheel hydraulic drum brakes.

The male half of a large die sits on the floor of the massive Dearborn Tool and Die Plant, ready to be moved to the Dearborn Stamping Plant. *Ford Photomedia*

Despite the officers' obvious lack of car manufacturing experience, Ford hired them and sent the 10 men out to investigate the workings of the Rouge Plant and other company operations. What they found was troubling. Ford's financial system was so arcane that no one could accurately measure its overall economic health or even make profit-and-loss projections. Their constant questioning earned Thornton's group the moniker "Quiz Kids," after a popular radio program in which grade school children won prizes for answering difficult questions. Later, they were called the "Whiz Kids."

Henry Ford II, though, didn't put all his faith in just one group of young executives. To Thornton's chagrin, young Henry recruited Ernest R. Breech, president of General Motors' Bendix Aviation Corporation subsidiary.

Breech was a longtime GM man, living like many auto executives in the Detroit suburb of Bloomfield Hills, north of Eight Mile Road, in Oakland County. Called a "real gentleman" by those who met him, Breech was comfortable at GM but was excited by the challenge of rebuilding Ford Motor Company. He took the job, becoming a Ford

The exterior was a radical, sleek design with a "bullet nose," nine body styles—including the Tudor, Fordor, and station wagon—and a 114-inch wheelbase. Because of the rush to design the car, the body didn't sit snugly on the frame, which allowed dust to intrude into the cabin. It was a flaw that couldn't be corrected until the next model changeover.

When the car debuted in dealerships in June 1948, it created such a sensation that an estimated 28 million people visited Ford showrooms in the first three days. Ford built an amazing 1.1 million vehicles that year, more than it had in any year since 1929, and its sales surpassed the Chevrolet's for the first time since 1937. Yet even with the 1949 Ford's success, the company's overall sales still lagged behind those of General Motors and Chrysler. Chevrolet retook the spot as America's number-one brand for the 1950 model year.

As planning for the 1949 model began, things began changing rapidly at Ford and the Rouge. For example, when people said "Mr. Ford," they were referring to Henry II rather than the company's founder. At first he was also called "Young Henry" or "Henry the

Reuther Shapes the UAW

"Walter Reuther is the most dangerous man in Detroit, because no one is more skillful in bringing about revolution without seeming to disturb the existing order of society."

—George Romney, president, American Motors Corporation, 1958

As World War II ended, about one-fourth of the nation's workforce (15 million people) was unionized. Labor leaders like Walter Reuther, however, were very much aware of history. Nearly 30 years earlier, after World War I ended, businesses successfully mounted an anti-union campaign. The same thing appeared to be happening again, but this time the unions fought back.

The first collision between the car manufacturers and the United Auto Workers occurred in November 1945, when Reuther demanded that General Motors boost wages by 30 percent, open its financial books to the union, and freeze prices. "Increased production must be supported by increased consumption, and increased consumption will be possible only through increased wages," Reuther stated, using logic reminiscent of Henry Ford's justification for the Five Dollar Day. But the car market was far different than it was 30 years earlier, and GM dug in. The result was a 113-day strike.

The situation was different at Ford when the UAW negotiators demanded the 30 percent wage increase. The company responded that it had been the victim of 773 wildcat strikes or slowdowns since 1941 and that the union should help crack down on members who caused such disruptions. As Ford and UAW negotiators went round and round for weeks, Henry Ford II adopted labor's jargon that "human engineering" was needed to reshape the management-union conflict. During a speech to the Society of Automotive Engineers in early January 1946, Ford first used the phrase "human engineering" and conceded that "labor unions are here to stay." Harry Bennett's "Service Department" had ceased to exist, and since the 1941 contract, Ford security guards wore uniforms instead of street clothes.

By the end of January, Ford had settled with the union for an additional 18 cents per hour—about half of what the UAW had asked for—and had the ability to fire workers who engaged in "illegal" work stoppages. Chrysler also settled with similar terms. (Along with national agreements, the UAW locals negotiated simultaneous agreements with their respective factory managers.)

Rival UAW leaders criticized Reuther, and as GM workers depleted their savings, they, too, demanded an end to the strike. Reuther finally settled with GM for roughly the same wage increase as Ford and Chrysler. He also gained a union dues checkoff and stronger clauses on defining worker seniority.

At first glance, the GM negotiations were a disaster, but Reuther became a martyr in the eyes of many UAW members. When delegates met in Atlantic City in 1946 to elect officers, Reuther campaigned hard against incumbent President R. J. Thomas, decrying his connections with communists. Despite rejection by Local 600, the redheaded Reuther gained the support of the anti-communist Association of Catholic Trade Unionists and won by 124 votes.

Although politically weak at first—the UAW executive board was stacked with opponents—Reuther placed loyalists, including his brother Victor, into key positions. His rise, however, was a blow to African-Americans—who had, by and large, been allied with Thomas.

As the UAW leaders squabbled, Republicans and conservative Democrats in Congress passed the Labor Management Relations Act of 1947 (also called Taft-Hartley) and rewrote the National Labor Relations Act to hamstring unions. Workers could no longer be forced to join unions, unions couldn't force employers to discharge a worker for failing to join, unions could not refuse to bargain collectively, and certain wildcat strikes and secondary boycotts were prohibited. The act also outlawed "closed shops," where only union members could be hired, but permitted "union shops," where new hires had to enroll in the union after a certain period.

Before the UAW's next election in 1947, a huge changeover occurred in the local leaderships as the rank and file ousted Reuther's opponents. Even the huge Local 600 flipped, and Reuther won a decisive victory, with his allies taking 18 out of the executive board's 22 seats.

That year's negotiations with Ford—the union and the automakers would soon switch to multiyear contracts—became the first in the industry to provide $100-a-month retirement pay. Many old-timers, like 71-year-old Walter Shaw of Dearborn, retired from the "long, tough grind."

Yet "human engineering" still needed adjusting, as Ernie Breech found out soon after joining Ford. While taking a tour of the Rouge with production executive Mead Bricker, the supervisor escorting them shoved a young man out of their path and then fired another worker who was reading a newspaper while waiting for more work. Angered, Breech told the superintendents that the culture of fear that had dominated Ford had ended. Such top-down directives, however, took many years to become reality.

The UAW worked in conjunction with the automakers in 1948 to create the "Torch Drive," which raised funds for the charities of the United Way. The union and Ford also worked to eliminate a carryover from the Harry Bennett era: gambling at the Rouge Plant. In 1948, Dearborn police chief Ralph Guy charged that a $10-million-a-year gambling racket was being conducted at the Rouge. There were also accusations of rigged elections at Local 600. After a grand jury investigation and subsequent arrests and prosecutions in the 1950s, the racketeering operation was virtually eliminated.

Around the same time Guy announced the investigations, Detroit was rocked by an assassination attempt on Walter Reuther the night of April 20, 1948. Reuther had just returned to his house on Apolline Road and was opening his refrigerator door when a shotgun blast shattered the kitchen window. The 12-gauge shot nearly severed Reuther's right arm. Witnesses saw a maroon 1947 or 1948 Ford sedan speed away.

Reuther was rushed to Grace Hospital, where he spent several weeks with his upper body in a plaster cast. Doctors saved his right arm, but he never fully recovered. The day after the shooting, the UAW board stated, "We are convinced that the person or persons who attempted to kill President Reuther are agents of the enemies of democracy and labor, and as such they could come from any number of economic or political groups of widely varying ideologies."

Several months after the shooting, Detroit police arrested Carl Bolton, the former vice president of UAW Local 400, which represented the Ford Highland Park workers. As Bolton was about to be brought to trial, however, Victor Reuther was nearly slain just before midnight

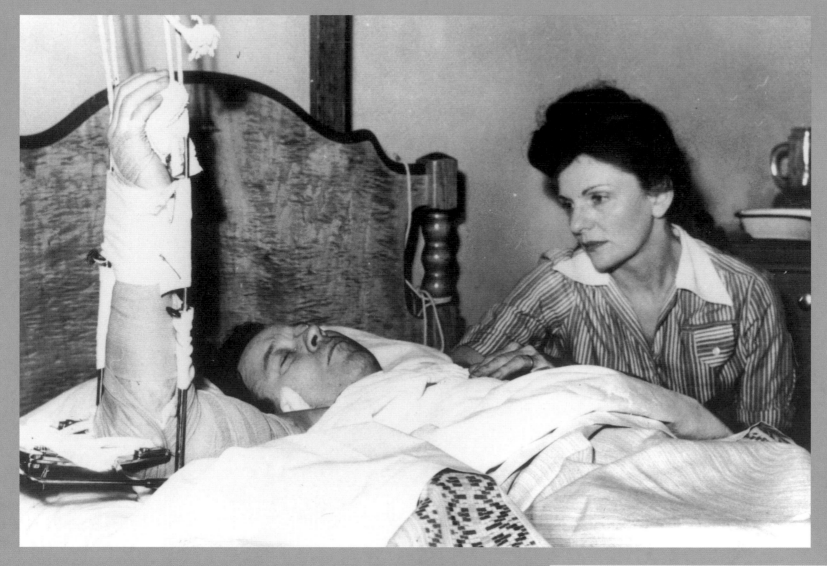

on May 22, 1949. As he sat in his living room, a 12-gauge shotgun was fired through the window screen, with the pellets ripping into Victor's face and chest. He was taken to Henry Ford Hospital, where his right eye was removed.

Witnesses saw a man leaving in a maroon sedan, and police recovered the shotgun, wiped clean of any fingerprints, at the scene of the crime. Although police theorized that one of Bolton's friends might have committed the second shooting, Bolton was released. Then, on December 22 that year, a *Detroit Times* reporter received a call that there was a bomb at UAW headquarters, located near the General Motors Building. Police found 22 sticks of dynamite hidden in a Christmas package near the back door. The fuses were defective.

The manhunt into the Reuther shootings took many twists and turns, with theories that the attacks had been ordered by the Mafia, communists, rival union leaders, or even corrupt auto executives. Several Local 600 members were arrested and released as the trail turned cold. The UAW charged that the police were incompetent or complacent and launched their own investigation, but the culprit was never found. After the shootings, the Reuthers hired their own bodyguards.

Three brothers who changed the face of the United Auto Workers—*(from left)* Roy, Victor, and Walter Reuther—as they appeared in 1937, soon after the UAW's successful sit-down strike against General Motors in Flint, Michigan. The three were all college educated, unusual in the labor movement. Walter went on to become the UAW president after a hotly contested election in 1946 and continued in that position until his death in a plane crash in 1970. *Walter P. Reuther Library, Wayne State University*

The year Walter Reuther was shot, Ford attempted to weaken the UAW by asking its hourly workers to vote to become an "open shop," but 90 percent of Ford workers voted down the request.

In 1949, the UAW and Ford again collided when John S. Bugas, the company's vice president for industrial relations, demanded an 18-month pay freeze, even as Ford's sales rebounded. Workers walked out for 24 days, and the union argued for higher wages, a company financed medical-hospital fund, and an end to assembly line "speed ups."

"Both my dad and my grandfather worked at the Rouge. The strike occurred when I was six, and I remember walking the picket line," Gilbert Rodriguez, of Local 600, recalled in 2003. "The forty-nine strike was very important, because it addressed one of the major problems in assembly plants—the adverse mix of product.

"You'd get convertibles, hardtops, cars with AC [air conditioning], no AC, premium sound, and so the workload varied, depending on the mix coming down the line. . . . The forty-nine strike settled what the company was supposed to do: either slow down the speed of the line, space the units apart with a larger gap, add manpower, or even stop the line intermittently to deal with the adverse mix."

Unrelated to union demands, the company quit its longstanding policy of paying workers in cash once a week and began issuing checks instead. In the past, pay wagons would pull up at various locations around the Rouge, and workers stood in line to receive fresh dollar bills. It was a good idea for a worker to count his pay right in front of the paymaster—if he walked away with too little money, he was out of luck. Once in a while, a Ford worker might get a "bonus" when two new bills stuck together.

By 1951, the UAW moved into a new international headquarters called Solidarity House, on East Jefferson, at the foot of Van Dyke in Detroit. The site included the property where Edsel and Eleanor Ford's first home had stood before they moved to Gaulker Point.

Under Reuther's leadership, the UAW picked up most of the members of the defunct Farm Equipment Workers union and gained a new, official name—International Union, United Automobile, Aerospace and Agricultural Implement Workers of America. While toying with the idea of creating a separate labor party, Reuther and virtually all union leaders allied with the Democratic Party, believing it was the best place to influence the course of political and social events to labor's advantage. Reuther also convinced leaders in the Congress of Industrial Organizations to merge back with the American Federation of Labor in 1955, creating the AFL-CIO. The new organization could claim up to 16 million members, leaving only about 3 million in independent unions.

Targeting the right auto company during contract negotiations became an art. If the UAW was after money, GM, with its deep pockets, could be targeted. If the union wanted to make a social statement, Ford would be the target. And Chrysler, the weakest of the Big Three, could least afford a strike. White-collar workers at GM, Ford, and Chrysler secretly cheered Reuther on, because if the hourly workers got a raise, their pay would rise too.

As the voice of the UAW, Reuther was mesmerizing when he spoke, leading George Romney, president of American Motors Corporation, to brand him "the most dangerous man in Detroit." During contract negotiations, he also knew how to entertain the media by regaling them with stories of his time at Ford.

When Soviet Premier Nikita Khrushchev visited the United States in 1959, the leader of the "worker's paradise" received a Reuther tongue-lashing about the Soviet's exploitation of East German workers. Soon afterward, rumors were floated that Walter had a wife in the Soviet Union and had fathered a child when he was there in the 1930s and had abandoned them. Reuther denied the charge, which was dismissed by most Americans as communist propaganda.

Reuther built bridges to the Kennedy administration and Martin Luther King Jr., but a growing rift between him and AFL-CIO President George Meany finally exploded over the issue of the Vietnam War. Meany supported President Lyndon Johnson's policy, while Reuther backed the antiwar movement. In mid-1968, Reuther pulled the UAW out of the AFL-CIO and allied with a former foe, James P. Hoffa, president of the Teamsters union.

By 1970, Reuther had been the UAW's president for 24 years. The union had purchased a large tract of land near Black Lake, in northern Michigan, to create the Family Education Center to train future union leaders and hold forums. On May 9, Walter Reuther and his wife, May, along with bodyguards, two pilots, and other passengers boarded a UAW-chartered jet to visit the incomplete center. The plane crashed after clipping a tree in a light rain just short of the Pellston airport, killing all aboard.

The UAW had gained a monopolistic control over the industry's labor, but Reuther's successors faced far different challenges as foreign auto companies made inroads into the American market.

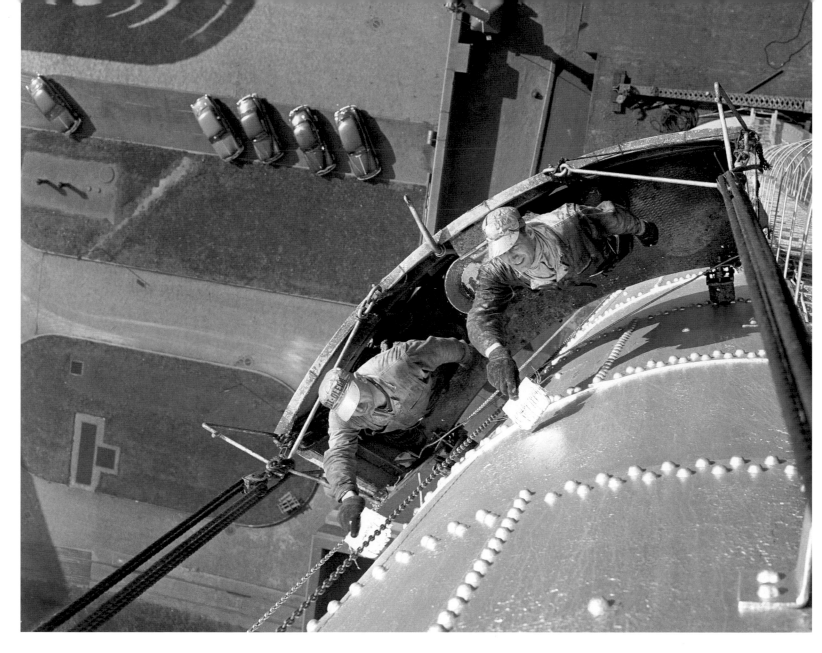

It's a long way down, but these two Ford painters seem unconcerned. They're working on one of the 333-foot-tall smokestacks of Powerhouse No. 1 at the Rouge Plant in either 1949 or 1950. First they would scrape off any rust, then apply a coat of Rustoleum, followed by gray paint. *Ford Photomedia*

Second." Only later did people start calling him "the Deuce" or, more rarely, "Hank the Deuce." The founder, on the other hand, was fading from view.

One of Henry Ford's last public appearances was at the Golden Jubilee of the Automobile Industry on May 31, 1946, at Detroit's Masonic Temple. Ford joined 13 other surviving car pioneers, including Frank Duryea, Charles King, and Ransom Olds. Each was presented with the 9-pound aluminum statuette called the "Charles Clifton Award," designed by the renowned sculptor Arvard Fairbanks of Utah, who also created the Dodge Ram hood ornament.

Henry had suffered another stroke in 1945, and his influence in the company was negligible. Many of his lieutenants, such as W. C. Cameron and the aging Ernest Liebold, had retired. His last hurrah came on April 7, 1947, when heavy rains caused the swollen Rouge River to spill over its banks. Near-record flood waters damaged Greenfield Village, created havoc around Dearborn, and knocked out

Fair Lane's generators, cutting off power. After touring the flood damage, Henry returned to his home, which was lit only by kerosene lanterns and candles, and took ill, complaining of a bad headache. Before a doctor could arrive, Ford died that night of a cerebral hemorrhage, at age 83.

"The world was horse-drawn when he entered it. When he departed, it was a world on powered wheels. He built for the 'great multitude' and they were both directly and by accident the beneficiaries of Henry Ford, master mechanic," a *New York Times* editorial said of his passing.

Henry Ford was laid out at the Edison Institute, and thousands came to see his body. The Rouge tours were suspended on April 10, 1947, the day of the funeral. When he died, he was the twelfth wealthiest American, according to a 1998 story in *American Heritage*. His $1 billion in wealth would have been the equivalent of $36.1 billion 50 years later. Clara Ford died at age 83 in 1950.

Ford's first postwar 1946 cars and trucks receive their final inspection in the Rouge's garage before being shipped out on October 17, 1945. The 1946 models were the same as Ford's 1942 vehicles, except for a few cosmetic changes to the grille. While Ford revamped its trucks for 1948, the cars were "phonied up" Ford V-8s. *Walter P. Reuther Library, Wayne State University*

"On the day of Henry Ford's funeral, we all shut off our machines, which was the first time they had been shut down except for maintenance," Samuel Cain recalled. "We all stood by our machines for one minute of silence. I looked forward to that moment. I heard that it cost the company about $1.7 million for that one minute."

Henry Ford's death marked the end of an era, and the Whiz Kids would shape the next one, but without Tex Thornton. Tex's dreams of quickly climbing the company ladder were crushed when he was fired in early 1948, after running afoul of Ernie Breech and Lewis Crusoe one too many times.

A year after Thornton left, Whiz Kid F. C. Reith interviewed a man who would rise to the pinnacle of the car company: Donald Eugene Petersen of Pipestone, Minnesota. Petersen had served a stint in the marines after the war. He was also a magna cum laude graduate of the University of Washington in 1946 and had just earned his masters in business administration from Stanford.

Petersen's first office was in the old Navy Training School barracks. During the summer months, he later recalled, a pungent odor drifted across the Rouge River from the Darling Soap Rendering Company's plant on the opposite shore, in Melvindale.

After World War II, the heart of the Rouge Plant became its steel operations. The demand for steel by rival auto companies and the construction industry was so great that Ford's only reliable source was its own Rolling Mill. Crews worked seven days a week to maximize production, while management passed out cigars and cigarettes every time a record was broken, and company photographers roamed the plant, snapping photos.

"In the 1950s, the crane operators made fortunes, working on market quotas and receiving incentive pay," said Bob Kreipke, Ford historian. "In 1958, with a high school education, some steel crane operators were making $90,000 to $100,000 per year. And Wilson Davis once told me that when Mr. Ford talked him into becoming a photographer instead of a crane operator, he lost $40,000 a year."

In November 1948, a third blast furnace fired up at the Rouge. Called the "William Clay Ford," or the "C" furnace, it was built in line with the "Henry" and "Benson" furnaces on land that had been set aside for just such a facility when the Rouge Plant was created. The "C" furnace was 104 feet tall, with a hearth diameter of 29 feet (versus 20 feet for the two original blast furnaces), and had nearly double the working volume of the other blast furnaces: 50,000 cubic feet versus 27,000 cubic feet.

In July 1948, a detailed statistical report of the Rouge Plant's operations was prepared prior to the lighting of the "William" blast furnace. Overall, this snapshot of the Rouge showed that it had 13.8 million square feet of floor space, 1⅓ miles of docks, 26 miles of roadways, parking spaces for 20,000 cars, 132 miles of conveyors, and employed 70,000 workers, with another 5,100 in the Administration Building and Rotunda. The Rouge railroad had 14 diesel engines and 4 steam locomotives that handled 50,000 freight cars a month, while 465 trucks also conveyed materials in the complex.

The storage bins had 1.5 million tons of capacity, with 550-foot-long "traveling bridges" with buckets that scooped up the raw materials and dumped them into the waiting scale cars on the adjacent ¾-mile-long "Hi Line." The scale cars weighed the raw materials, insuring a proper mixture, before transferring the materials to a skip car that took them up to the charging bell on top of the furnaces.

The 92½–foot-tall "Henry" and "Benson" blast furnaces, which produced heat in the range of 2,700 degrees Fahrenheit, had an average casting time of 5 hours and could produce 1,500 tons of iron per day. The Rouge steel plant made 73,000 tons per month and used 1.9 million gallons of oil and 600 million gallons of cooling water. The

183 Kopper-Becker coke ovens consumed 4,500 tons of coal per day and made 45 million cubic feet of gas, 30,000 gallons of tar, 3,300 tons of coke, 11,000 gallons of crude light oil, and 95,000 pounds of ammonium sulfate.

The Glass Plant had 60 grinding units and 100 polishing units and made 3¼ miles of glass per day, in sheets 53 feet wide and 3/16 inch thick. The plant's most photographed building, Powerhouse No. 1, consumed a combination of 2,500 tons of pulverized coal and blast-furnace and coke-oven gas per day while producing 60 million pounds of steam and could power the domestic needs of a city with a population of 1 million. In fact, Ford used to sell its excess power to Detroit Edison at peak usage times.

The 10,000 employees in the Production Foundry made 6,000 V-8 cylinder blocks per day, using 1,500 tons of new sand for the molds and 65,000 gallons of oil per month. The Motor Building had 10,500 workers, 7,000 machines, and 15 miles of conveyors; 135 worker-minutes were required to assemble one engine.

"B" Building, renamed the Dearborn Assembly Plant, built 500 cars every 8-hour shift, and the line speed was set at 22 feet per minute, giving workers about one minute to complete their tasks. The Rouge

Above left: The rear body panels, with doors attached, for the new 1949 Ford hang on an overhead conveyor at the Rouge Plant on November 8, 1948. *Walter P. Reuther Library, Wayne State University*

Above: The body of a blue 1949 Ford is dropped onto a chassis. Due to the rush to get these cars into production, the bodies never quite fit right, allowing dust to infiltrate the cabins. Despite its flaws, the '49 was a sales success, helping to push the company's overall sales above 1.1 million units for the first time in 20 years. *Ford Photomedia*

A forklift driver stacks tailpipes at the Rouge Plant in 1948. Forklifts were a vital part of the factory, moving materials from the receiving docks to storage and then out to the assembly line. *Walter P. Reuther Library, Wayne State University*

had a full-fledged hospital, with a total staff of 203, including 27 nurses and 20 first-aid stations scattered around the complex.

About the time the report on the Rouge was issued, John Bugas was involved in the yearly contract negotiations with the UAW. Henry Ford II wanted better relations with the union, but Bugas faced the enormous task of building his "Industrial Relations" organization from the ground up. "There was nothing to build on but ashes," Bugas said in a story printed in the 1948 *Ford Rouge News*. "As a matter of fact most of the few files that did exist were burned by our predecessors [Bennett] as they departed."

The Dearborn Assembly Plant nearly became ashes that year, when a fire broke out in the balcony that housed the upholstery department a few minutes before 6 p.m. on Wednesday, December 15. Employee Cesidio Volpe noticed the blaze and sounded a general alarm as the flames spread rapidly. Some employees stayed long enough to put the wheels on 10 Fords and 20 Mercurys, both on parallel assembly lines, and push them out of the factory, while others hurriedly drove 300 finished cars out of the garage.

Fifteen fire companies responded, rescuing three men trapped in the upholstery department and six women in a restroom, as the blaze consumed 200 cars, damaged one-third of the assembly plant, and cracked the huge sawtooth skylights before it was brought under control. The fire caused an estimated $500,000 in damage, and the company scrambled to produce the hot-selling 1949 Ford at its other assembly plants until Dearborn Assembly resumed operations in January 1949.

After "B" Building was repaired, Ford bought for $7 million the five war plants that had been erected at the Rouge. The Aircraft Building was temporarily used as a warehouse, while the armor-plate and ordnance production buildings were converted to steelmaking.

The Administration Building was also renovated by the late 1940s, with a revamping of the executive offices and the addition of an F-shaped, concrete-block annex to the back, to increase office space. Edsel Ford's old office was turned into the boardroom, and bleached mahogany replaced the dark walnut paneling. Herculite clear glass doors separated the outer offices from the hallway.

A laundry service was even added to the Rouge in 1950, installed in Powerhouse No. 3, one of the complex's oldest buildings. It employed about 40 employees, who laundered 50,000 garments a week, including coveralls, shop coats, jackets, and work pants in 10-foot-tall washers. These employees also inspected the garments, sewing and patching them as needed.

As Ford continued its restructuring efforts, international events colored the development of the Rouge. One overarching worry was the Cold War, which turned hot on June 25, 1950, when 60,000 North Korean troops crossed into South Korea. The United States and several allied nations sent troops under a United Nations–approved "police action" that lasted three years and saw some of the most intense fighting experienced by American soldiers.

Unlike World War II, the federal government did not suspend civilian car production but did issue war contracts and place quotas on car manufacturing. Ford built M-151A1 Jeeps for the Korean conflict, but in Chicago, not at the Rouge. Instead, the company accepted a $40 million contract to make tank engines and spare parts at the Rouge's former magnesium smelter factory.

After 31 years of service, 73-year-old Walter Shaw of Dearborn carries his lunch box across the Gate 4 overpass for the last time. In March 1950, he became one of the first workers to retire under the union's negotiated pension plan, which entitled him to $100 a month. Shaw had emigrated from England to work at the Highland Park Plant in 1919. He later transferred to the Rouge, where he worked a number of jobs, including in the Body Shop and the tool room. *Walter P. Reuther Library, Wayne State University*

In September 1951, Ford announced it would spend $100 million to modernize the Rouge for defense production. Improvements included building 37 new coke ovens across from the boat slip, to increase steel production by 190,000 tons per year; adding 200,000 square feet of floor space to the Dearborn Iron Foundry; and converting the old Aircraft Building into the Dearborn Engine Plant. The aging Motor Building, described as the last factory at the Rouge that resembled something out of Charlie Chaplin's movie *Modern Times*, was retired.

When its conversion was complete, the Dearborn Engine Plant could make 4,660 V-8s in a single day. Demolition of the old Motor Building began in 1954, to provide room for new three-story, air-conditioned office building to house the Rouge Division's staff and a communications center. The 525-foot-long building faced Miller Road and had two adjoining wings, each also 525 feet long, creating 365,000 square feet of floor space for its 2,500 office workers.

Another facility added near the Rouge River was kept secret for more than a decade. Built partially underground with thick concrete walls, it was a gunnery range, where 20-millimeter aircraft cannons and 30-millimeter tail guns for B-52 bombers were test fired as part of Ford's defense work.

While the Korean War and its aftermath influenced the boom-bust cycles of the economy, which impacted the auto industry, the fate of the Rouge Plant itself was directly affected by Ford's "decentralization" strategy and Del Harder's desire to automate Ford's car plants.

Decentralization meant several things to the automaker in the 1950s. First, Ford copied General Motors' corporate structure and replaced Henry Ford's one-man rule by spreading out decision-making authority. When it came to the Rouge Plant, several Ford executives thought the company was trying to do too much at the complex. When Ford opened a new state-of-the-art transmission plant in 1952, it was in the city of Livonia, nearly 17 miles from the Rouge.

Ford spent $2.5 billion in the 1950s to build or modernize 20 factories in the United States, including adding the Mercury plant (Wayne Assembly) in Wayne, Michigan, a new glass plant in Nashville, Tennessee, and new stamping plants. Only a portion of this money went into improving operations at the Rouge, as it became less of a nexus for Ford as the company disposed of its extended properties. The Brazilian rubber plantation, now superfluous with the demise of the Tire Plant, was sold at a loss in late 1945. Many of the Village Industries and soybean processing plants were also discontinued. But in 1947, the company laid plans to create a modern engineering complex near the old Ford Airport in Dearborn, just down Rotunda Drive from the Rouge.

Another casualty of the changing times was Ford's 31-year-old Iron Mountain–Kingsford plant, which made wooden station-wagon bodies; the company announced its sale in August 1951. Wood had been a major component in the Model T's construction when the Rouge was created, but by then steel had replaced wood for most uses, because it was stronger and lighter.

The Rouge also lost its tractor production, to Highland Park in 1949, but that was due to production problems with the farm machine. In the meantime, the Ford-Ferguson venture had fallen apart, and Harry Ferguson sued the automaker for $251 million, alleging that Ford was trying to harm his business. The case was eventually settled out of court in a deal that exonerated Ford of most of the charges but awarded the Irishman $9.25 million in patent royalty payments.

Automation was the next force that radically altered the Rouge Plant. "Automation is the word that has caught the fancy of engineers. It means the automated handling of materials between machine operations," proclaimed the Ford News Bureau in a March 1952 press release. But the automaker's automation efforts had actually started in 1947, when Del Harder created the "Automation Department."

Working in a maze of pipes, this plumber/pipefitter installs, repairs, and replaces plumbing systems that provide water, oil, gas, steam, and air to the massive Rouge factory complex. *Ford Photomedia*

RIVER ROUGE

A motorized crane rolls down a row of steel girders in the Rouge Plant's outdoor storage yard for its steel products in 1952. Just like a warehouse, each area is numbered, so the crane operator knows what parts to pick. The steel, however, might be stored outside for months, allowing rust to form long before it's turned into a finished product. *Ford Photomedia*

Automation greatly increased mass production while reducing the number of employees needed to make cars. For example, the time it took to make a V-8 engine plunged 3.25 hours to 14.6 minutes. As machines took over more of the process, gone were assembly lines with dozens of workers in tightly compact groups. Automated plants also worked better, by consolidating all production on one floor rather than requiring multistoried buildings, such as Dearborn Assembly. Of course, these new facilities required more land, so many newer factories were built away from the Rouge.

By 1951, on the tenth anniversary of the UAW's victory in organizing Ford, Carl Stellato, president of Local 600, blamed decentralization and the "speed up" (automation) for cutting the Rouge's workforce from 85,000 active members to 55,000. Ford was also "farming out" work to supplier companies.

Two years later, when the country slipped into a post–Korean War recession, the Local 600 paper, *Ford Facts*, stated that Ford's decentralization program and automation meant that the company would "employ a considerably fewer number of employees" and that many laid-off workers would not have a job to return to. However, Henry Ford II said that the layoffs would be temporary. Ford was partially correct. By 1958, the Rouge payroll rose back to 65,000 people.

Yet the union's worries in the early 1950s point to the first signs of the breakdown of vertical integration and the Rouge's diminishing role from Ford's showcase plant to just one of many manufacturing sites.

Despite the recession, 1953 was a special year for Ford as the company celebrated its fiftieth anniversary. It started with President Dwight D. Eisenhower dedicating the company's new Research and Engineering Center in May, via a television link. The main celebration was held June 16, when the Rotunda, decorated as a birthday cake with 50 "candles," reopened to public.

And Ford's cars for that year—offered in the Mainline, Customline, and Crestline styles—featured a special medallion with the Ford crest. Buyers had the choices of V-8 and V-6 engines and could get one of three transmissions: conventional, overdrive, or an automatic called the "Fordomatic." While the 1953 model cars and pickup trucks were still built at Dearborn Assembly, the assembly work was becoming more complicated as the cars became larger and had more standard and optional equipment. Also, Ford abandoned its founder's strategy of producing the lowest-priced cars in its segment and adopted prices comparable to those of General Motors.

Competition with GM became much more intense (Ford had surpassed Chrysler in sales, retaking the number-two spot in 1952) when Chevrolet introduced a new six-cylinder engine that delivered more horsepower than Ford's V-8s and launched the two-seat Corvette sports car. No longer could Ford be complacent with its engine technology or content to offer one basic car model. The Ford division responded to Chevrolet, in part, by bringing out the two-seat Thunderbird in 1955,

which was built at the Rouge. The Crestline was renamed the "Fairlane," adopting the name of Henry and Clara Ford's mansion. It was also given a wraparound windshield, a lower silhouette, a flatter hood, and a longer rear deck than other 1955 models.

The Thunderbird had been in development since 1951, and Lewis Crusoe pushed the design forward. The original car had a 102-inch wheelbase, a removable hardtop, and a 292-ci V-8, but hardly any of the early T-Birds were equipped with either overdrive or automatic transmissions. Porthole windows were added in the hardtop for ventilation the following year.

The first two-passenger T-Bird rolled off Dearborn Assembly on September 9, 1954, but when T-Bird profits proved unacceptable, the car was phased out on December 13, 1957, and the two-passenger car was replaced with the four- passenger "square bird."

Ford sales seemed on a roll in the mid-1950s, but a marketing disaster was brewing in Dearborn. As early as 1952, a committee led by Jack Davis had advised that Ford needed another car, code-named the "E car." Instead of creating the E car, however, Bill Ford was placed in charge of reintroducing the Continental nameplate as a separate division.

This worker in the Rouge Engine and Foundry Division has little to do as he monitors this LaPointe machine in December 1953. This photograph was taken to publicize Ford's complete automation of the 1954 overhead-valve engine line. *Ford Photomedia*

Another example of automation taking over tasks that once required dozens of workers is this Motch & Merryweather wrist pin, connecting rod, and piston assembling machine that could make more than 4,000 engine components per day. *Ford Photomedia*

The company's fortunes changed in February 1955, when 38-year-old Whiz Kid Jack Reith, who had successfully restructured Ford's French operations, unveiled a proposal to separate Mercury from the Lincoln Division for the 1957 model year. He also proposed using the E car to create an entirely new division to launch in late 1957. Reith's report had the backing of Ford Division executive Crusoe.

It was an audacious plan that left little time to design an entirely new Mercury lineup, let alone create a new division. Cars at the time were body-on-frame designs, which allowed automakers to change the shell with relative ease, especially with the nascent regulations concerning vehicle safety. If the plan worked, Reith hoped to succeed Crusoe, who was in line to replace Breech.

The Ford board of directors accepted the Crusoe-Reith plan. Despite the misgivings of the Ford family, Breech and other Ford managers thought it would be fitting to name the new division in honor of Edsel Ford. With the separation of Lincoln and Mercury, Benson Ford was shunted into handling company-dealer relations, and the poor-selling, limited-production Continental Division was folded into Lincoln. Bill Ford was given the title "vice president, styling." As it became clear that young Henry wasn't going to share power with his brothers, Benson began a battle with alcoholism. William bought the Detroit Lions football team in 1961 as an outlet for his passions.

Breech was elevated to chairman of the company's board of directors. Crusoe moved up to executive vice president, Car and Truck Division, which essentially gave him control of all vehicle assembly and distribution. McNamara became head of the Ford Division.

As the executive changes took place, other events were inexorably moving the company's center of attention away from the Rouge Plant and toward financial and global matters. The company prepared to take its stock public and commissioned a new headquarters building, miles from the manufacturing complex.

Henry Ford had viewed his minority shareholders as parasites who may have helped launch the company but who had done little to earn their yearly dividends. His descendents, though, had little choice but to turn to Wall Street if the company were to obtain the financing it needed to grow and "beat Chevy."

Because of the massive federal "death" taxes enacted during the Great Depression, Henry and Edsel Ford had created a charity called the Ford Foundation in 1936 to help their heirs avoid huge bills upon their deaths. The foundation ended up owning 88 percent of the company's nonvoting Class A stock. The family retained control of the company with its Class B voting stock but had a significantly lower financial stake than the charity. Not content with one source of income, the foundation's administrators wanted the ability to sell some of its Ford stock. A plan was developed whereby the family's Class B stock would give them 40 percent of the shareholder voting power. When the Class A stock went on sale in January 1956, its price rose from $64.50 to $70.50 a share.

The result was that Ford Motor Company was no longer a private fiefdom where money-losing ventures could be tolerated, such as having 5,000 workers devoted to cleaning and painting a manufacturing complex. More than ever before, the company had to pay attention to the whims of Wall Street brokerage houses and investors.

Another blow to the Rouge Plant as the center of Ford's empire came when the 12-story glass-and-steel-sheathed Central Office Building (COB) opened on September 26, 1956, near the intersection of Michigan Avenue and Southfield Road in Dearborn (later the Southfield Freeway). The COB, later called Ford World Headquarters and nicknamed the "Glass House," was 2 miles from the Rouge. The vast heavy-industrial complex was still in sight from the windows but now at a comfortable distance from the executives.

The Ford Division moved into a new building constructed at Rotunda and Southfield, two miles south of the COB. The new Mercury Division moved into the Administration Building, and Reith took over Ford's old office, with a sprawling view of the Rouge complex. Reith didn't have much time to sit back and look out his window, however, because Mercury sales had nosedived in 1956, and the new cars, including his Turnpike Cruiser, were launching that fall with many quality problems.

As the American economy slumped into a recession in 1957, sales of small cars experienced a significant uptick, while Mercury sales sagged. Instead of gaining market share, Mercury was losing ground. After Crusoe suffered a massive heart attack and was forced to take an early retirement, Breech and McNamara picked apart Reith's overambitious plans. When the final sales tallies were in, Mercury had sold only 136,000 cars instead of the 423,000 Reith had promised. McNamara's Ford Division, on the other hand, beat Chevy in sales for the first time since 1949.

Reith was removed as head of Mercury and, realizing that his path to the top of Ford was closed, quit to join another company instead of accepting a lesser post. Trouble followed Reith at Avco Manufacturing, where he ran the troubled Crosley Division. Pressures mounted as the Crosley Division faltered, and he took his own life on his son's birthday, July 3, 1960.

An apprentice inspector is in training at the Rouge Engine and Foundry Division as the white-haired veteran shows him how to use a "miking" gauge to examine the dimensions of a crankshaft. *Ford Photomedia*

The front clip of a 1958 Fairlane four-door, hardtop sedan is lowered into place. The Rouge was the only automotive factory complex in the world where raw materials could be transformed into a finished automobile in 28 hours. *Ford Photomedia*

Right: A dream machine is born as the clamshell lowers the body of a 1955 Thunderbird onto the waiting chassis. *Ford Photomedia*

Below: One man stoops as if getting ready to lift the bottommost instrument panel from the rack, while another worker appears to be installing a headlight on a Ford Thunderbird. *Walter P. Reuther Library, Wayne State University*

Mercury was folded back into Lincoln, and when the new Edsel Division launched with extremely poor sales, McNamara, now vice president of the Car and Truck Division, combined it with Lincoln-Mercury to briefly create Mercury-Edsel-Lincoln (M-E-L). By 1959 Edsel had sold fewer than 111,000 cars after two years on the market, and Henry Ford II announced that the car line would be discontinued. The failed Edsel brand had cost Ford $250 million, and the name "Edsel," in the public's mind, became synonymous with failure.

Ford Division got a boost in 1959 when the Rouge's Engine and Foundry division developed the thinwall casting process, which substantially reduced weight and costs—so much so that the automaker abandoned efforts to make aluminum engines. Cast iron had superior strength and rigidity, greater corrosion resistance than aluminum, and could withstand higher temperatures. The engines of very early cars weighed 25 pounds for every 1 horsepower they produced. That figure had dropped to 9 pounds per horsepower by World War II, but the thinwall casting process shaved the ratio further, to 2½ pounds per horsepower.

In 1959, the Ford Galaxie was born and immediately became the crème de la crème of the division. It, too, would go into production at the Rouge Plant. Unlike the Mercurys and Edsels of the late 1950s, the Galaxie was well received and was offered with four engine choices,

from a 145-horsepower six-cylinder all the way up to the 300-horsepower 352 "Thunderbird Special" V-8. It also came with numerous options, such as air conditioning, multicolored wheel covers, a power front seat, power steering, and power windows.

At the other end of the scale was the compact car influenced by McNamara: the 1960 Ford Falcon. The base model offered simple transportation and harkened back to the ideal of the Model T, with a six-cylinder engine that offered 30 miles per gallon fuel economy on the highway, single-color paint, a tight fit for six passengers, and little ornamentation. The 1960 Ford Falcon and its sister model, the Mercury Comet, were also the first vehicles to use Ford's thinwall cast engines. The "plain Jane" car would sell more than 400,000 units in its first year and about one million in two years. While the Falcon was not produced at the Rouge initially, it was four years later when a derivative model came out: the Mustang.

Henry Ford II was also asserting more and more control over the company, countermanding Breech's orders, until he finally told his chairman that he had "graduated" and didn't require a teacher any more. Breech retired as chairman in July 1960 but remained on the Ford board of directors until April 1967. Ford held the titles of both president and chairman until 1960, when he chose Whiz Kid McNamara to become his president but retained the chairman's post.

McNamara, however, had a short reign as Henry's chosen one. After just six months as Ford's president, he accepted the offer of U.S. president-elect John F. Kennedy to become secretary of defense, leaving Ford little choice but to chart another new course.

Chapter Seven

Home of the Pony Car, 1960–1976

"I grew up in the shadow of the Rouge, and my grandfather worked there, and so did my father. My father said to me, 'I'm going to get you into the Rouge. It's the best thing a father can do for a son. It will be a job for life.' Although he didn't succeed, eventually, I worked in the assembly and engine plants."
—Ishmael Ahmed, Arab Community Center for Economic and Social Services (ACCESS) president, interviewed 2003

Dearborn's "South End," which was part of the old city of Fordson, was the red-light district in the 1920s and 1930s, and its neighborhoods were run as much by Harry Bennett as by the racketeers. The residents there still live in the shadow of the Rouge Plant, feeling its every rumble, smelling its smells, and hearing its noises.

"It is a very powerful presence. The Rouge just towers over you," said Ishmael Ahmed, who grew up in the South End, worked at the Rouge after serving a tour in Vietnam, and later helped found the Arab Community Center for Economic and Social Services (ACCESS) in the 1970s. "I can remember watching them pour steel when I was a little kid, or going out to the clothesline where my mother had put the clothes to dry, and they were so filthy from the dust that we'd have to wash them again.

"As a kid, I went to the Rotunda to see Santa Claus, the only place a Muslim kid was going to see that. I used to play around Local 600, and one day I found a house with the old Socialist Party hall in the basement. There is so much industrial history around here."

By the 1940s, according to *Ripley's Believe It or Not*, 52 languages were spoken in Dearborn and southeast Detroit, with immigrants from Western and Eastern Europe, Turkey, and Mexico, plus Arab Christians and Muslims from Lebanon and Syria. Arabs were first drawn to Detroit by the promise of the Five Dollar Day. More came when the River Rouge Plant opened.

Arab immigration slowed in the 1930s, due to congressional limits on non-European immigrants, especially those of Asian descent, such as the Chinese, but there was an upswing after several pivotal court decisions, including one classifying Arabs as "whites." Still, relatively few Middle Easterners moved to Detroit until the late 1960s, when many fled wars and disasters in their home countries.

Immigrants came in waves from 1967 through 1972, in 1975, and again in the 1970s and 1980s. Chaldeans came from Iraq; Palestinians from Egypt; an estimated 3,000 to 7,000 Lebanese came to America per year during the Lebanon civil war of the 1970s and early 1980s; and when the Yemeni government allowed women to leave, many Yemeni families left their country, bound for Detroit.

Many Arab immigrants found work at the Rouge or at the Dodge Main Plant. Some worked on management's side, others for labor. One of the most famous Arab-Americans was Steve Yokich, who worked his way up through the UAW under Walter Reuther and eventually became president of the union.

But Arabs faced some seemingly hostile pressure from city hall. From the 1950s through the 1970s, the South End's residents, many of them Arabic, fought against the "urban renewal" plans of Mayor Orville Hubbard and Ford Motor Company, which were really attempts to turn their neighborhoods into an industrial park. But at the beginning of 1960, Ford was too distracted by Robert McNamara's departure to the Kennedy administration to worry about concerns in the local community.

There was no clear successor to McNamara. Although Whiz Kid Jim Wright was as much responsible for the Ford Division's success as McNamara, he had only been vice president of the Car and Truck Division for a few weeks. Lee Iacocca, who had gained fame for his marketing strategy of selling Fords for $56 a month in 1957, likewise was too inexperienced.

Burning coke is pushed out of one of the Rouge Complex's 183 ovens and into a waiting skip car, which will then rush down to the quenching tower, where the flames will be smothered with water. *Walter P. Reuther Library, Wayne State University*

A sonar device is used to check cylinder-wall thickness on a Ford 406-ci engine in March 1962. The operator at the Dearborn Engine Plant uses a probe to send sound waves through one side of the cast-iron cylinder wall and receive echoes from the other side. The tiny time lapse is read as wall thickness from a scale on a cathode tube. *Ford Photomedia*

Henry Ford II chose John Dykstra, one of the General Motors men recruited by Ernie Breech in 1946. Born in the Netherlands, Dykstra's father was a master coppersmith who had brought the family to Detroit when John was four. Dykstra didn't have a college degree, and his rough-and-tumble personality was cast in the mold of Charles Sorensen. To his credit, Dykstra had improved vehicle quality since the Mercury and Edsel disasters, but he lacked the management and leadership qualities Henry wanted to instill in the company.

Once Dykstra reach mandatory retirement age in 1963, Ford created the "Executive Office," where he remained chairman, while elevating Whiz Kid Arjay Miller to president and Charles Patterson, a manufacturing executive, to executive vice president. After being passed over a second time by Ford, Wright resigned, leaving only four of the original ten Whiz Kids at the company: Miller; Ben Mills, the general manager of Lincoln-Mercury; Charlie Bosworth, purchasing director for the Ford Division; and J. Edward Lundy, who controlled financing.

In the post-Edsel era, Lundy recruited top MBAs from universities around the country for Ford's burgeoning finance staff, which watched how the pennies and dollars were spent. It was an austere environment that forced marketing creativity but sacrificed long-range quality and performance innovations.

Iacocca was disappointed by the slim profit margins on the Falcon, despite 417,000 units sold in 1960, but he couldn't make major changes to it when faced by Lundy's bean counters. Instead, he created special packages to jazz up the car, such as the 1961 Falcon Sports Futura, which offered bucket seats, air conditioning, and power steering. For 1963, Iacocca offered the Falcon with an optional V-8 engine. Within two years and 46 days from its introduction, the Falcon sold one million units, setting a Ford postwar sales record for one vehicle. In large part, Iacocca's efforts kept the Falcon's sales propped up as car buyers turned back to larger vehicles with more options and horsepower.

After Chevrolet altered its Corvair into a sporty-looking vehicle by adding bucket seats and other trim and rebadging it the Monza, Ford designers created a prototype car with a long hood and a short deck that was given the code name "Allegro." When a two-seat convertible prototype was shown off at the 1962 Watkins Glen Grand Prix, it attracted enormous public interest. Iacocca lobbied Henry Ford II, saying that the car would appeal to the growing youth sports-car market, but Henry II rejected the proposal four times. Finally, he stopped by the design studio one day and marched up to Donald Frey, the Ford Division product manager. "I'm tired of hearing about your [expletive] car," Ford said. "Build it, but it's your ass if it doesn't sell."

The company went through several proposed names for the car, including "Cougar" and "Torino," before naming it after the famed P-51 Mustang, the fighter aircraft that helped win World War II in Europe. To keep manufacturing and development costs to a mere $51 million, the Mustang was built on the existing Falcon chassis, giving it an overall length of 181.6 inches and a wheelbase of 108 inches, and borrowed many parts from other vehicles. The Mustang had a starting price of $2,368, came in coupe or convertible body styles, and initially offered four engines, ranging from the base 101-horsepower inline six-cylinder to the 289-ci V-8 with 271 horsepower.

Although Ford finance forecast that the company would sell only 80,000 Mustangs during its first year, Iacocca not only dedicated production space at Dearborn Assembly but had the San Jose, California, and Metuchen, New Jersey, assembly plants prepared to build the car. The Rouge was also geared up to build the 1965 Falcon and the Ranchero, the pickup-truck-like derivative of the Falcon. The first Mustang production model, a white convertible, rolled off the Dearborn line on March 10, 1964.

The Mustang was formally unveiled April 17, 1964, at the Ford Pavilion at the New York World's Fair. On March 2, 1966, the one-millionth Mustang rolled off the Rouge assembly line, less than two years after the first production model was finished, beating the Falcon's record. *Time* and *Newsweek* featured Iacocca and the Mustang on their covers. GM and Chrysler responded with competing models, including

A diemaker at Dearborn Tool and Die in April 1963 works on a newly installed machine that finishes dies to an accuracy of a thousandth of an inch by electronically eroding away the tough alloy steel, one molecule at a time. In making a set of stamping dies, the punch half is formed to the finished dimensions by a skilled diemaker. After the second half of the die set was rough-cut, this Cincinnati machine finished it by flowing electrical current from the punch to produce matching contours on the second half. *Ford Photomedia*

Death of the Rotunda

When the Rotunda reopened to the public during Ford's fiftieth anniversary in 1953, it had received a number of ultramodern renovations, in keeping with the Atomic Age.

During the reopening ceremony on June 16, 1953, hundreds gathered at the edge of the Rouge Plant to watch as Bill Ford Sr. used a wand tipped with a small amount of radium to turn on the 50 huge birthday "candles" placed along the rim of the circular building. Inside, the building included numerous updates, most notably the 93-foot-diameter, 106-foot-high geodesic dome that turned the central courtyard into a "Dream Garden" of tropical plants designed by Dearborn florist Harry Miller.

The dome was a technological marvel created by inventor R. Buckminster Fuller. A conventional glass-and-steel dome would have weighed 320,000 pounds and crushed the Rotunda's steel framework, but Fuller's plastic-and-aluminum design weighed only 17,000 pounds and allowed the central courtyard to be used year-round.

Various car displays dotted the interior, and the south wing housed a 388-seat theater, while the north wing held the 9 million documents and 450,000 pictures of the Ford Archives. Outside was the "Roads of the World," a mile-long test track on which visitors could ride in the latest Ford cars, traveling over gravel, cobblestone, and corduroy pavement with chuckholes, a simulated railroad crossing, a small climbing hill, and inclines where cars could be accelerated up to 60 miles per hour.

"People wanted to have rides in a number of Ford cars, including Thunderbirds and Galaxies, but no one wanted a ride in a Falcon," noted Jim Sanderson, who was hired as a Rouge Plant tour guide and Rotunda test-track driver in the early 1960s, while taking classes at the University of Detroit.

The free Rouge and Rotunda tours were available year-round, except for the two weeks of model changeover during the summer. The tours became so popular that they attracted larger crowds than Niagara Falls and Yellowstone Park. During the winter, there were special nighttime tours. For years, more visitors went to the Rotunda than went on the Rouge tours.

Two tours of the Rouge were available: visitors went either to the engine and assembly plants, which took two hours, or on the much longer trek through the steel operations.

"On the steel division, you got to watch the red-hot ingots get rolled back and forth and rolled out to sheet metal. You could smell that steel and feel that heat," Sanderson said. "When we went through where they made the castings for the engine blocks, the heat in there was unbearable, and it was dirty. The engine and assembly plants were both very clean, and the assembly plant had a feeling of everything being new."

The Rotunda's annual "Christmas Fantasy" was immensely popular and included "Santa's Workshop," where elves built vehicle toys on a miniature assembly line, and a nativity scene. Topping off the display was a large Christmas tree.

Just before 1 p.m. on November 9, 1962, 118 students from South Bend, Indiana, had finished their tour of the Rotunda, which was mostly decorated for Christmas, when someone on the school bus looked back at the building and cried out, "There's smoke."

An infrared heater had ignited tar being applied to the roof as weatherproofing. An employee on the ground floor noticed the blaze and sounded the alarm, allowing the 60 other people inside to hurry out as workers on the roof scrambled to safety.

Although firemen responded quickly, the blaze had already entered the structure. The heat weakened the steel girders, and the building groaned, giving a dozen firemen enough time to flee before the Rotunda's walls collapsed inward. The Rotunda was gone before 2 p.m., but firefighters kept the blaze from consuming the Ford Archives.

Ford tore down the remains of the Rotunda and donated most of its archival material to the Edison Institute/Henry Ford Museum. To the disappointment of many Dearborn residents, Henry Ford II decided not to rebuild the structure, but the Rouge tours continued out of the Central Office Building. Finally, on August 5, 1974, for the fiftieth anniversary of the tours, Ford opened a new Visitors Center across the street from the Henry Ford Museum & Greenfield Village.

The last tour for more than 20 years was held on July 27, 1980. The program was halted in part to cut costs—but also because many Ford executives were no longer proud of the Rouge. The public tours, which had started August 5, 1924, were interrupted only by World War II and strikes and had drawn more than 22 million people. Smaller, private tours still went through parts of the complex, but it wasn't until May 3, 2004, that Ford reopened what was left of the Rouge to the public.

The top of the Rotunda collapsed in a devastating fire that started during a roof re-tarring project on November 9, 1962. Firefighters in this photograph seem to be directing their attention to the wing where the Ford Archives department was housed. Had their efforts not been successful, this book and many others would not have been possible. Watching the fire from his bicycle near the red car at the bottom center of the photograph is the young Michael Birrell, future fire chief of Dearborn.
Ford Photomedia

The Basic Oxygen Furnace was one of the latest developments in steelmaking by the mid-1960s. One of two refractory-lined vessels, each 34 feet high and 24 feet in diameter, operates at a time, producing 250 tons of steel an hour, while the other vessel undergoes maintenance. Each furnace "charge" consists of 400,000 pounds of molten iron and 170,000 pounds of scrap steel, along with measured quantities of burned lime, fluorspar, and ore pellets. *Ford Photomedia*

the Pontiac Firebird, Chevy Camaro, and Plymouth Barracuda, creating the "pony car" market segment.

As Mustang production galloped ahead, the Rouge saw the first fruits of the company's $1.6 billion "Modernization and Quality Program" first announced in 1959. The first new factory to open was the Basic Oxygen Furnace, which fired up in 1964. The "BOF" was built on the west side of the boat slip and covered 23 acres. Inside were two pear-shaped cauldrons, 34 feet high and 20 feet in diameter. The cauldrons were charged with molten iron from the blast furnaces and scrap metal and received an injection of pure oxygen. In less than an hour, the two vessels produced 250 tons of molten steel, or nearly 3 million tons annually. The facility replaced the Open-Hearth Building, which closed, and included a multimillion-dollar dust collector, making it one of the cleanest such factories in the world.

The Dearborn Frame Plant was also given a 200,000-square-foot addition, to make the new "torque box frames" for the 1965 Fords and Mercurys, which allowed the car bodies to sit in the frames rather than on top of them. When the Frame Plant expansion was announced in September 1964, Ford also said it would build a state-of-the-art stamping plant. When Woodhaven Stamping opened in 1965, 14 miles from the Rouge, it took over the prominence that had once been given to Dearborn Stamping, signaling yet another decline of the Rouge.

In 1965, however, Henry Ford II also announced that the automaker would again modernize its steelmaking operations at the Rouge. "The purpose of the program is to enable the company to maintain its ability to produce about half its own steel tonnage in the expanded vehicle markets of the future," Ford said. Some Rouge workers later argued that the company still did not put enough money back into the operation, as evidenced by the fact that the original blast furnaces were kept in operation even as Japanese steelmakers expanded using continuous casting furnaces.

Among the improvements the Rouge received were three new high-speed "pickling" lines and a new hot-roll "flat-pass" mill to make steel sheets and coils. Pickling is the process that cleans the surface and improves the finish of hot-rolled steel. The new pickling lines were also equipped with an acid regeneration facility, to drastically reduce water pollution.

The Rouge's 1935 Open-Hearth Building was demolished to make way for a new 290,000-square-foot Slabbing Mill and storage building.

Molten iron from the blast furnaces pours into torpedo-shaped ladle cars, which have a thick lining of ceramic brick to retain heat. The metal remains molten while Ford Railroad engines push the ladle cars to the Basic Oxygen Furnace. *Ford Photomedia*

The Slabbing Mill opened in 1969 and replaced the 30-year-old Blooming Mill, converting ingots into 32-foot-long, 24-ton steel slabs for use in the Hot Strip Mill. The Rouge's 1935-era Hot Strip Mill was supposed to have been replaced by mid-1969, but completion was delayed until 1974, because its design was enlarged and more pollution control equipment was added.

While the Rouge steel facilities received badly needed updates, Ford also modernized its glassmaking facilities. The Dearborn Glass Plant had produced Ford's first curved-glass safety windshields in 1951. Three years later, its floor space was nearly doubled.

In 1964, Ford acquired a license from Pilkington Brothers, Ltd., of England, to produce the latest technology, "float" glass (Pilkington had helped Ford develop its original glassmaking processes in 1919). In

March 1967, the Dearborn Glass Plant became the first factory in the world to make ⅛-inch glass for laminated windshields. Ford was the third largest producer of float glass in the United States by 1973, also making products for windows and doors, and the only automaker to manufacture its own glass.

"The Pilkington method was a revolutionary way of making glass," said Jim Sanderson, who worked as a quality control inspector at the Glass Plant in 1965 during a co-op program while attending the University of Detroit. "Before it came in, you had to extensively grind and polish the glass. With the Pilkington method, the glass floats out clear, but defects can crop up."

To check for "critical distortions" in the windshields, Sanderson took pictures through the glass using a Polaroid camera. As an inspector,

This giant dipper pours 400,000 pounds of molten iron into the mouth of the Basic Oxygen Furnace, where the iron will be converted into steel. The finished molten steel is then poured to form huge ingots, which are rolled into bars and sheets, ready for fabrication at the Dearborn Stamping Plant. *Ford Photomedia*

he had the power to shut the line down if he noticed a defect, but there was enormous pressure to keep production going no matter what. "I had to be right," Sanderson said, explaining that he did shut the glass line down twice because of problems but was still chewed out by the plant manager, a cantankerous German named Rudy.

The late 1960s were a tumultuous time in the United States, and the Rouge was no exception. As older workers retired, the younger generation coming in wasn't satisfied with the status quo, distrusting both the company and the union.

Detroit was the fifth largest city in the U.S. but had started declining as the growing interstate highway system helped create new suburbs. The automobile had become the choice of transportation for many workers, since the city's streetcar system was discontinued in 1955, leaving buses as the only practical mass transit alternative.

Race riots had broken out in several U.S. cities, but Detroit Mayor Jerry Cavanaugh, an Irish-Catholic Democrat, was confident that his city of 1.65 million people—40 percent of whom were black, many of them homeowners—would remain calm. But racial tensions reached the boiling point on July 23, 1967, following a police raid by predominantly white officers on an illegal nightclub filled with black patrons. A large crowd gathered as police were leaving, and someone threw a bottle. That act ignited the nation's bloodiest and most sustained riot.

Above: Duward LaFortune *(left)* of Wayne and Stanley Albinger of Allen Park, workers at the Glass Plant, make sure a rearview mirror just heat-inducted onto the glass stays in place. *Ford Photomedia*

Right: In the wake of the devastation of the 1967 Detroit riot, Henry Ford II joined other community, industrial, and religious leaders in extending a helping hand. Here, throngs of people, called the "hard core unemployed" by the *Detroit News*, line up at a Detroit facility to apply for jobs at the Rouge Plant and other nearby Ford factories. *Walter P. Reuther Library, Wayne State University*

As Detroit burned and looters ran rampant, Governor George Romney declared a state of emergency and ordered 7,300 National Guardsmen into the city, but the riot continued. At 3 a.m. on July 24, Romney asked for federal assistance, but it wasn't until eight hours later that President Lyndon B. Johnson ordered 4,700 paratroopers from the 101st and 82nd Airborne Divisions deployed to the city.

At the end of the week, with the insurrection finally quelled, 44 people were dead and more than 300 were seriously injured. About 5,000 residents were left homeless, and more than 7,300 were under arrest as Belle Isle was converted into a temporary prison compound. Entire city blocks had burned to the ground, with some 1,300 buildings destroyed. Dearborn Mayor Orville Hubbard issued an order for police to shoot looters on sight if violence broke out there.

Following the riot, Henry Ford II, UAW President Walter Reuther, and others created an organization called New Detroit to "build bridges" between whites and blacks. Henry promised to open jobs at the Rouge and other factories to Detroit's "hard core" unemployed. But the result of the riot was "white flight" from the city to the suburbs. Many businesses fled Detroit, too, because of its crime rate. Within 30 years, Detroit's population dropped below 1 million, and its population was more than 80 percent black. Metropolitan Detroit received the dubious distinction of being one of the nation's most racially segregated regions.

Henry Ford II shook up the company's management in January 1968 when he replaced Arjay Miller with an outsider from General Motors—Semon E. "Bunkie" Knudsen. Bunkie was the son of William Knudsen, the former Ford production man who had risen to become president of General Motors. "Big Bill" had given his son the odd-sounding nickname because their relationship was so close, they were like "bunkmates."

Ford had tried to recruit Knudsen back in 1963, but Bunkie thought he had a chance to follow his father's footsteps to the top office on GM's "fourteenth floor." By 1968, however, Bunkie was passed over at GM and accepted the Deuce's new offer. Unlike Ernie Breech, Knudsen brought few GM managers with him and found himself undermined by Iacocca on the product side and by Whiz Kid Lundy on the financial end. By September 1969, Henry told Bunkie that "things had not worked out" and that he was fired.

Ford divided the president's duties between Iacocca, who became executive vice president and president of Ford North American Auto Operations; Robert Stevenson, president of Ford International Operations; and Robert Hanson, president of Non-Automotive Operations. This "troika" arrangement lasted for a little more than a year before Henry II named the cigar-chomping Iacocca as the company president.

Nineteen sixty-eight and 1969, however, were not bad years under Knudsen. Ford sold cars about as fast as it could make them, and the company hired as many people as it could. Even convicts were brought

in to work at the Rouge, causing a spike in crime at the complex. And the personnel office at Gate 4 wasn't too careful about checking the ages of applicants, as when 16-year-old Brian Olind of Dearborn conned his way into a job.

Although underaged, Olind wanted to help his parents pay for his education at Detroit Catholic Central High School. After borrowing his older brother Mike's identification, Brian trekked down to the Rouge to stand in the employment line for nearly three hours. "I asked if I could get a job cutting the lawns," Olind said. "The guy who did the interview said, 'This is an auto plant. We have jobs in either the Assembly Plant or the Engine Plant. They pay $3.25 in the Assembly Plant and a nickel less in the Engine Plant—what do you want?' I thought I had died and gone to heaven."

A specialized but bulky pneumatic tool allows this Dearborn Assembly worker to simultaneously tighten all the lug nuts on a 1967 Mustang wheel. *Ford Photomedia*

A quality controller checks the body-side of an incomplete 1967 Mercury Cougar clamped in a jig. *Ford Photomedia*

Workers in the spray booth on the second floor of Dearborn Assembly apply finishing enamel to 1967 Mustangs and Cougars. In this pre-OSHA era, not everyone is wearing a dust mask, despite the enormous overspray and paint fumes that must be present in this confined space. *Ford Photomedia*

the right number of rpms," Olind said. "Then they let them run for 8 to 10 minutes, go to the next engine, and start it. While they were starting those 12, I'd be completing work on the other 12 engines."

The engines ran without mufflers, so it was constantly noisy. Once the inspectors were done, Olind removed the equipment from the hot engines, occasionally getting blasted by steam.

Just before he turned 18, Olind's falsified application nearly cost him his job when his brother Mike went to work at the Livonia Transmission Plant. A manager met with Brian to tell him it was against policy to let employees hold two company jobs. "I came down to fire you, but you've never been late and never missed a day here or at Livonia and had perfect attendance. So I wanted to meet someone who could work two jobs," the man told Brian.

Brian never revealed that he had falsified his application. Shortly after he turned 18, he rehired into the Rouge under his own name. His brothers Mike and Norb also worked in the different plants at the complex.

The Rouge was still fairly clean, but forklifts (Hi-Lo's) constantly moved around. At the Stamping, Frame, and Engine plants, Hi-Lo drivers picked up tottering stacks of parts, running along like Indy drivers. Occasional accidents hurt and even killed workers and foremen.

Decades of workplace accidents and union pressure led Congress to pass the Occupation Safety and Health Act (OSHA) in 1970, one of a number of pieces of legislation enacted during the 1960s and 1970s that radically changed how the auto industry functioned. But 1970 was also a watershed year, because the National Highway Traffic Safety Administration (NHTSA) was established and the Nixon administration and Congress worked together to create the Environmental Protection Agency (EPA).

Even the UAW supported stronger environmental controls. Union leaders, like many people, believed that "Detroit"—GM, Ford, and Chrysler—cried wolf far too many times when safety and environmental regulations were proposed. Along with creating the EPA, Congress passed the Clean Air Act of 1970. This legislation banned lead in gasoline and the fuel additive to eliminate engine knock. It also mandated significant advancements, including the use of catalytic converters, electronic engine control systems, fuel injectors, and sensors to control vehicle emissions such as hydrocarbons, carbon monoxide, and nitrogen oxides. Factories fell under the more stringent air and water pollution laws, too.

By no means was Ford alone in facing this challenge, but by 1971, the company had already invested millions of dollars installing pollution controls at each plant, including massive dust collectors on the

Olind worked in the Engine Plant's hot-test facility on Mondays and Fridays—the days many full-time union members were taking "long weekends." The finished engines were hung from an overhead conveyor, and the "stick men," who used a long stick to reach the overhead chain, directed the engines into the 24 testing bays. There, Brian attached temporary starters, water and fuel lines, and flexible pipes to the engines.

"There were two inspectors behind us who actually started the engines, set the timing and balance, and revved them up until they hit

Final inspections of the Mustang are made on the Dearborn Assembly line in 1968. These popular sporty cars launched the "pony car" segment, as rivals GM and Chrysler fielded their own models, such as the Pontiac Firebird and the Plymouth Barracuda. *Walter P. Reuther Library, Wayne State University*

Rouge's Basic Oxygen Furnace, Powerhouse, and Sinter Plant. After an oil slick on the Rouge River caught fire in the 1960s, Ford added an "oil eating" pontoon boat that operated in the boat slip.

Frank Kallin, environmental control manager, said at the time that older plants like the Rouge were the toughest to renovate to meet the new regulations. "Adding pollution reduction facilities to twenty-five-year-old plants is like putting in the plumbing after the house is built. . . . The Rouge is the largest industrial complex in the world. We want to make it the cleanest."

Yet the creation of the EPA and growing environmental regulations didn't stop the 1971–1973 U.S. Army Corps of Engineers project, which reshaped the Rouge River as dramatically as the scheme that had straightened the waterway back in the 1920s. By the early 1970s, most Detroiters viewed the river, which regularly overflowed its banks, as an open sewer. Over the protests of ecologists, who posted signs along the river saying "Rape of the Rouge," the federal government constructed a concrete channel that encased the river between Michigan Avenue and the Rouge Plant's turning basin. The channel greatly reduced flooding but created an eyesore.

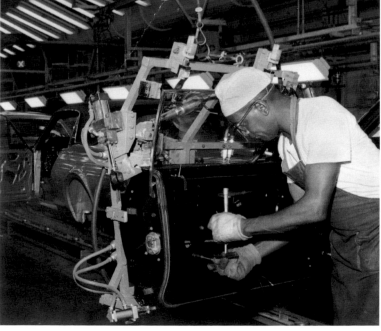

A worker installs glass with the aid of a jig that fits up against the door. *Ford Photomedia*

General welder James Stasie drives the "welding buggy" he helped create in the early 1970s for use in the Dearborn Stamping Plant. Stasie received a $6,000 award for suggesting the creation of these buggies to carry welding equipment, grinders, and other tools he might need for on-the-spot die repairs. *Ford Photomedia*

Ford started a number of projects at the Rouge to address the tightening federal air and water quality regulations while boosting production. In the late 1960s, the aging Dearborn Iron Foundry received six new cast-iron molding lines. The foundry made 1,800 molds per hour and manufactured more cylinder heads, intake and exhaust manifolds, and transmission case housings than ever before. On the environmental side a high-efficiency ventilation system and dust precipitators were installed on the foundry's cupolas to wash and purify furnace gases. A new laboratory was installed at the foundry to test the chemical and physical properties of all materials. Even with these updates, when the iron foundry celebrated its fiftieth anniversary in 1970, its days were numbered.

"Through the years, Dearborn Iron Foundry has had many improvements, renovations, and facelifts, but it just hasn't been able to keep up with the times," said John Perkins, the foundry manager at the time.

Ford decided to build a new state-of-the-art facility called the Michigan Casting Center, with 25 acres under one roof and five molding lines. Like the Woodhaven Stamping Plant, this new facility was not placed at the Rouge but was nearly 17 miles away, in Flat Rock, a few miles south of the Woodhaven plant. Michigan Casting partially

opened in 1972 and was fully operational when the Dearborn Iron Foundry closed for good in 1974.

The iron foundry had poured more than 50 million cast-iron engine blocks, including some 33 million V-8s. By late 1977, Ford announced that the shuttered plant would come tumbling down, to be replaced by a landscaped berm. A park-like plaza with trees and benches was added to the Gate 4 bus stop, while the historic overpass also met the wrecking ball. Scrap metal from the foundry was fed into the basic oxygen furnaces.

The Michigan Casting Center, however, didn't have the longevity of the old iron foundry, closing when the economy slipped into two deep recessions in the late 1970s and early 1980s. Eventually, the Flat Rock factory was converted into AutoAlliance, a joint-venture assembly plant between Ford and the Japanese automaker Mazda.

With the iron foundry on a path toward obsolescence, Ford added capacity to the Dearborn Specialty Foundry's crankshaft molding lines, building a $1.3 million wastewater treatment plant in 1971. The plant used a series of grit-removal tanks and chemicals in a 75-foot-diameter clarifier tank to remove solid wastes, which were disposed of in a landfill.

Environmental concerns altered the design of the Rouge's new Hot Strip Mill. The new design used reheating furnaces fired by natural gas, which virtually eliminated pollutants from the smokestacks. The facility also recycled great quantities of water, using a walnut-shell filtration system and a wooden cooling tower. This reduced the Rouge's need for fresh water and cut down toxic discharges into the river. When it finally opened in 1974, about five years after original projections, the mill became one of Ford's largest steelmaking facilities. Capable of producing 3 million tons of hot-rolled steel annually, it was more than one-third of a mile long, with 525,000 square feet of floor space, and employed 6,000 workers.

In the Hot Strip Mill, steel slabs were heated in a "walking beam" furnace to 2,300 degrees Fahrenheit. The white-hot slabs then went through a series of "roughing" mills that reduced them from 6 inches to less than 1/10 inch, to make 72-inch wide coils.

The new Electric Furnace Melt Shop opened in 1976, on the site of the old navy school, adding three-quarters of a million tons of raw steelmaking capability to the Rouge. At that time, Ford projected that the United States needed an additional 25 to 30 million tons of raw steel capability by 1980, a prediction that proved to be far too optimistic.

At the time, Ford received most of its iron ore from the Eveleth Taconite Company in northeastern Minnesota. Eveleth Taconite was a joint-venture enterprise Ford formed in 1963 with the Oglebay Norton Company, to crush low-grade iron ore (taconite) and separate the metal from the waste rock, using a magnetic process. This left a fine powder, which went through a bonding mixture in rolling drums to create iron pellets. The process had revived the Mesabi Range as a key source of iron. The Ford Steel Division also operated extensive material reserves and mines in Kentucky and Michigan.

At Dearborn Assembly, the Mustang continued after production of the Falcon and Ranchero was moved elsewhere following the 1967 model year. Replacing them on the line were the Mercury Cougar from 1966 to 1973 and the Ford Maverick and Mercury Comet for the 1972 and 1973 model years. With bigger engines, however, the Mustang had gotten 600 pounds heavier and was less nimble. The 1971 model was 8 inches longer and offered a plusher interior. But when the 'Stang's sales plunged in 1972 to their lowest level, Ford began working a smaller version, based on the Pinto subcompact platform.

The Mustang's downsizing came just in time, because on October 6, 1973, Syria and Egypt launched a surprise invasion of Israel that became known as the Yom Kippur War. After the tiny Jewish state beat back its larger Arab neighbors, Libya shut off oil exports to the United States. The Organization of Petroleum Exporting Countries (OPEC), with the urging of Saudi Arabia and the Shah of Iran, followed Libya's lead by launching oil embargoes against the United States, Canada, Western Europe, and Japan. The economy slid into a recession as gasoline prices in America doubled, then quadrupled. The Nixon administration exacerbated matters by imposing a national 55-mile-per-hour speed limit and standby gasoline rationing.

Sales of large American cars plunged—GM's total dropped by nearly 1.5 million units, Ford's dipped by 500,000, and Chrysler's fell by 300,000—causing massive layoffs at the Rouge and other automotive plants as buyers turned toward small, fuel-efficient cars. Many buyers discovered that the cars from Toyota, Datsun (Nissan), and Honda were not, after all, poorly made for the price. With American-made cars averaging less than 15 miles per gallon, Congress passed the first Corporate Average Fuel Economy (CAFE) law, which raised the average new car's fuel economy to 18 miles per gallon by 1978 and 20 miles per gallon by 1980. Automakers that didn't comply faced "gas guzzler" taxes.

The quandary the Big Three automakers found themselves in was that much of the existing technology to cut tailpipe emissions and improve passenger safety actually harmed fuel economy. The only choice was to downsize car designs, reducing the amount of steel needed, cutting horsepower, and offering far fewer big cars, even if buyers wanted them. Because pickups were considered "work trucks," the federal fuel and safety standards were lower for them.

When the slimmer Mustang II was introduced in September 1973, it weighed about 700 pounds less than its predecessor, was shorter than the original car, and became the only model built at Dearborn Assembly. The car offered an overhead-cam, four-cylinder engine—which, after the enactment of the CAFE laws, came off the line sporting the white letters "MPG" to signify that it obtained 34 miles per gallon on the highway and 23 in the city. Buyers could also get a V-6, but the V-8 option had disappeared and would not resurface until 1978, as a 5.0-liter option on the King Cobra. The convertible also vanished from the Mustang's lineup.

Despite Ford's updates to the Rouge and the Mustang, executive Donald Petersen was about to learn that many of the complex's factories were obsolete. Petersen's career had taken a few twists since he was last at the Rouge, in an office in the old navy barracks, including becoming vice president and general manager of truck operations in 1971. Petersen said that while he was at the truck division, where executives not on the fast track were exiled, he learned how to pay attention to customer needs and improve products rather than play corporate political games.

In 1975, Petersen was placed in charge of Diversified Products operations, a hodgepodge of different businesses. Several of the Rouge factories, including the Steel Division and the Glass Plant, reported to his office. At that time, the Boston Consulting Group finished a study that presented a dark outlook for the future of the Rouge.

"Boston Consulting's study looked at growth versus the profitability of our operations," Petersen recalled. "In some cases, we had operations where high growth and profitability were predicted. In others, we were making a lot of money then, but the business wasn't growing. Or there were operations where we were losing money and the business was going nowhere."

Ford wanted to know what businesses to keep and which operations might be better performed by outside suppliers. Many of the

The main channel of the Rouge River was altered south of Michigan Avenue to the Rouge Complex in the early 1970s. This picture, taken July 11, 1973, where Rotunda Drive crosses the river, shows the U.S. Army Corps of Engineers flood control project that straightened the river, turning it into a concrete channel. As a result, southeastern Dearborn, the Rouge Complex, and neighboring communities no longer suffered from the river overflowing its banks, but it was a severe blow to nature and aesthetics. *Walter P. Reuther Library, Wayne State University*

Rouge factories ranked at the bottom of the study. The Steel Division's general manager, George Ferris, was trying to upgrade his factories to stay competitive, but the American steel industry faced extreme pressure from foreigners.

After Petersen delivered the Boston Consulting Group's recommendations to Henry Ford II and Lee Iacocca, the automaker tried giving the Rouge a reprieve from its day of reckoning. On July 9, 1976, Ford announced that the factory complex would receive yet another multimillion-dollar renovation. Employment at the complex, though, had dropped to a little more than 26,000 workers.

In some cases, the renovations amounted to window dressing. The gray bricks and exposed pipes and windows of the 58-year-old "B" Building were covered by a façade of white-over-pale blue aluminum siding, and rows of saplings were planted around the complex. The warehouse (old Tire Plant), Steel Mill, Dearborn Specialty Foundry, and the Employment Office on Miller Road were similarly renovated. The complex's roads, parking lots, plant grounds, and railroad

Above: The Dearborn Stamping Plant had grown tremendously by 1973. The space between the former Pressed-Steel and Spring and Upset buildings was long ago filled in by additions, as the plant bumped into the steel mill to the south. Yet the Stamping Plant's place in the company had been eclipsed by newer, larger factories, including Woodhaven Stamping, located 14 miles from the Rouge by rail or truck. *Ford Photomedia*

Right: The north end of the storage bins displays a touch of greenery after Ford's multimillion-dollar renovation of the complex in the early 1970s. The shovel of the nearest of the three transfer cranes hangs just above the ground. The boat slip is just out of frame, to the right. *Walter P. Reuther Library, Wayne State University*

tracks were cleaned, repaired, and painted, while unused facilities were demolished.

The Dearborn Engine Plant was scheduled to receive a 227,000-square-foot addition by 1980, which would give it 1.8 million square feet of floor space. When it was renovated, it produced new four-cylinder inline engines for a new family of small cars, the 1981 Ford Escort and Mercury Lynx, while phasing out truck and small engine production. While this change preserved jobs, it was another sign that the Rouge was becoming less and less integrated. The engines would be shipped down Michigan Avenue to Wayne Assembly rather than to Dearborn Assembly, which would get its engines from Ford's engine plants in Windsor, Ontario.

At the end of America's bicentennial year, Henry Ford II had set events in motion to replace Iacocca, but few realized that the American auto industry's bright-looking future would grow considerably dimmer before the decade's end.

Above: The gray bricks and exposed pipes that dominated the front of the 60-year-old Dearborn Assembly Plant along Road 4 are visible to the left. The former location of the three massive Eagle Boat doors is evident from the placement of the windows. In the mid-1970s, in one of several facelifts made to the factory throughout its history, the façade was covered by aluminum siding, and a row of trees was planted along the front. *Ford Photomedia*

Left: Not much seems different between the *Detroit News* photo taken of the Rouge coke ovens made on May 8, 1946, and the color photograph from the 1970s on page 119. *Walter P. Reuther Library, Wayne State University*

Chapter Eight

The End of an Aging Giant?
1977–1998

"We are faced with the dilemma of that tradition on the one hand, and the fact, on the other hand, that by nature and by the movements in technology, much of the Rouge is getting old. So we're faced with the dilemma of what to do with the Rouge, or perhaps in different terms, what to do with the individual components that make up the Rouge. The bottom line for any organization is that it must be competitive on the world scene."

—Allan D. Gilmour, Ford chief financial officer, Dearborn Press & Guide, 1987

As Ford Motor Company prepared for its seventy-fifth anniversary, the Rouge Plant was losing its spot as the company's manufacturing showcase. Employment slid below 30,000 workers during the economic doldrums of the mid-1970s, and getting a job in the auto industry became a lot harder for unskilled laborers. Some doubted that venerable factories like the Rouge would even survive.

"There were massive changes that happened here in the 1970s, with the iron foundry closing and then the Specialty Foundry. It seemed like it was only a matter of time before Ford shut the whole thing down," said Jerry Sullivan, president of UAW Local 600 since 1997. "We used to build the Capri, the Mustang, the Maverick, and the T-Bird, and all we were left with was the Mustang and a lot of quality problems.

"The old story is that Local 600 was so strong that it almost ran Ford Motor Company, and it was the largest local in the UAW, so the company and the union agreed to destroy the local. Think about it: the only major reinvestments were done outside the Rouge. They totally gutted the Engine Plant, and people were scattered everywhere. I think they wanted to close up every plant in the Rouge."

There are no documents to support the charge that the UAW and the automaker conspired to thwart the power of Local 600. Donald Petersen, who became Ford's president in 1980 and served as chairman from 1985 until 1990, said he never heard of such a plan.

Yet there could be a shred of truth to the "old story," noted Wayne State University business professor Charlie Hyde. "No one in the union or Ford Motor will ever admit that, but Local 600 was the largest, most communist-leaning local in the UAW," he said. Since the Rouge not only assembled cars but also manufactured parts for other plants, a wildcat strike by the local or a disaster there could shut down the entire company.

"With dilution of the Rouge's power, the local lost much of its clout over the years," Hyde said. "I think that Walter Reuther had developed a particular dislike to the local's leaders. He certainly didn't object when Ford started moving jobs elsewhere."

Jerry Sullivan hired into the Rouge in 1971 at age 24, nearly two years after he returned from a tour and a half in the army's 1st Infantry Division in Vietnam. He still remembers the cold looks from people at the airport when he returned from the war. Sullivan kept his background to himself and didn't find out about fellow workers who were also Vietnam veterans until a couple of years later.

Starting as an apprentice electrician, Sullivan experienced animosity from some older workers of the World War II generation who didn't like the changes brought in by the new generation. About this time, for example, the company newspaper began running stories about how workers should deal with drug abuse and racism.

"There was a lot of pressure from older guys, and it was not an easy job, with situations that could put someone's life in jeopardy," continued Sullivan, who narrowly avoided a serious injury during his first year on the job. He was ordered to take a motor off an unused welding machine, but the power switch could not be locked in the "off" position and someone accidentally turned the machine on while Sullivan was inside. After that incident, and when he was reprimanded for taking time off around his father's death in 1974, Sullivan started becoming active in the union.

These 1979 Mustangs appear trapped after a heavy snowfall during the winter of 1980, symbolic of the domestic auto industry's winter of discontent, with the country sliding into recession. Ford would be forced to take drastic steps to reduce its workforce amid questions about whether the Rouge would survive. *Ford Photomedia*

Superintendent Ralph Wood checks out the day's production schedule against the background of the 20-foot-wide exhaust ducts of the new Electric Furnace Shop's air purification system in 1977. *Ford Photomedia*

Ford dismissed Iacocca's supporters, and on April 14, 1977, he knocked Iacocca down to the number three position in the company by creating the three-member Office of the Chief Executive. Iacocca continued as president and took on the title of chief operating officer, but he now reported to Philip Caldwell, who was named to the new position of vice chairman. Caldwell had served on Admiral Chester Nimitz's staff during World War II and had hired into the company just after Iacocca. Under his tutelage, the truck and international divisions blossomed.

The day after Iacocca's first tumble, Henry Ford II dedicated the Detroit Renaissance Center, a castle-like office tower complex. Reminiscent of his grandfather, the Deuce had become engrossed with real estate ventures. The RenCen, as it was called, was built along the shore of the Detroit River, nearly on the spot where Alexander Malcomson's coal yard had been. The RenCen was Henry's effort to help Detroit rebuild after the 1967 riot, but he arm-twisted a number of suppliers and even rivals GM and Chrysler into contributing to the $500 million project. Ford Motor Company, though, footed much of the bill.

Many visitors—and even tenants—got lost in the circular Renaissance Center. Detractors pointed to the RenCen's two massive concrete berms placed between the front entrance and Jefferson Avenue, calling them "tank traps," as if to ward off the city's rabble from the glittering edifice. The office towers, though, housed a two-floor office suite, complete with fireplace, for Henry and became the new home for the Ford and Lincoln-Mercury divisions, which vacated their offices in Dearborn. The company's parts division occupied the old Rouge Administration Building until moving out in 1993, leaving the building vacant.

Addressing the problems of "human engineering" at the Rouge was not at the top of Henry Ford II's agenda in early 1977. He was going through a messy divorce with his second wife of 10 years, Cristina Vettore Austin Ford. His marital problems came to light in February 1975, when he was arrested for driving while intoxicated in California. With him was a blonde model, 35-year-old Kathleen DuRoss. When reporters asked him about the incident, the Deuce replied, "Never complain, never explain."

More troubling to Ford II was the heart trouble he suffered in early 1976, followed by the death of his mother, Eleanor, the family matriarch, that October. Henry's brother Benson also had heart problems. Henry II decided it was time to plan for a successor.

His heir apparent was Lee Iacocca, but the Deuce was not pleased with Iacocca's flamboyance and popularity, which rivaled his own. He suspiciously viewed Iacocca as a usurper like Harry Bennett. Also, evidence was mounting that the Iacocca-fathered Pinto and its sister car, the Mercury Bobcat, had a design flaw that left their fuel systems susceptible to leakage in rear-end impacts, often leading to fires.

Another 1977 event that would impact the Rouge Plant was a lawsuit filed by the Environmental Protection Agency to stop pollution at the Detroit Water and Sewerage Plant, then the largest such facility in the world. The case was heard by U.S. District Court Judge John Feikens, who gradually expanded the scope and goals of the lawsuit to involve three southeast Michigan counties and 48 communities. It called on every business and resident along the 126-mile Rouge River watershed to reduce "point" sources of pollution, such as wastewater discharges by factories, and "nonpoint" sources, which included debris, oils, and chemicals that washed into sewers and then into the river. Feikens' rulings helped lead to a rebirth of the river then considered one of the dirtiest waterways in the Midwest.

Nineteen-seventy-eight was Ford Motor Company's seventy-fifth anniversary and the year the new Mustang was scheduled to come out of Dearborn Assembly, but it also signaled the end of Iacocca's career at Ford, and probably the last time anyone thought a job at the Rouge Plant was secure for life. Also that year, the Ford family suffered a tragedy when Benson had a fatal heart attack on July 27.

Sales of Ford cars had dipped slightly since 1977, mostly because of bad news about the Pinto, but Lincoln and Mercury cars were selling well, and the next phase of renovations at the Rouge was about to begin. In this seemingly secure time, Henry Ford II decided to take Iacocca down another notch. On June 8, just days before the company's anniversary gala, Caldwell was promoted to deputy chief executive officer, while Bill Ford Sr. was named chairman of the executive committee and joined the Office of the Chief Executive. The move dropped Iacocca to number four in the company.

Henry II also told the press he was going to retire within three years and that Caldwell would become the new CEO and brother Bill Sr. the new chairman. Another bombshell dropped the day after the Deuce's announcement. The automaker notified the public that it was recalling 1.5 million Pintos and Bobcats, to install a shield to protect their fuel tanks. The company was facing increasing government pressure and numerous lawsuits, many of which it would lose, including a $125.8 million judgment—later reduced to $6.5 million—for Richard Grimshaw of California, who suffered disfiguring injuries in a fiery 1972 accident.

The axe finally fell on Iacocca the night of July 12, during an emergency meeting of the board of directors. Henry II delivered an ultimatum to several reluctant members who didn't want to fire Lee: "It's him or me!" The board gave the Deuce what he wanted.

Iacocca later reported in his autobiography that he received a call from Keith Crain, publisher of the trade newspaper *Automotive News*, the same night. Crain tipped him off to the board's actions and said, "Say it isn't so."

Iacocca went into the Glass House the next day and had an uneventful morning and lunch. But at three o'clock he was summoned to Henry Ford's office, where, with Bill Ford present, the Deuce told him, "I think you should leave. It's best for the company." The only explanation Henry gave Iacocca was, "Well, sometimes you just don't like somebody."

A deal was worked out where Iacocca would officially resign by October 15, his birthday, so he could preserve his pension benefits. The day after his birthday, Iacocca was shuffled off to an office at the Detroit Parts Distribution Center on Telegraph Road in Redford Township, a warehouse nearly 9 miles from the Glass House. Management's only preparations for his arrival were to hire an extra security guard. The office's previous occupant was none other than Ernie Breech, who had died earlier that year. After retiring from Ford, Breech had chosen the office and had stayed there 18 years, including while serving as chairman of Trans World Airlines.

After seeing the cracked linoleum floor in the secretary's office and getting coffee from a machine in the hallway, Iacocca left, never to return. In November, he accepted an offer to become president of the ailing Chrysler Corporation. While eager to upstage Ford, Iacocca and

During Ford's multimillion-dollar renovations of the Rouge Complex in the 1970s, this peppermint-striped, canopied snack area with tables and brightly colored stools, reminiscent of a Parisian sidewalk café, was added to the middle of Dearborn Assembly. *Ford Photomedia*

his fellow Ford expatriates faced several difficult years at Chrysler, requiring them to seek a $1.5 billion federal loan guarantee and help from new UAW President Douglas Fraser.

At the time the Deuce gave Iacocca the boot, Ford launched the 1979 Mustang and its "twin," the Mercury Capri, which was built at the Rouge until 1985. The unveiling was one of the Rouge Plant's last shots in the corporate limelight for nearly a decade.

The car was based on a modified Fairmont chassis, called the "Fox" platform within the company. The Fox Mustang was larger than the

Lee Iacocca, Henry Ford II, and Philip Caldwell (*from left*) announce the creation of the Office of the Chief Executive during a May 1977 press conference at the Glass House. Ford made Caldwell vice chairman of the board, effectively dropping Iacocca, the president, to third rank. *Walter P. Reuther Library, Wayne State University*

RIVER ROUGE

Pinto, with a wheelbase 4 inches longer, but was lighter and had an edgy, angular look that came in coupe and hatchback body styles. It offered two 2.3-liter four-cylinder engines—the standard overhead cam (OHC) and the 140-horsepower turbocharged version—plus the 2.8-liter Cologne V-6 and a 5.0-liter V-8. The suspension was all new, with MacPherson struts in front and coil springs in back.

Sales of the new pony car roared ahead, and despite the chaos caused by Iacocca's demise, the company reported record profits for 1978. But the American economy and the Rouge's fate were altered by events in Iran, customer expectations of car quality and value, and actions of the U.S. Federal Reserve. On January 13, 1979, Iran was taken over by Muslim extremists who rallied around the Ayatollah Khomeini. Soon, Iranians would be calling America the "Great Satan," but there was a lull before Khomeini confronted President James Earl Carter more directly.

In the United States, the economy was on the skids, with inflation hitting more than 13 percent by the year's end and unemployment rising. Initially, it was business as usual at the Rouge, with the 1979 Mustang selling 369,939 units (about 269,000 of which were made at the Rouge, the rest at the San Jose plant) and Ford bankrolling renovations of the Dearborn Engine Plant and planning to expand the Steel Division.

But the mass-production system popularized 65 years earlier by Henry Ford was failing. Fordism relied on assembly-line workers to do one or two simple tasks, while foremen rarely took a hand in completing tasks. Quality inspectors worked at the end of the line, looking for defects and having vehicles reworked before they were shipped to dealers. Union-negotiated rules had ossified many workplace procedures, creating hundreds of job classifications that reduced production flexibility. Many managers blamed the high cost of unionized labor for their problems, saying that it made the Big Three uncompetitive, but didn't take their own share of the blame.

Decades of cost cutting, instituted by Whiz Kid J. Edward Lundy and his protégés, had sacrificed long-range innovations and finally caught up with Ford. Petersen noted that vehicle quality had stagnated during the 1970s, while the Japanese had kept improving. The media bombarded the public with stories of the vaunted Japanese quality and cars built there by "subservient" employees who worked at an "inhuman" pace. Lundy retired from his post as chief financial officer in June 1979, with the automaker's fortunes in decline.

Looking for answers, Ford tried to form a joint venture with Toyota, but it fell through after Arab countries warned the Japanese automaker that it would face a boycott of its products. (Ford had opened manufacturing operations in Israel, one of the company's many gestures to atone for its founder's anti-Semitism. When Arab countries initiated a boycott of Ford-made products, Henry Ford II refused to back down, and the boycott remained in force for years.) After being rebuffed by Toyota, Ford signed an agreement on November 1, 1979, to purchase 25 percent of the Japanese manufacturer Toyo Kogyo, which became Mazda Motor Corporation.

That October, Caldwell had officially become Ford's chief executive officer, just as the U.S. Federal Reserve implemented its "tight money policy." The Fed hiked interest rates to 21 percent to halt runaway inflation, but the policy also slammed the brakes on the economy. Then, on November 4, some 500 Iranians stormed the U.S. Embassy in Tehran, taking 52 hostages. President Carter responded by embargoing Iranian oil imports and freezing Iranian assets in the United States. Iran, though, persuaded OPEC to hike oil prices, which skyrocketed from $12.46 per barrel to $35.24. America fell into a deep recession and, except for a brief respite around the time Ronald Reagan was elected president, didn't climb out again until 1982.

As large, higher-priced American-made cars piled up on dealership lots, Henry Ford II had a shock for his brother Bill, who was prepared to become chairman. About an hour before the annual shareholders' meeting on March 13, 1980, Henry told his younger brother that Caldwell would become chairman and CEO, while Don Petersen would became president.

Bill Ford asked, "Where does that leave me?"

Above: When Ford announced in 1978 that it would hire an additional 1,300 people at the Rouge to help assemble the hot-selling Mustang II, throngs of people lined up outside Gate 4, requiring the Dearborn police to handle crowd control. *Walter P. Reuther Library, Wayne State University*

Left: The Dearborn Glass Plant received a new system for laminating safety glass windshields in 1979. *Dearborn Historical Museum*

Left: Fred Diiacovo, working on a "man mate" machine in Dearborn Assembly, peers through the passenger-side body panel of a 1979 Mustang. No longer based on the Pinto platform, the car has an all-new look for the 1980s, as fuel economy and emissions regulations put a bite on the Big Three. *Ford Photomedia*

Below left: Workers install engine components on the new 1979 Fox-platform Mustangs at Dearborn Assembly as the cars run sideways down the assembly line. *Walter P. Reuther Library, Wayne State University*

"Well, I guess it leaves you vice chairman," the Deuce answered. Henry, while officially retired, retained his seat on the board of directors and chaired the important finance committee, which still allowed him to influence the company's operation.

It was the first time a Ford family member was not to be atop the company, but as brutal as Henry's action was, it was a brutal year that saw the company's sales plunge. Yet, six days after Caldwell's elevation, Ford announced a $44.7 million program, most of it slated for new machinery and equipment, to boost the Rouge Steel Division. The remaining $1.2 million was for building improvements. At the time Ford, said the renovations would allow the division to produce high-strength and other specialty steels for lighter cars in the 1980s. In reality, Ford wanted to make its steelworks appealing to potential buyers.

Some of the improvements were at the Hot Strip Mill (one of the highlights of the soon-to-be discontinued public tours), where 32-foot slabs of reheated steel were rolled into strips a half mile long and then wrapped into coils. To boost production and make thinner steel, the plant received a seventh finishing stand and the 7,000-horsepower motors on two stands were replaced with 9,000-horsepower motors.

Sulfur removal equipment was added to the Basic Oxygen Furnace (BOF), to improve steel quality and save energy. Sulfur was a contaminant that could get into the molten iron from the coke used in the blast furnace. If not removed, it resulted in brittle steel. Previously, the Steel Division had added limestone to the taconite (iron) pellets and coke, to remove the sulfur in the form of slag.

Additional railroad tracks were built outside the BOF to handle more flatcars, called buggies, which held molds of molten high-strength and specialty steels that needed more time to solidify.

Around the time Ford announced the Steel Division renovations, the company cut 250,000 cars from its production schedule as the economy worsened. Harold "Red" Poling, who became head of Ford North America in 1980, toured company factories to tell hourly and salaried employees that consumers didn't believe Ford could produce cars of the same quality and cost as the imports. Poling wanted the workers' input to help fix Ford.

One bright spot at the Rouge in 1980 was the $650 million renovation and expansion of the Dearborn Engine Plant (DEP), unveiled in

September. The plant would build the company's new Compound Valve Hemispherical (CVH) four-cylinder engines for the "world car," the 1981 Ford Escort, and its Mercury sibling, the Lynx. Extending nearly 10 football fields in length, the plant had the capacity to make 1 million engines by 1982, a level it hit by the end of 1981.

Employing 2,500 workers, the renovated DEP featured six automated "cold test" and 34 automated "hot test" stands. During cold tests, the engine's crankshaft was rotated while the equipment checked engine noise and vibration, the manifold vacuum, and oil pressure. Hot tests were more extensive, as each engine ran for 5 minutes, 6 seconds to analyze the exhaust gases, spark plug load, and other parameters prior to shipping.

Ford, however, lost $1.5 billion in 1980, as the Big Three's total vehicle production in America slid from about 9 million units two years earlier to 6.4 million units. Japanese automakers surged forward to produce about one-fourth of all vehicles made that year, approximately 7 million units. For the first time, Japan eclipsed the United States as the world's leading automotive manufacturing country. Its less expensive, fuel-efficient cars captured an unheard-of 25 percent of the American market. American buyers also rediscovered that Japanese vehicles had fairly high production standards compared to those of the Big Three.

Massive layoffs—many of them permanent—ensued in the U.S. auto industry. Ford closed seven factories, including one of its newest plants in Mahwah, New Jersey, and the Michigan Casting Center in Flat Rock, Michigan. The Rouge also saw its workforce trimmed as Ford cut its worldwide employment level from 515,000 to 375,000.

As gasoline prices peaked at $1.31 a gallon in 1981, the Mustang's V-8 engines were reduced to 4.2 liters and lost 21 horsepower. Production of the pony car plunged to 182,562 units, all made at Dearborn Assembly. In 1982, Ford rationed V-8s to meet federal CAFE standards, making only 5,000 available for sale.

Detroit became the symbol of the "Rust Belt," and the aging Rouge Plant, despite its updates, became a poster child for this image. Adding to the sense of gloom, Detroit had also earned the moniker of "murder capital" of the United States by the late 1970s. With few prospects, young adults and families began an exodus from Michigan. One joke was, "Will the last person to leave Detroit please turn off the lights?" As the 1980s rolled on, there were also rumors that General Motors would move its headquarters to New York City or next to its technical center in Warren, Michigan.

Even as the Big Three floundered, they continued to unlock the secrets of "Japan Inc." Henry Ford and Charlie Sorensen would have

Right: The Rouge's last remaining gas tower, near the coke ovens, still sports the blue oval. Before the end of the decade, however, Ford sold its steelworks, breaking the complex in two, and the oval came down.
Ford Photomedia

RIVER ROUGE

Extending nearly 10 football fields in length, the Dearborn Engine Plant is pictured in February 1980, just after a major renovation. It was gutted to its metal beams to prepare it to build the new, in-line four-cylinder engines for the 1981 Escort and Lynx. The plant's 67 automated stations included torquing positions, an analysis system to monitor the quality of fastened joints, and test stands to uncover misassembled engines. *Ford Photomedia*

Dearborn Engine Plant employees assemble the new 1.3- and 1.6-liter four-cylinder engines for use on the Ford Escort and Mercury Lynx. The Rouge Complex is becoming de-integrated, since the new Fox Mustang will use 2.3-liter four-cylinder engines, 2.8-liter V-6s, and 5.0-liter V8s constructed elsewhere. *Walter P. Reuther Library, Wayne State University*

recognized many of the Japanese concepts that became fashionable in the 1980s American auto industry. One such concept was *kaizen*, or "continuous improvement" of the product and the manufacturing techniques. The Japanese system, though, stressed teamwork between workers and managers and finding and fixing the root causes of defects—even if that meant shutting down the line for extended periods.

Toyota, the most successful of Japanese automaker, also used a concept called *kanban*, or "just in time" (JIT) delivery of parts to assembly plants. Developed by Taichi Ohno, the Toyota's vice president, this technique allowed the automaker to save millions of dollars by cutting down on inventory waiting at its assembly plants. Although interruption of these deliveries could shut assembly plants down, JIT saved so much money that the entire auto industry eventually adopted it. When asked how he came up with JIT, Ohno said it was from studying vertical integration at the Rouge Plant and heavily modifying it to fit Toyota's needs.

Looking to reverse their fortunes in the 1980s, Ford, GM, and Chrysler also turned toward an American consultant revered by the

One of the 34 automated hot-test stands installed at Dearborn Engine Plant during its renovations. The computerized stands put each 1.3- and 1.6-liter four-cylinder engine through a 5½-minute test cycle to simulate in-car operating conditions and decide if their performance was acceptable. Before getting to this point, the engines were cold-tested to check their oil pressure, manifold vacuum, and noise, and to isolate any problems. *Ford Photomedia*

RIVER ROUGE

Not all products from the Rouge Glass Plant were for cars. Ford supplied one million square feet of high-quality glass for the mirror-surfaced heliostats at Southern California Edison's solar power plant, near Barstow, California. The image of power company research engineer Paul E. Skvarna seems to be suspended above him in space in this January 1982 photo. *Ford Photomedia*

Japanese since the 1950s but mostly ignored by the Big Three: W. Edwards Deming. Born in 1900, Deming studied electrical engineering, mathematics, and mathematical physics before working at the Department of Agriculture and the Bureau of the Census. By World War II, he had learned how to improve quality control using mathematical statistics—a technique pioneered by physicist Walter Shewhart at Bell Laboratories.

Although American manufacturers turned a deaf ear to Deming, the Japanese sought him out after World War II as they rebuilt their war-torn country. In 1951, the Japanese even created the "Deming Prize" for companies that achieved high quality. Emperor Hirohito officially recognized the Iowa native in 1960.

Deming's teachings made many at Ford realize that so-called "random" quality issues were not unusual and could be fixed, because they were the result of manufacturing processes, Petersen said. Even though Deming's stature rose in the American auto industry, it took Ford employees years to implement his lessons and, at times, the automaker's management would seemingly forget his teachings.

A change also occurred in the industry's traditionally confrontational labor-management relations, starting with the 1982 agreement negotiated by UAW Vice President Don Ephlin and Peter J. Pestillo. Pestillo had started as Ford's vice president of labor relations in 1980 and sought to build a strong relationship with labor. Ephlin was eager

to prove that American workers could compete against the Japanese if they were empowered and treated as partners. Ford and the UAW built a new rapport nearly 35 years after Henry Ford II adopted labor's "human engineering" term.

With the recession continuing and the company on its way to $7 billion in losses over three years, Ford implemented the proposals of the Boston Consulting Group, first selling its tractor business, then preparing to sell its steelworks—at the time, the eighth largest steel producer in the United States.

On New Year's Day 1982, the Steel Division became the Rouge Steel Company, a Ford-owned subsidiary. In July, the Rouge steelworkers, many of them World War II veterans, received a rude surprise when Ford announced it was talking to a consortium of Japanese companies headed by Nippon Kokan KK, Japan's largest steel producer, a consortium that included Mitsubishi Corporation.

Despite a promising beginning, negotiations between Ford and Nippon Kokan fell apart by May 1983, when the UAW refused to accept pay cuts or adopt Japanese work rules. The Japanese, for their part, found the Rouge steelworks antiquated. With the collapse of the sale, Ford stretched out the maintenance shutdown of the "C" coke battery

A Rouge Steel employee sprays sand into a mold at the Ingot Mold Foundry. This plant was closed and demolished once Ford's steel subsidiary opened its continuous caster. *Ford Photomedia*

and "C" blast furnace, indefinitely shut down the ingot mold and electric arc furnace, and reduced manpower in the oxygen plant.

The Dearborn Glass Plant celebrated a bleak sixtieth anniversary in September 1983, with its workforce slashed to one shift. Work was also cut to one shift at the Stamping and Engine plants, as 9,500 workers, some with 13 years of service, were indefinitely laid off.

Dearborn Assembly faced closure when sales of the 1983 Fox Mustang slid to 116,120 units. Its future had also been threatened in 1982, when Ford began a joint venture with Mazda called the SN-8 to replace the Fox Mustang. The SN-8 was scheduled to be built on the same platform as the Mazda 626 at Mazda's Flat Rock assembly plant (formerly Michigan Casting) by 1987.

But the Mustang and Dearborn Assembly had a white knight, in the form of Ford's new Special Vehicle Team (SVT). One day, SVT's John Coletti saw a clay model of the SN-8 while walking through the Ford Design Center and was told it was going to be the next Mustang. "I then made some off-the-wall remark like, 'That car may be a lot of things, but it's not the new Mustang,'" Coletti recalled. "The car ultimately became the Probe."

SVT began offering engine improvements and performance packages that spurred U.S. Mustang sales to 131,762 units in 1984 and 159,741 units in 1985. Dearborn Assembly even made 224,410 cars in 1986 (though U.S. sales reached only 175,598 units) before domestic sales slid to 159,145 units the following year. In 1988, Mustang sales rebounded to 211,225 units.

The Rouge was given a stay of execution in 1983, thanks to an economic rebound and a cap on Japanese imports. Protectionist legislation that was slowly winding its way through Congress had prompted Japan to voluntarily reduce car exports to the United States. As the economy recovered, Ford recorded a $1.9 billion profit in 1983 and invested $500 million in Rouge Steel, including a new $200 million Continuous Slab Casting Plant.

When the plant's two continuous casters came online in 1986, they allowed Rouge Steel to bypass the ingot-making process, thus sharply reducing costs. Now, molten steel from the Basic Oxygen Furnace and the Electric Furnace was poured into a ladle and moved by a huge, rubber-tired carrier to the handling bay at the Continuous Slab Casting Plant. An overhead crane transferred the ladle to a conditioning stand, where the steel was stirred with an injection of inert gas, to homogenize the liquid metal's chemistry and temperature.

From the conditioning stand, the crane moved the ladle to one of two turrets above one of the giant casting machines. The turret rotated 180 degrees, placed the ladle over the caster, and poured the molten steel into a reservoir called a tundish. When a slide gate valve opened, a river of metal flowed from the tundish into the molds. For maximum production, a second ladle was placed on the other turret and began pouring once the first ladle was finished.

Next, a "dummy bar" was inserted into each mold at the beginning of the cast. When the mold was filled to the desired height, the dummy bar was slowly withdrawn at the same rate more molten steel was poured in. The dummy bar pulled a strand of steel with it down conveyor rollers.

The "chilling" effect of the mold caused an outer shell, or skin, to form on the steel so it retained its shape as it was pulled out. To prevent the shell from sticking, the mold was oscillated during the casting. Water was sprayed on the strand as it proceeded down the rollers to the cutting bay, where torches cut it into slabs that were painted with identification numbers. From there, the slabs were taken to the Hot Strip Mill for additional processing.

By 1985, Ford was on sounder financial footing. Philip Caldwell, then 65, wanted to remain chairman but was overruled by Henry Ford II. Petersen took over as chairman on February 1, in one of the smoothest transitions in the company's history, even though Caldwell was barely on speaking terms with his successor.

Just before his retirement, Caldwell unveiled the new Ford Taurus. The sedan was one of a number of new products Ford launched following the dark days of the recession, and it became the automaker's top-selling vehicle. But the new showcase car was not slated for the Rouge—it was built at Ford's Atlanta Assembly Plant, which had opened in 1947. Indicative of the Rouge's fall from grace, Petersen said in 2003, "We didn't have a 'crown jewel' plant at that time, but I'd say we were very proud of our Atlanta plant."

Although, Rouge Steel kept piling up losses and facing increased competition, producing just 2.7 million tons of finished steel in 1986, its continuous casters came online, as did the electrolytic galvanizing line and the Double Eagle plant on Miller Road, a joint venture with U.S. Steel. Electrolytic galvanizing allowed the steelmaker to coat one or both sides of its cold-rolled steel with zinc, improving corrosion resistance. The steel enterprise supplied 40 percent of its output to Ford and the rest to about 500 customers.

Last Voyages of the Fleet

Following World War II, the Ford fleet was reduced to a mere two ships, the *Henry Ford II* and the *Benson Ford*, after the company sold off its remaining ships, tugs, and barges. Ford still needed ships to haul new cars along the nation's waterways but contracted this service out instead.

Henry Ford II removed Harry Bennett appointees from the company's Marine Office, which was folded into the Rouge's Transportation Office. Clare J. Snider, who had been working as a clerk in the Marine Office, was given responsibility for scheduling the *Henry* and *Benson* and outside shipping companies to haul the Rouge's "annual buy" of raw materials while avoiding delays.

"In the back of his mind, the dispatcher had to remember not to ever schedule [departures] on a Friday," Snider wrote in his 1994 book, *The Ford Fleet*. "This was one superstition never ignored in the Ford Fleet; a captain would gladly depart the dock on the first trip at 12:01 a.m. on Saturday—but never two minutes earlier on a Friday."

Snider compiled annual reports on the company's Marine Operations, which showed executives that Ford's two ships were economical when compared to outsourcing shipping. As the Rouge's need for raw materials grew, Ford decided in 1951 to build a new ship, the 647-foot *William Clay Ford*, to supplement its fleet. The keel for the $5.3 million *Clay* was laid on April 19, 1952, at Great Lakes Engineering, and the ship was launched on May 5, 1953. With a 70-foot beam and a 7,000-horsepower steam turbine, the *Clay* was twice as powerful as the *Henry* and *Benson* and could carry 19,000 tons.

With a crew of 35, the ship was equipped with the most modern equipment, including radar, a fathometer, a gyrocompass and gyropilot, and ship-to-shore telephones. (Radar was later added to the *Henry* and *Benson*, so they wouldn't have to anchor during fog.) The *Clay* also had no more than two crewmen to a cabin and was one of the first vessels on the Great Lakes to provide interior tunnels, so the crew didn't have to walk across the deck in storms.

While the *William Clay Ford* was being built, the Rouge Plant started receiving Brazilian and Liberian iron ore, portending the flood of 1,000-foot-long international deepwater freighters that became common sights on the Great Lakes after the St. Lawrence Seaway opened in 1959.

The process of unloading ore freighters at the Rouge changed when one of its two Hulett unloaders was struck and destroyed by a departing ship in the early 1950s.

The ships of the Ford fleet were painted during the winter season. Working conditions in the cold were extremely difficult, but it was the only three-month period in which the ships were laid up. The stern of the *Ernest R. Breech* can be seen down the dock. *Ford Photomedia*

Ford decided to replace its remaining Hulett with three large clambucket-type machines that could unload 17,000 tons of ore in nine hours. The clambuckets, however, tended to damage ships' cargo holds.

Throughout the remainder of the 1950s, Ford's three vessels hauled 75 percent of the Rouge's raw material needs during the year. In a 1959 speech, Snider, by then promoted to Marine Operations manager, reported that freighters delivered 2 million tons of iron ore, 500,000 tons of limestone, and 2.5 million tons of coke to the Rouge's 2,300-foot-long dock, which unloaded an average of two ships a day.

All three Ford ships had passenger quarters, in addition to the crew's and officers' quarters, and during the summer carried many company guests. Because of the limited space, however, requests to use the passenger rooms had to be signed by the company president or an executive vice president.

Ford crewmen typically worked seven days a week from the last week of March through the middle of December, standing four-hour watches twice a day. Crewmen might swab the decks or scrape and paint the ship while the stewards cooked. In port, crew members were free to leave if they weren't on watch. Ford ships often plowed the Great Lakes on 1,500-mile trips from the Rouge to Duluth, Minnesota, and back, but they also traveled to other ports in Michigan, Wisconsin, and Ontario. During the winter months, the ships were laid up in the Rouge boat slip for maintenance, which was difficult in the freezing temperatures.

Until the United Auto Workers' victory over Ford in 1941, all Ford fleet employees were nonunion. After 1941, the seamen joined the National Maritime Union, an affiliate of the American Federation of Labor, to the consternation of the rival Congress of Industrial Organizations. The ships' officers remained non-unionized after an abortive attempt to launch the Foreman's Union at the Rouge in 1947. (The foremen had wanted their own union because many of the UAW members resented them, but Ford didn't really considered them part of management.) The Foreman's Union fell apart after a two-month strike, when Ford used salaried employees and higher-level managers to keep operations running.

In 1962, the *Henry* became the first Ford ship outfitted with bow thrusters. Located below the waterline at the bow and powered by diesel engines, the thrusters allowed the ship to turn by jetting water to either side, so it could navigate around the Rouge turning basin or tie up and leave the dock without the assistance of tugs. The bow thrusters were such a success that the *Benson* and *Clay* were similarly equipped the following year.

The fleet nearly doubled in size in 1962, when Ford bought the nine-year-old *Charles L. Hutchinson*, a 642 x 67–foot ore carrier, from the financially troubled Pioneer Steamship Company of Cleveland for $3.4 million. With a 4,000-horsepower steam turbine, it could carry 18,700 tons. Though slower than the *Clay*, it was an economical ship to operate. It was refurbished in 33 days and re-christened the *Ernest R. Breech* on April 10. The *Breech* also received a bow thruster.

Later that year, Ford discovered that no other steamship lines were available to handle its winter coal-shipping needs from Toledo, Ohio, to the Rouge. Instead of contracting to use more coal trains, which were expensive, Snider found a deal. Pioneer was about to scrap its 53-year-old, 500-foot *W. H. McGean* ore carrier, which Ford bought for a mere $80,000. The automaker spent $15,000 to refurbish the freighter and rechristened it the *Robert S. McNamara*. While the *McNamara* was expected to last only a year, it continued in operation until 1972, when it was retired.

The Rouge Marine Office was moved to the head of the boat slip in 1965, having bounced around in different buildings since its inception. The fleet had a total of 166 officers and men, with ships capable of hauling 6 million tons of raw materials annually. The next year, the fleet expanded to six ships when the company bought the *Joseph S. Wood* from Northwest Mutual Life Insurance Company for $4.6 million and renamed it the *John Dykstra*. The latter was the same age as the *Breech* and had similar capabilities.

At the time the *Dykstra* was purchased, Ford was in the middle of its "corporate identity" program to standardize the signage and look of Ford properties. The block-letter "FORD" name on the Glass House was replaced with the "blue oval," and large signs were added outside the Rouge Plant. The company also wanted to change the color of the ships' hulls from black to blue. Snider argued, however, that blue-hulled ships would be unsafe, because they would blend with the color of the sky and water, making them hard for other ships to see. A compromise was reached whereby the ships retained their black hulls and white pilothouses but everything above the cabin level was painted blue.

Ford modernized its ships over time to keep up with increasing U.S. Coast Guard regulations and to take advantage of new technology. When the *Henry Ford II* needed an overhaul, it was outfitted between November 1973 and August 1974 to become the fleet's first self-unloader. A long belt loop was placed into the cargo hold, while a "reclaimer" pushed the coal onto the belt, so crewmen didn't have to do the hazardous work. By 1975, the Ford fleet, by then reduced to five ships, was able to handle all the Rouge's iron ore, coal, and limestone needs. The freighters were sometimes chartered out to haul cargos for other companies too.

In 1978, the *Clay* was dry-docked at Fraser Shipyards in Superior, Wisconsin, and cut in half, so a 120-foot-long section could be added. When the overhaul was completed in May 1979, the *Clay* was 767 feet long and was equipped with a 7,000-horsepower steam turbine. The ship could now carry 23,900 gross tons at speeds up to 16 miles per hour, fully loaded.

The Ford fleet, however, was showing its age when the 1980 recession hit. At the end of the 1981 sailing season, the 57-year-old *Benson* was mothballed and put up for sale. The ship was eventually scrapped. Ford also created Rouge Steel, and its ships went under the control of the new enterprise.

The *Benson* name lived on for a short while longer with the renaming of the *Dykstra*. Even with the loss of the old *Benson*, however, Ford found that it had a great excess of cargo-carrying capacity. The recession, coupled with the auto industry's drive to reduce steel use to comply with federal CAFE standards, had greatly cut Rouge Steel's appetite for raw materials. The *Breech* was contracted out to haul grain, and the *Clay* was retired and sold for scrap after the 1984 sailing season. Its pilothouse became part of the Dossin Great Lakes Museum on Detroit's Belle Isle.

Replacing the *Clay* were two self-unloading freighters, the 42-year-old, 826-foot *Walter A. Sterling* and the 32-year-old, 767-foot *Edward B. Greene*. The *Sterling* was renamed the new *William Clay Ford*. The *Benson* was sold for scrap in 1987, and the *Greene* was renamed, becoming the third ship to be called *Benson*.

The aging *Henry* was chartered to International Salt (now known as AKZO), which led to severe corrosion of its cargo hold. It was laid up and scrapped, while the *Breech* was sold in 1988. On March 13, 1989, Ford announced it was selling its remaining two ships and that Rouge Steel would sign long-term transportation agreements to fulfill its shipping needs. After nearly 70 years, the Ford fleet had taken its final voyage.

A crewman aboard the *Benson Ford* throws a line to a man on shore. *Dossin Great Lakes Museum*

At the end of the 1978 sailing season, the *William Clay Ford* was taken to the Fraser Shipyards in Superior, Wisconsin, where it was cut in half and a 120-foot section was added, along with a 7,000-horsepower steam turbine engine. The overhaul of the *Clay* was completed in May 1979, and the ship was back at work the following month. *Dossin Great Lakes Museum*

Ford announced a record net profit of $3.3 billion for 1986, surpassing General Motors for the first time in 62 years and capturing 26.6 percent of the North American market. GM actually saw its total revenues surpass $100 billion that year, but its market share dropped to 33.8 percent, while its net profit plunged to $2.9 billion, mostly a result of a wild spending spree by GM Chairman Roger Smith.

Back at Ford, sales of the Mustang slowed to 163,392 units, and Rouge Steel's decision to close the coke ovens, eliminating 400 jobs, prompted rumors of the Rouge's demise. The coke ovens were obsolete by this time, and Ford's steel managers figured that buying coke from suppliers would be cheaper than making it on their own. It was a classic case of seeking short-term profit while ignoring the long-term outlook for prices.

An April 9, 1987, story by *Dearborn Press & Guide* reporter Cheryl Eberwein that looked into the Rouge Complex's future wasn't promising. Dearborn Assembly had outdated equipment and could be closed by 1988 or 1989. Dearborn Frame and a portion of Dearborn Stamping were also outdated and at high risk of being shuttered. The Rouge factories were operating independently of each other, shipping parts around the world, rather than operating as one vast plant to reduce costs through integration. Then-UAW Local 600 President Bob King told the *Press & Guide* that vertical integration had died at the plant because there was no central management and each factory ran as a separate entity. "They don't make the best use of the integration of the facilities that could be made."

Alex Trotman, Ford chairman, president, and chief executive officer, greets Dearborn Engine and Fuel Tank Plant employee Robert Cooper during a visit to the plant. Just behind Trotman in the white shirt and glasses is Ron Gettelfinger, then a UAW-Ford vice president. *Ford Photomedia*

The loss of the Rouge would devastate Dearborn, noted its mayor, Michael Guido, who had been in office little more than a year. The complex provided $90 million of the city's $2 billion tax base. "In a worst case, if the entire Rouge closed . . . I would have to cut the basic services by 80 percent. And it's very hard to find former industrial sites that have been renovated once closed," Guido told Eberwein.

In October, Rouge Steel offset some of the feeling of doom by announcing it would spend an additional $100 million on various improvements. One was the installation of computer process controls at the Hot Strip Mill. Another was converting the boilers at Powerhouse No. 1 to run on cleaner-burning natural gas in addition to pulverized coal and blast-furnace gas.

The complex limped along, but the company as a whole did well, posting a record $4.6 billion profit. Yet 1987 also marked the end of another era with the death of Henry Ford II, 70, on September 29. When he announced his retirement at the 1979 annual shareholders meeting, Ford had said, "If any other member of my family achieves a senior position in the company, it will be through merit and by a decision of the board of directors. There are no crown princes in the Ford Motor Company."

The family, though, was still very much involved in the company. Bill Ford Sr. remained vice chairman until 1989. After retiring, he stayed on the board of directors and chaired the finance committee until 1995. In addition, two younger Fords had been proving themselves in the company—the Deuce's son, Edsel B. Ford II, and Bill's son, who had dropped his child's nickname of "Billy" and went by Bill Ford Jr. Both cousins had their eyes on advancement.

Over Petersen's objections that they were still too young, Bill Sr. had his son and nephew elected to the board of directors on January 14, 1988. As the Ford crown princes rose in the company, Rouge Steel's fortunes were on the upswing. After eight years of losses, the steelmaker earned a modest $40 million profit for 1988, and a buyer finally came knocking on Ford's door: Marico Acquisition Corporation.

The head of Marico was Carl L. Valdiserri, 53, the retired chief operations officer for Weirton Steel of West Virginia. His partners included Worthington Industries, a Columbus, Ohio, steelmaker with a minority stake in Marico. Ford sold Rouge Steel to Valdiserri's group below book value, for a pretax loss of $561 million, completing the deal on December 13, 1989. Initially, Ford retained a 20 percent interest in the steelmaker.

The remnants of the Ford shipping fleet had been sold in March, and as Rouge Steel took ownership of the boat slip, docks, Hi Line, storage bins, and all the steelmaking facilities, Henry Ford's vertically integrated plant was finally torn asunder. Ford kept about half the complex's property, some 600 acres.

The steelmaker also took 60 percent ownership of Powerhouse No. 1. The railroad, fire department, and other operations were also split between the two companies, but a clean divorce was problematic, because the factory complex had been designed to function as one vast plant, with interconnected electrical relays, steam pipes, and telephone systems. Rouge Steel maintained its headquarters alongside Ford in the Miller Road office building.

The bottom line was that Ford management felt that a company devoted to the steel industry could better run Rouge Steel and provide job security to its 4,500 employees. Of course, an unmentioned side benefit was that Ford no longer had to worry about maintaining Rouge Steel's "dirty" factories in the face of ever more stringent pollution standards.

As part of the deal, Ford agreed to purchase 40 percent of its U.S. and Canadian steel requirements, about 800,000 tons annually, from Rouge Steel for 10 years, while Worthington would purchase 700,000 tons. The deal hit a snag, however, when 750 salaried employees protested to prevent Ford from transferring them to Rouge Steel. UAW Local 600 also had the foresight to demand that employees at Rouge Steel at the time of the sale be granted the right to transfer back to Ford at a later date in the event of bankruptcy.

As the sale of Rouge Steel was hammered out, the Mustang's production at Dearborn Assembly again appeared to be in trouble. Despite Ford's record profits, the American economy was on increasingly shaky ground since the stock market collapse in 1987. Unemployment was climbing, though modestly in comparison to the 1970s, and economic growth slowed from an annual 5 percent to an anemic 0.9 percent. Ford looked at ways to cut the cost of new car programs, whose price tag was more than $1 billion. The Mustang was slated for extinction because of its relatively low volume compared to the Taurus, and due to traditional car development costs—typically five years of designing, engineering, and tooling—which added up to more than $1.5 billion. That's when a Scot named Alex Trotman stepped in.

Trotman had started his career as a purchasing trainee at Ford of Britain in 1955 and had earned a reputation as both a solid engineer and manager. He had just taken over Ford North American Operations, but even as a European, he recognized the value of the Mustang name. In the summer of 1989 he put out the call to save the model and the factory that produced it. UAW Local 600 was also working with management to save jobs at the Rouge Complex.

John Coletti recalled that one August afternoon his manager, Ken Dabrowski, met with him and asked if he wanted to put together an affordable program for a new Mustang. At first Coletti was dumbstruck. He knew that only a select few people in the auto industry ever had a chance to shape a new car. "I didn't answer right away, so Dabrowski said, 'So, what's your answer?' I said, 'I'd be honored to,'" Coletti said.

For about four months, Coletti and a team of eight others met in his office after hours on Tuesday nights to put together a proposal. During that time, however, a radical change took place at the top of Ford.

Donald Petersen, highly respected by the automotive press and the business community, had planned to retire as chairman in 1991. Many considered chief financial officer Allan D. Gilmour his likely successor. But Petersen had rubbed the Ford family the wrong way one too many times. The company announced unexpectedly in November that Petersen was retiring by February 1990 and that Red Poling, not Gilmour, would take his place. Officially, Petersen said he retired to avoid the chaos of having three of the company's top executives leave at the same time, but other company sources said that the board of directors forced him out.

In February 1990, Coletti's group showed Trotman their proposal. The only wrinkle was that they could not meet the goal of making the new Mustang for only one-third the price of a typical new car program. "I figured at that point we had failed," Coletti said. "But then, Trotman said, 'Well, what can you do it for?' It turned out that it was about half [$700 million]. He said, 'I'll take it.'"

Coletti's "Team Mustang" moved into an old Montgomery Ward warehouse on Southfield Road in Allen Park, within 2 miles of the Rouge, and assembled a program that appealed to the cost-conscious Poling. While they saved money by heavily modifying the Fox platform, improvements were made to Dearborn Assembly.

Workers use a jig to apply pinstriping to the side of a 1989 Ford Mustang as the pony car celebrated its twenty-fifth anniversary. The company had been threatening to kill the car and thus probably close the Dearborn Assembly Plant. *Ford Photomedia*

An autoworker attaches the famous badge to the grille of a black 1994 Mustang, nearly 16 years after the emblem last graced the front of the car. The substantially restyled Mustang saved Dearborn Assembly for another decade of production. *Ford Photomedia*

The new Mustang was given the green light, even as America's economy fell into another recession. Adding to the economic uncertainty was Iraq's invasion of neighboring Kuwait in August 1990 and fears that Saddam Hussein's army would continue marching southward, taking over the oilfields of Saudi Arabia. President George H. W. Bush's administration put together "Operation Desert Shield," a massive air- and sealift of troops and equipment to the Persian Gulf.

Despite strong opposition in Congress, "Operation Desert Storm" was launched on January 17, 1991, when Hussein refused to pull out of Kuwait. The resulting month-long bombing campaign, followed by a three-day ground war, expelled Iraqi troops from Kuwait, and Iraq signed a truce by March. By then, America was already sliding into a recession.

U.S. light-vehicle sales fell by 23 percent, from a peak of 16 million new cars and trucks in 1986 to a low of 12.3 million by the end of 1991, as Ford posted losses of $3.2 billion. GM and Chrysler also recorded high losses, and Michigan's jobless rate hit 9.3 percent, far higher than the national average of 6.8 percent. Four out of five hallway lights were turned off in Ford's office buildings to cut electricity costs, but the Mustang program survived, because it was a bargain Poling just couldn't refuse.

By 1993, Ford was preparing to launch the fourth-generation Mustang just in time for the car's thirtieth anniversary (Ford doesn't count the brawny 1971 model as a Mustang generation). Eliminating many of its angular lines, the car took on a more rounded look,

inspired by Ford's "bubble car," the Taurus. Gone, too, was the hatchback, leaving only the two-door coupe and convertible styles. The car did, however, retain its "long hood, short deck" theme, with a bold, galloping pony emblem in the center of its grille and faux side air intakes just behind the doors. (Engineers determined that the base models didn't require real intakes, which would only have increased wind noise.)

Under the hood, the 3,140-pound car offered a choice of engines, ranging from the 3.8-liter V-6, producing 145 horsepower, to the Mustang GT's 215-horsepower, 5.0-liter V-8, to the SVT Mustang Cobra (released midyear), with a 240-horsepower V-8. (In two years, the Mustang would receive the all-new 4.6-liter modular V-8 as an option).

Ford conducted some limited hiring at the Rouge. From the late 1970s throughout the 1980s, the domestic automakers, in general, added few new workers. Laid-off workers were enough to fill any openings, and the UAW had negotiated clauses in the national and local contracts to favor those laid-off members. "When we were laying people off here at the Rouge, they were hiring people down the road at Wayne Assembly and Michigan Truck," Jerry Sullivan explained. "We had to make sure our people had the right to transfer over and fill those jobs."

Despite its age, the Rouge Complex still had a visual impact on those few new hires who saw it for the first time, such as Penny Cauzillo. "On my first day here, I went to labor relations at Gate 4. It was six o'clock in the morning in July 1993, and it was still dark," said Cauzillo, who in 2003 worked in Dearborn Assembly as a team leader in the chassis department. "I saw the blast furnaces at Rouge Steel, and they looked smoky and dirty. I thought of the Doctor Seuss story about the Lorax, where they cut down a forest of beautiful trees to put up a factory. When I walked in that day near the Body Shop and it was dirty and the floor was all cracked, people were wearing big, green coveralls, and sparks were flying from the welding machines."

Cauzillo was a graduate of the University of Detroit, where she had played on the girl's basketball team and earned a bachelor's degree in criminal justice. She started working at the Rouge for the same reason countless others have been enticed to work there: the money.

"I was undecided on whether I wanted to go to law school or be a cop or even be a teacher," she said. "So my friend's mom said that they were hiring at Ford and I could make some decent money while I was deciding on what to do. Now, ten years later, I'm still here."

Initially, Cauzillo felt trapped at her job—she worked nights for three years, starting her 10-hour shifts at 5 p.m. and not returning home until 5 a.m. She started in the Paint Shop, earning about $17.50 an hour, and admits that some of her first duties were fairly easy. On some days, all she had to do was use an air hose to blow dirt off the cars.

"When I started in paint, the smells and the heat were unbelievable," Cauzillo said. "I must have lost 20 pounds in less than a month from

By 1994, robots, not people, performed most of the critical welding on Ford Mustangs at Dearborn Assembly. The car bodies were picked up by clamshells and shuffled from station to station for nearly 100 feet. The welding machines were located on the factory's first floor. It was loud, and sparks mostly flew against protective plastic shields, although some went into the nearby aisle. *Ford Photomedia*

the heat alone. Then there are the sounds. There are bells that ring 'nah-nah-nah-nah.' There are buzzers going off, and bells. My first week, every time I heard a noise, I'd ask, 'Was that a fire alarm?' I didn't know."

In October 1993, Red Poling drove an appropriately colored red fourth-generation Mustang off the line for the car's official rollout. He stepped out, handed Alex Trotman the keys, then announced to the gathered workers that Trotman would become the new CEO. Trotman had earned the distinction of becoming the first foreign-born executive to lead Ford.

Allan Gilmour was passed over for promotion yet again. He was highly intelligent, a respected voice on Wall Street, and had been a protégé of Whiz Kid J. Edward Lundy. There had reportedly been a nasty behind-the-scenes campaign to discredit him as a "closet homosexual." After retiring from Ford in 1995, Gilmour admitted he was gay and became an advocate for the cause. Although it seemed to be the end of his career at Ford, he would be back within seven years.

In the 11 years during which the fourth-generation Mustang was built, the pony car recorded far better than expected sales, Coletti said. Originally, production had been set at only 110,000 units per year, but sales actually hit 130,000 to 150,000 units annually, making it one of Ford's success stories for the 1990s.

Under Trotman, the automaker started a program called "Ford 2000," to consolidate power in Dearborn by integrating the company's American operations with its foreign branches. The initiative, however, threw parts of the company's bureaucracy into chaos as managers

slowly began taking their eyes off the ball: improving existing vehicles and making sure new ones were coming up properly.

Several members of Ford's senior management were jockeying to become Trotman's successor: Jacques "Jac the Knife" Nasser, who took over Ford North American Operations, Ford marketing executive Robert Rewey, and Ed Hagenlocker, whose efforts at the Ford Truck Division had whipped General Motors. While this was happening, GM decided to shake Ford up. Instead of renovating its aging, Albert Kahn–designed headquarters, GM pulled a coup in 1996 by purchasing the Renaissance Center for a mere $70 million from the real estate firm that owned it and giving Ford two years to move 1,800 employees elsewhere. The bust of Henry Ford II was removed from the RenCen's lobby, and Ford Division moved back to Dearborn, into a Ford-owned building north of the Glass House.

Rewey convinced the board of directors that the future of Lincoln-Mercury (which soon dropped the hyphen as a marketing move) would be best served in California. The move, Rewey successfully argued, would inject fresh thinking into the stodgy division, allowing it to better compete against Toyota, Honda, and Nissan, which then dominated the California new-car market.

By the end of the 1990s, UAW Local 600 had won commitments from Ford to reinvest in its half of the Rouge Complex. The Rouge would be reborn as a modern vision of twenty-first century manufacturing, but not before several cataclysmic events sent Rouge Steel into a tailspin from which it never recovered.

Last Ford Train to Nowhere

The Ford Rouge Railroad (FDRX), with its 106 miles of track, all confined to the 1,200 acres of the Rouge Plant, was often called the "railroad that goes nowhere," but it promptly delivered engines, radiators, tires, doors, fenders, and panels to the Dearborn Assembly Plant (DAP). The railroad also transferred sand from ships, pig iron from blast furnaces, and steel slabs to the pre-heat mill.

Although the FDRX was confined to the Rouge, about 20 other Ford assembly plants around the country depended on its smooth operation to get components when they needed them.

When other parts of the Rouge were updated in the late 1940s, the FDRX received its share of new equipment. In 1950, "Old No. 30," one of the first four Ford steam locomotives, built in 1923, became the last of its kind to retire. In 27 years of continuous service, the company estimated that Old No. 30 had traveled about 300,000 miles, nearly all of it within the Rouge. The last enginemen to leave it were Albert Melbus, 61, and Harry Copeland, 60, who transferred to one of Ford's new diesel-electric switching units, No. 6606.

With 19 diesel engines and 481 men, the railroad added three more locomotives in 1954. Eight were powered by twin 500-horsepower Cooper Bessemer engines, 11 had 600-horsepower engines, and 3 had 300-horsepower engines. All were equipped with two-way radiotelephones.

In the 1950s, the FDRX handled more than 1,000 railcars a day from the seven outside rail lines that connected to the complex: the Detroit, Toledo & Ironton; Michigan Central (New York Central); Detroit Terminal; Wabash; Pere Marquette; Grand Trunk; and Pennsylvania. In most cases, Ford locomotives met trains outside the complex's grounds to haul incoming cars and switch outgoing cars to the commercial lines. The railroad could move parts from the plant's perimeter to Dearborn Assembly in a matter of minutes.

Ford also owned 622 hopper cars, 416 gondolas, 14 frame gondolas, 40 air dump cars, 9 steel tanks, 10 steel flatcars, 6 scale cars (to weigh incoming loads), 50 hot slab cars, 24 slag ladle cars, and 9 hot metal (torpedo) ladle cars. The company repaired its rolling stock on a "rip track," where it converted its wooden-frame cars into steel units and rebuilt rusting steel cars from the wheels up.

In its heyday, the FDRX employed about 100 section hands to maintain the track. They laid approximately 10 miles of replacement rails per year, using 156,000 spikes and 7,000 ties. The maintenance exceeded that of most commercial railroads but was necessary due to the heavily loaded freight cars. By the 1970s, the maintenance crews were replacing about 2 miles of track per year, or more when needed, and keeping about $750,000 worth of inventory on hand. After 1989, it trimmed its inventory to $500,000.

The Rouge railroad offered plum jobs that many outside railroad men, such as Jerry Mattias, vied for. Mattias had a job on the New York Central but left to join FDRX's "extra board" in 1964. "Being on the extra board meant that when they needed you, they called you," he said. "That usually meant that I ended up working 40 hours a week."

Mattias grew up in southwest Detroit and remembers seeing the great haze around the Rouge foundries and the smoke rising from its other factories. His father had worked there during the Harry Bennett days, and when he joined the FDRX he briefly worked alongside his father-in-law. After 1965, however, Mattias became a full-time Ford employee when he left the railroad and became a skilled tradesman at Powerhouse No. 1.

"In the Rouge itself, there were three [rail]yards: one at the open hearth, where cars were brought in with scrap metal; the middle zone, that took care of the blast furnaces; and the West Yard, where they switched cars for the assembly, engine and frame plants," Mattias said. "The open hearth needed switching every eight hours, because that's how long it took to make the molten metal."

The locomotives pulled the torpedo cars—called "Treadwells" after the company that made them—filled with molten iron from the blast furnaces, to the Open-Hearth Building and, later, the Basic Oxygen Furnace. Slag from the furnaces was dumped into the cooling pits, where it would be recovered and sold to cement companies. Parts from the Dearborn Stamping Plant and engines from the Dearborn Engine Plant went into boxcars that were shipped out to Ford plants around the country. And when the Rouge still made transmissions in the 1950s, the leftover metal shavings went onto a conveyor that took them to a hopper. Once the hopper was filled, the shavings went into a spinning machine that extracted the oil for reuse by the cutting machines. The railroad took the shavings back to the Open-Hearth Building where they were melted down to make new steel.

In the early 1960s, the FDRX had five-man crews, consisting of the engineer, fireman, conductor, fuel man, and head pin, who turned the switches. All the railroad workers were members of the United Auto Workers rather than an outside railroad union.

Three new GMD (General Motors) locomotives, painted in the Ford Rouge Railroad's orange livery, are shown in Flat Rock, Michigan, being taken to the Rouge by a DT&I "puller" on December 29, 1975. For years, Ford refused to buy locomotives from its automotive rival, preferring Alco, Baldwin, and General Electric engines. *Ernest B. Novak Collection*

The interior of the Rouge Complex's locomotive shop during the 1990s. The diesel-electric engines are painted in a "highway orange"-over-yellow scheme, for high visibility. *Ford Photomedia*

A Ford Railroad engine passes the stove towers to the Rouge Steel blast furnaces in the early 1990s, in this photograph taken from Miller Road. *Kenneth Borg Collection*

Ford added "direct wire" remote controls to the locomotives in 1965 that allowed an engineer to control the throttle, brake, horn, and sand speader. By the mid-1908s, radio remote controls were added so the locomotives could be operated from outside.

The FDRX dipped to 16 locomotives and 730 cars in 1966 but still employed 237 men, including 51 engineers, and remained the largest privately owned railroad in the country. Also during the 1960s, the railroad's colors were changed from red over dark blue to an ashen white as part of Ford's new "corporate identity" program. In the mid-1970s, the railroad's colors changed again, to orange over yellow.

For years, Ford preferred to buy locomotives from Alco, Baldwin, and General Electric, but by 1975, management decided to purchase three new General Motors GMDs, Nos. 10021 through 10023. Through the early 1980s, Ford bought about a half dozen other new and rebuilt locomotives from GM's Electro-Motive Division.

In 1977, Ford press releases reported that the FRDX had 20 diesel-electric locomotives and 85 miles of standard-gauge track and that it moved 455,000 freight cars annually. With the creation of Rouge Steel in 1982, more than half the track and rolling stock went with it, but the steelmaker contracted with Ford to handle its rail needs.

In 1997, eight years after the sale of Rouge Steel to Marico, Rouge Industries (as the steelmaker was now called) took over its own railroad needs, leasing locomotives from CANAC, originally a subsidiary of Canadian National (CN) railroad. In 2003, the steel company switched to leased engines from Relco Locomotive.

The Ford Rouge Railroad, however, declined precipitously during the late 1980s and 1990s. By 1998 it had five diesel-electrics in operation, primarily engaged in switching 30 loaded tri-level freight cars of completed Mustangs per day, Monday through Friday, sending them out around 2 p.m. The practice of just-in-time delivery to the Rouge's automotive factories had killed the railroad's use as part of the complex's conveyor system. Truck deliveries, which were much more flexible, took the railroad's place.

The final blow to the FDRX came when CN stopped loading railcars at Dearborn Assembly, instead trucking the completed automobiles to the AutoAlliance plant in Flat Rock,

where they were loaded onto tri-levels. In November 2002, Ford announced that it would exit the railroad business. Yard and maintenance duties at the Rouge were contracted out to Canadian National on December 1. The remaining Ford Railroad workers either retired or were absorbed into other jobs at the car company, and its three remaining engines were put up for sale.

The Ford Railroad is no more, but Canadian National will have a more visible presence at the Rouge. While the truck plant was built, CN constructed a new vehicle-shipping yard with a multilevel dock and eight tracks so it can stock 80 vehicles at a time.

Rouge Steel engine No. 1514 pulls eight coke cars near the Miller Road T-Bridge in the late 1990s. *Kenneth Borg Collection*

Chapter Nine

From Tragedy to Rebirth, 1999–2004

"We're calling from Salina School. The Rouge Plant just blew up. Something just blew up, and it's all in flames and smoke."

—*Unidentified caller to Dearborn police, February 1, 1999*

After more than a decade of rumors that the Rouge Complex was headed for extinction, the workers finally got some good news when UAW Local 600 and Ford Motor Company signed the "Rouge Viability Agreement" in 1997. Details of the compact were not fully revealed, but word leaked that Ford had allocated $2 billion to renovate the Rouge, including $500 million to upgrade the Dearborn Engine and Fuel Tank Plant, $71 million for Dearborn Stamping, $88 million for Dearborn Frame, and money to replace the aging Powerhouse No. 1.

One of the first revelations of the agreement was that a new $1.25 billion Paint Shop would be completed by the fall of 1999. It would replace Dearborn Assembly's existing paint shop and be capable of handling upward of 250,000 vehicles annually—a far greater number than the Rouge had produced in decades. Residents of Dearborn's South End protested, however, noting that if the facility ran at full tilt, its emissions would be greater than those from the existing Dearborn Assembly Plant. Members of the Arab Community Center for Economic and Social Services (ACCESS) argued that Ford should install more expensive water-based paint technology.

"We made a major additional investment in water-based technology to address their concerns," said Timothy O'Brien, who was director of Ford's Environmental Quality Office at the time. "This was a good example of community collaboration, because it cut the total emissions from the plant . . . and it pointed out an economic interest we had. The emissions are from paint that didn't get stuck on the vehicle, and car paint costs between $100 and $120 per gallon."

The Paint Shop opened in 2000 and became the site of a pilot program where volatile organic compounds (VOCs) in the paint fumes were captured and concentrated into a mixture of hydrocarbons. This chemical brew was sent through a reformer to create a hydrogen-rich gas that fueled a small cell, which generated about 5,000 watts of elec-

tricity. The program was such a success that a larger fuel cell system was installed in 2004, to generate up to 100,000 watts.

The South End residents also convinced Ford and Rouge Steel to tone down the new power plant to significantly reduce pollution, noted Ishmael Ahmed, president of ACCESS. Unlike the 1920s—when Henry Ford turned to his own people, such as William Mayo, to build Powerhouse No. 1—the automaker and Rouge Steel sought out DTE Energy (formerly Detroit Edison) and CMS Energy Corporation (formerly Consumers Power) to jointly create, own, and operate the plant, called the Dearborn Industrial Generation (DIG) Project. DTE, however, eventually backed out of the venture.

The proposed 550-megawatt plant was supposed to become partially operational in July 1999 and replace Powerhouse No. 1 the following year. Tragically, events forced the power companies to accelerate their timetable, as we shall see.

A different kind of tragedy occurred in early 1997, when the old Albert Kahn–designed Administration Building was demolished. Kahn had said it was made to last a thousand years, and Henry Ford had indicated he wanted it preserved. However, the structure, with its asbestos insulation, had been empty for years. Ford management decided that the building wasn't worth saving, although it did salvage some items, such as stone from the front façade with the Ford Motor Company name carved into it.

Rouge Steel (owned by the Rouge Industries holding company since 1996) was moderately profitable throughout the mid-1990s. It had mothballed the "Henry" blast furnace and its Electric Melt Furnace, but it altered its two remaining blast furnaces to reduce casting time from 4 hours to 2 and boost steel production.

But the American steel industry was consolidating. More than a hundred small and medium-sized companies went bankrupt in the face

Powerhouse No. 1 represented the might of American industrial power. It was also one of the most photographed structures of the complex, with its eight towering smokestacks, seen in this 1946 picture taken from the south side of the building. *Ford Photomedia*

of growing foreign competition and regulations requiring costly pollution-control equipment. A flood of imported steel began in 1998, dropping prices dramatically.

Imported steel was one of a series of misfortunes that beset the Dearborn steelmaker. In addition, coke prices were rising and impinging on profits, but Rouge Steel couldn't restart its mothballed coke ovens, because they needed prohibitively expensive pollution-control equipment. If they had remained in operation, they would have been covered by grandfather clauses in federal regulations.

As plans for the Rouge's future were worked out behind the scenes, Ford was riding high, with impressive sales of its Explorer sport utility vehicle, the F-Series pickup truck, and the regenerated Mustang. Cash reserves were up—and, because Ford's manufacturing costs were lower than those of General Motors, the company posted higher profits than GM did. Also, as Japan's economy took a nosedive, "Japan Inc." no longer seemed so formidable.

Success blinded Ford executives to the fact that sales of its redesigned Taurus and many of its other cars were lackluster, even as Toyota and Honda opened more factories in North America and dominated the car market. The good economic times of the 1990s, however, seemed like they would never end. The business community wasn't concerned with the political battles between President Bill Clinton and the Republican-controlled Congress; instead it went gaga over the Internet, dot-com companies, and other "new economy" trends. The siren song of some analysts was that the boom-and-bust economic cycle had been broken.

Wall Street and the media became enamored of Chrysler, saying it was more nimble than either Ford or GM because it was the least vertically integrated and relied on outside suppliers for many of its vehicle components. In response, GM placed many of its captive parts plants under a new entity called Delphi Automotive Systems. Ford similarly formed Visteon Automotive Systems, announcing the new enterprise September 9, 1997, at the Frankfurt Motor Show. Both Delphi and Visteon were destined to be spun off into separate companies. Many at the Rouge feared that some of their plants would be transferred to Visteon, but it didn't happen.

Chairman and CEO Alex Trotman was also riding high, but like many a Ford executive before him, he tangled with the family whose name was on the building. The ambitious Bill Ford Jr. had taken his father's place in 1995 as chairman of the powerful finance committee on the board of directors. Bill, a friend of Michael Braungart, a Greenpeace chemist and cofounder of Germany's Green Party, began pushing for the automaker to adopt a more ecological agenda, but Trotman paid more attention to the bottom line.

Ford executives, however, weren't tone-deaf to environmental concerns. In 1990, a member of Ford's Corporate Strategy Staff, Andrew G. Acho, had initiated the Recycling Action Team, nicknamed the "Rat

Above: Wearing protective gear, an autoworker applies a coat of paint to the front of a red Mustang convertible at the Rouge's new Paint Shop. Using water-based primer and base-coat paint systems, along with advanced abatement equipment, the new shop has significantly reduced emissions. *Ford Photomedia*

Right: The Paint Shop has been equipped to capture the volatile organic compounds in paint fumes and convert them into hydrogen-rich gas. The gas then feeds a fuel cell, a device that converts chemical energy to electricity. This fuel cell can generate up to 100,000 watts. *Ford Photomedia*

Patrol," to find ways to incorporate recycled materials into Ford cars. Acho's family had fled Iraq after an uncle was killed for being a Christian, and he started working as a quality control engineer at the former Engine and Foundry Division in 1960.

The Rat Patrol followed two guidelines. "The recycled product had to be as good as or better than the one it replaced in terms of durability, quality, or reliability," Acho said. "Second, it had to cost the same or less than an existing product." One improvement was the creation of "returnable containers"—shipping packages that could be collapsed and returned to the supplier after use—which saved Ford $3 million to $14 million per year.

Despite the company's successes, Trotman's "Ford 2000" program was unraveling, and the family-controlled board of directors didn't like his chosen successor, truck executive Edward Hagenlocker. Eventually, they settled on Lebanese-born Jacques A. Nasser.

Nasser's father was an entrepreneur who had moved his family to Australia when Jac was four years old. There, he faced racism while growing up. Nasser joined Ford of Australia in 1968 and spent 30 years working in Australia, Latin America, and Asia, and ran Ford of Europe. He had a passion for vehicles but was also known for ruthlessly cutting costs and being tough to work for, earning the nickname "Jac the Knife."

Since Nasser was still a relative unknown, the board extended Trotman's term as chairman from July 1998 to January 2000, but Bill Ford Jr. and Jac the Knife had other plans. The young Ford had impressed many other board members (though Trotman wasn't captivated), who reportedly started referring to him as "Prince William."

By September 1997, Nasser and Bill Ford convinced the board that the 52-year-old Nasser, with his greater experience, could take on the day-to-day grind of being CEO and president, while Ford, 41, who was also president of the Detroit Lions football team, could be chairman and watch out for the shareholders. It was déjà vu, like a replay of how Henry Ford II worked with Ernie Breech.

When the board approved the transition, forcing Trotman to retire on January 1, 1999, an angry Alex reportedly told Ford, "So now you have your monarchy back, Prince William."

With Trotman's departure came the retirement of Edsel Ford II, who had desired to run Ford Motor Company but had realized there was room for only one family member at the top. He retained his seat on the board and officially became a paid consultant.

The Ford public relations machine celebrated the return of a Ford to the head of the company and played up the close relationship between Jac and Bill. An astute observer of human ego wasn't fooled. "I think it would be a miracle if they last two years. One wants to be the hero of the environment. The other wants to be the hero of shareholders," retired Chrysler Vice Chairman Robert A. Lutz predicted in an interview for *Fortune* magazine in April 2000.

Left: This woman appears to be applying a filler compound on a Mustang at the new Paint Shop. This area of the line is well lit and almost antiseptic. *Ford Photomedia*

Below: Albert Kahn said that the Administration Building had been built to last a thousand years, but it was demolished in early 1997. The executive garage and part of the main building have already been reduced to rubble. The fourth floor was the site of the executive dining room, while the third window in on the basement level marks the location of Harry Bennett's former office. *Ford Photomedia*

Above: A worker installs the driver-side door glass on an early-2000s Mustang. *Ford Photomedia*

Above right: Two operators were required to control the throttle valves for the powerhouse's two General Electric high-pressure steam turbines in this 1930s photo. Huge, 100-foot-tall boilers provided the steam for the turbines, and the boilers were fueled by blast furnace gas and pulverized coal. *The Henry Ford*

Nasser purged rival executives, starting with Hagenlocker, who became one of the first forced into "retirement." Then Jac cherry-picked executives from other auto companies, creating a cadre of loyalists. He offered a glimpse of his distrust of the many Ford careerists below him in his keynote speech to the *Automotive News* World Congress in January 1999, when he departed from his prepared speech and noted how, when he ran Ford Automotive Operations (FAO), other executives had nicknamed it "for accents only."

Nasser also moved fast to consummate a deal to buy the car division of the Swedish vehicle manufacturer Volvo, which was announced on January 28. It would be one of several acquisitions as the company used its nearly $25 billion in cash reserves to expand.

But it was one of Bill Ford Jr.'s first meetings as chairman that profoundly impacted the development of the Rouge Complex. Architect William "Bill" McDonough, who was also a friend of Braungart, met with Ford Jr. to explain how the automaker could design its buildings to save money and be "green" too. "I had a 15 minute appointment," McDonough recalled. "Once we started the meeting, however, it went all afternoon. He had to do other business, but he just kept telling me, 'Stay here.' And we'd do another meeting in his office, and we just kept talking."

Two weeks after that meeting, while Ford was still contemplating how to rejuvenate the Rouge into an icon of twenty-first-century manufacturing, a symbol of twentieth-century industrial might was about to die.

Powerhouse No. 1 was the heart of the Rouge. It also provided low-pressure steam, high-pressure (1,250 psi) steam, compressed air, and mill water for the steel factories, and it powered the air blowers for the blast furnaces. Covering a little more than six acres, the seven-story brick, concrete, and steel structure (with a three-story basement) was topped by eight steel smokestacks that towered 320 feet in the air. One was capped, because it had no boiler under it—ever since Henry Ford's time, the space had been left open for a spare boiler that was never installed. The powerhouse had been modified a number of times, including the addition of massive steel dust collectors that mushroomed from the roof of the building.

The main structure was broken into four connected buildings. On the west side of the powerhouse was the two-story, 216 x 76–foot turbo blower building; then came the seven-story, 227 x 216–foot boiler house, the 216 x 68–foot generator building, and the 197 x 68–foot electrical building.

The first photo (*far left*) shows one of the powerhouse control rooms in 1931. While it may have resembled a spaceship control center in a 1930s sci-fi movie, the white-suited operators could control the turbines and switching power to substations around the Rouge Plant and to the outside. Each of the powerhouse's seven boilers had its own control rooms, one of which is seen in this photo from the 1990s (*left*). Except for the fluorescent lighting, the controls and gauges looked as much as they did 60 years earlier. After the 1999 powerhouse explosion, much of the building's interior was gutted by fire, including the control rooms (*below left*). *The Henry Ford; Joseph Cabadas Collection*

An overhead conveyor connected the powerhouse to the seven-story Pulverizer Building, located 80 feet away, near the Hi Line. Coal was fed into a bunker at the top of the Pulverizer Building before falling into the 12 high-speed mills that crushed it into a talc-like powder, which allowed it to burn more efficiently. The conveyor then took the powdered coal to the powerhouse, where it was fed into the seven boilers that also used blast furnace gas or natural gas.

Many of the 140 powerhouse workers had worked there a decade or more. Over time, many maintenance procedures had become so routine that, in some cases, there were no written checklists. Some workers later told an investigative team lead by Dearborn fire marshal Richard Polcyn and investigators for the Michigan Occupational Health & Safety Administration (MI-OSHA) that maintenance had gotten lax since 1989. There were allegations that the service tunnels were deteriorating, gas valves were leaky, and coal dust had built up in places, ranging from a thin dusting to "six inches thick," Polcyn's investigators reported.

On Friday, January 29, 1999, workers began shutting down Boiler No. 6 for its annual maintenance. Although it was built in 1965, it was one of the newest and most efficient of the seven boilers and was rarely offline.

The 100-foot-tall, high-pressure Babcock & Wilcox generated 500,000 pounds of steam per hour. It had been equipped with a "fire-eye" safety system to automatically shut down its fuel supply if a problem occurred. However, the fire-eye had been disabled in 1966, because it interfered with normal operation.

Shutting down the massive boiler took time. First, the south blast furnace gas line was turned off, using a method called "blanking,"

where a solid piece of metal was inserted into the gas line after the valves had been turned off. Next, the pulverized coal feed was turned off, so that eventually, only a residual amount remained in the boiler's bunker. Meanwhile, three other boilers were fired up to make up for the lost steam production.

The maintenance crew reviewed the shutdown procedure on the morning of Monday, February 1—a sleety, blustery day. Then they blanked the north blast-furnace gas line and closed the two manual natural-gas valves. The indicator on one of the manual gas valves, however, had broken years earlier. It was impossible to know if the valve was open or closed unless one physically tried to turn it, the Dearborn Fire Department later reported. In Control Room No. 6 (each boiler had its own control room, with more than 100 gauges and switches), the indicator showed that the gas flow was off.

161

Above: Emergency personnel work amid billowing smoke and steam at the Ford River Rouge Complex. An explosion and fire had rocked the power-generating plant just after 1 p.m. on Monday, February 1, 1999. The explosion killed one man instantly; five other men died from their injuries during the next six weeks, and more than 20 other workers carry their scars for life. *AP/Wide World Photos/ Tom Edwards*

Right: The force of the natural gas explosion in Boiler No. 6 on Monday, February 1, 1999, shattered the powerhouse's concrete roof. Slabs and chunks of concrete hang down by their weakened rebar, adding a degree of danger for the firefighters who went in during the blaze to search for victims, as well as investigators afterward. *Joseph Cabadas Collection*

By approximately 10:30 a.m., the boiler's fires were out, and the water valves were closed, to vent steam pressure inside the boiler. Because it would take 12 hours for the interior of the boiler to cool, the crew broke for lunch.

Just after lunch, Jerry Mattias walked out of the powerhouse to the parking lot at the northeast corner of the building. He had worked at the facility for 30 years after transferring from the Ford Railroad, and,

like many of the old-timers, was marking time toward retirement. He was not involved with shutting the boiler down that day. Instead, he met a foreman and drove out to the Stamping Plant.

Inside the powerhouse, the maintenance crew continued working on No. 6, and an operator in the control room opened the "Bailey controls," to purge any remaining gas in the lines before they were blanked. Suddenly, the natural gas chart showed a sharp increase. The manual valve for the 10-inch mainline on the east side of the boiler had been left partially open, and natural gas flowed into the boiler at a rate of 6,000 to 9,000 cubic feet per minute for one or two minutes.

Just before 1 p.m., the operations supervisor walked into control room, looked at the control board, and noticed something amiss. "Someone left the valve open," he reportedly said. Then he and a worker left the room. A minute later, there was a gigantic explosion.

Virtually all of the powerhouse windows were blown out, with fragments later found 100 feet away. The northern masonry walls failed, with debris blowing into the control room, a locker room, a lunchroom, and a stairwell. The blast shattered the concrete roof. Large chunks of concrete, some weighing more than 50 pounds, were thrown upward, landing in the parking lots or raining down from the ceiling. Asbestos insulation was blown off pipes.

The investigation committee under the Dearborn fire marshal later concluded that a natural gas explosion had been sparked by an unknown source—either static electricity or hot fly ash caught in the electrostatic precipitator (the steel dust collectors atop the building). The committee members disagreed, though, on whether the coal dust in the powerhouse had ignited, causing a secondary explosion.

A worker on the second floor later told investigators that he saw the explosion start near the east valve, heard the blast, and "saw red come out of the flange; then everything was red like a fire pit."

The explosion knocked down many of the workers near the boiler. As they got back up, they noticed they were on fire or had their hair and eyebrows singed off. At least one man appeared to have been blinded. Another man didn't get up. Donald Harper Sr., a 35-year Ford employee who was just shy of retirement, had been killed at the scene.

Two Rouge Steel firefighters and other steelworkers inside the training center at Gate 2, on the south side of the powerhouse, ran out after the explosion and rushed to help the wounded streaming out of the shattered building. Some of the steelworkers said they saw people they had known for years but didn't immediately recognize, because their skin was burned off. Some of the wounded were screaming, "I want to die!"

At the Ford firehouse, alarm box 2-2-2 rang at 1:02 p.m., and then the phones started ringing. "Within two hours, we were going to have a couple guys go to the powerhouse for the monthly inspection," said former Ford fire captain Gary Dell. "There were only three of us on duty at the time, so we responded with our ambulance and pumper truck."

Near the Stamping Plant, Mattias and his foreman heard the explosion and turned their car around, returning to the powerhouse. Near the "C" blast furnace, Mattias saw that the cars in the parking lot he had just left had been crushed by debris.

About a mile from the powerhouse, in the bowels of the Dearborn Assembly Plant, the lights flickered and went out, plunging the interior into darkness until the emergency lights snapped on. Albert Kahn's skylights and the side windows had been blacked out during World War II and further covered after the 1948 fire and 1970s renovation. "People were happy and started hollering, because they thought they'd be able to go home early. We didn't hear the explosion or feel any shaking," said Penny Cauzillo, who was working on the line that day.

The mood in the plant changed to panic when the workers were told to evacuate because of a fire. Some thought the plant was on fire and ran out. As Cauzillo exited the building, she saw police and fire engines outside, and her cellular phone began ringing as friends and family tried to reach her, to find out if she was okay.

Another Rouge Steel fireman (the third of the three who worked for the steelmaker) joined Dell's group as the Ford firefighters drove out to the north side of the powerhouse, near Gate 4, where they saw the hellish display before them. "One of my initial thoughts at that time was, 'My God, that fire's going to track into the Pulverizer Building,'" Dell said. "The Pulverizer had blown up three times before." At that point, though, the force of the explosion had already caused fire to race through the conveyor between the two buildings and had blown out the back wall of the Pulverizer.

As Dell and his partner, Tonya Ecckles, put their air packs on, a man came running around the powerhouse to tell them there were wounded on the south side of the building. The two Ford firefighters drove around the debris to get to the Rouge Steel training center, leaving the pumper truck to meet up with the Dearborn Fire Department.

Some 3 miles away, at the main Dearborn firehouse, word came in about the explosion, and the engines began rolling. Because a Rouge Steel train had damaged the Rotunda Drive connecting bridge to Miller Road six months before—and it had not been repaired—the fire engines rolled down to Gate 9, off Schaefer Road.

Turning onto Road 4, the fire trucks drove through the middle of the darkened complex to get to Gate 4, taking the tunnel under the Stamping Plant, and were set up within 10 minutes. Gate 4 was the site of the recently built Ernest Lofton Center for Physical Fitness and had become the Rouge's main medical facility after the old hospital closed several years earlier. The Fitness Center, however, had mostly lost power.

Back at the powerhouse, the Rouge Complex's medical van just happened to be sitting outside the building, near Gate 2, at the time of the explosion. About 10 of the burned and injured workers stumbled into the van and the driver rushed them off to the fitness center at Gate 4.

The powerhouse's generator room was also heavily damaged by fire after the 1999 explosion and would never run again. *Joseph Cabadas Collection*

In the meantime, someone at the Rouge Complex began calling fire departments and hospitals around the area, notifying them of the disaster. One call came into the aero unit of the University of Michigan Trauma Burn Center in Ann Arbor, said Dr. Paul Taheri, division chief of the Burn Center. "We sent the helicopters out before we were officially informed," Taheri recalled. "Then we made the traditional preparations . . . making sure that only the sickest of the sick were there."

Finally arriving at Gate 2, Dell and Ecckles went into the Rouge Steel training building to help set up a triage, while several workers inside the burning powerhouse formed a human chain to escape down a smoke-filled stairwell from the fourth floor. One man with third-degree burns to his hands had climbed out of the powerhouse onto a fifth-floor catwalk and walked over to an adjacent tower on what was called the "water deck," where he would remain trapped for an hour and a half.

Michael Birrell, then the training officer for the Dearborn Fire Department, arrived in his Ford Crown Victoria at the north side of the powerhouse. "The entire building was obscured by black smoke, and in the smoke, I believe I saw flames about 200 feet up," Birrell said. "Then I saw a phenomenon that I've only rarely seen, called a 'rollover.' That's when smoke accumulates at the ceiling of a structure and there's a bunch of unburned combustibles. When you get the right mixture of heat, fuel, and air, you'll get a flame rolling across the ceiling." The whipping winds must have created a ceiling effect and knocked enough of the smoke down to cause a rollover outdoors.

In the chaos, someone had initially told the firefighters that all the wounded had been evacuated to the Fitness Center, but then they heard there might be casualties on the south side of the powerhouse. Birrell was ordered to take a look. Driving between the powerhouse and the Pulverizer Building, Birrell arrived at the south parking lot and noticed piles of burned debris on the ground. "Then I realized that some of these 'debris' were moving and were injured people," he said.

Powerhouse No. 1 barely resembles its pre-explosion appearance in this view at the south wall. Its towering steel smokestacks have been removed, and the building sits abandoned and open to the elements. *Ford Photomedia*

The Dearborn Fire Department took over the disaster scene. Inexplicably, a supervisor ordered the gathering Ford firefighters, who could have helped Dearborn in the initial stages, to remain at the Rouge firehouse for nearly half an hour before sending them to the powerhouse, according to the Dearborn Fire Department and reports from Rouge Steel workers.

A large contingent of firefighters from Detroit and several Downriver cities arrived, but the Dearborn Fire Department determined there wasn't much they could do and stopped them from trying to go into the powerhouse to look for workers, leading some Rouge Steel and Ford workers to accuse the department of cowardice.

Birrell, who later became Dearborn fire chief before retiring in 2004, defended the department's decisions. None of the other departments was familiar with the layout of the powerhouse, and they operated on a different radio frequency than Dearborn, meaning there would be no way to coordinate their activities. There was also a fear that the 320-foot smokestacks might collapse or that several of the 6,000- to 10,000-gallon tanks of hydrogen, acid, and other chemicals next to the building might explode. It was better to keep firefighters out of the way.

Finally, there was no purpose risking lives for a building that was already destroyed, Birrell said. "In any fire, you're playing catch-up. But to put out a fire in a 300,000-square-foot building like the powerhouse, you'd have to put 100,000 gallons of water per minute on it. The typical pumper might only do 1,500 gallons per minute. We didn't have 200 fire trucks available."

By that time, a Ford powerhouse supervisor handed Birrell a list of all the workers who had been in that day. The supervisor had the presence of mind to mark off all the workers he saw outside, determining that approximately 70 of the 100 who had been in the building were accounted for.

Teams of three or four Dearborn firefighters joined Rouge Steel and Ford firemen to search specific areas of the burning powerhouse for trapped workers. Over their heads, sections of broken concrete ceiling, some measuring 4 x 8 feet, were suspended by weakened rebar. A baseball-size chunk hit one fireman.

The search for victims was suspended by 11 p.m. and resumed the next day. By early evening, three more search teams were sent in, supported by Michigan State Police dogs trained to find cadavers. One dog was injured when the flooring collapsed below it. Other than Donald Harper, whose body was recovered the next day, no one else had died in the building or been trapped there.

As events unfolded at the Rouge, Bill Ford Jr. left Ford World Headquarters the afternoon of February 1 to personally inspect the devastation. Later, he went to Oakwood Hospital to visit some of the victims. Ford said that he considered all of the company's employees to be "members of my extended family" and that he was deeply saddened and sickened by what he saw. He also met with the victims and their families at the University of Michigan Hospital, Detroit Receiving Hospital, and the St. Vincent Medical Center in Toledo, where the most critical patients were taken. Ford Jr. made a personal connection to the company's workers and "came into his own," noted Keith Crain, publisher of *Automotive News*.

The University of Michigan Trauma Burn Center received 9 of the 19 powerhouse victims—roughly equivalent to 5 percent of its average number of patients per year—within 30 minutes of one another, Taheri said. Burn victims need tremendous amounts of blood, anywhere from 10 to 20 units per operation, and many of the injured powerhouse workers needed several operations within the first couple of days, taxing southeast Michigan's normally low blood supplies. Jerry Sullivan, president of UAW Local 600, quickly contacted the Red Cross to set up emergency blood drives. Hundreds of donors appeared, including Jennifer Granholm, then Michigan attorney general, who came unannounced and without fanfare, Sullivan said.

Before the end of the month, however, five more powerhouse workers died—Cody Boatwright, Warren Blow, John Arseneau, Ron Moritz, and Ken Anderson.

With its victims removed, the coal bunkers smoldered for months, even with dry ice constantly layered over the debris. For all intents and purposes, the powerhouse that had been the pride of the Rouge was gone. Parts of the gutted hulk, such as the turbo blower room, needed to be rebuilt, if only to operate the blast furnaces. But more immediately, power and steam had to be restored to the complex, or its nearly 10,000 Ford and Rouge Steel employees would be out of work, not to mention those at other Ford plants that needed parts.

Ford brought in a number of generators and portable boilers to provide steam, while DTE Energy workers ran temporary electrical feeds to connect the auto plants back to the power grid. The Detroit Fire Department's boat, the *Curtis Randolph*, tied into the boat slip and connected its pumps to Ford's water distribution system. It was time-consuming to get the plants back up and running, because a number of circuit breakers and fuses had blown throughout the complex. There were also any number of dangerous situations, such as hydraulic presses at the Stamping Plant that were under load, ready to come down, that had to be reset. It was estimated that the explosion—the deadliest at an automotive complex in 50 years—and restart efforts cost more than $1 billion, making it one of the most costly industrial accidents in American history.

The automotive plants were back up and running to some degree after a week, but Rouge Steel faced a far more difficult path, reporting a $76 million loss by May. Its facilities were shut down for 93 days, and to fulfill orders, it bought steel from other companies as its own production dropped from 797,000 tons to 237,000 tons for the first quarter of 1999.

The old powerhouse claimed one more life, and two more injured when a rebuilt turbo blower exploded. Shrapnel from the machine was embedded in the walls and ceiling, and the force of the explosion cracked the 4-inch-thick metal case of the turbine next to it.

The remaining coal for the powerhouse was sold off, and the Pulverizer Building was torn down. In 2002, the eight steel smokestacks were dismantled, one at a time. The shattered building still existed as of 2004, awaiting final demolition.

A corridor in Local 600 was turned into the "Wall of Pain," where sympathy cards and banners were hung. On the annual "Workers Memorial Day," April 28, 1999, the Ford cousins, Bill Jr. and Edsel II, along with Nasser, were among those who participated in services at the union hall. "It's been very, very devastating for all of us here," said Sullivan at the time. "To date, there are 23 kids that are fatherless as a result of the explosion. There are many heart-tugging stories in regards to each and every one of the fatalities."

About a month before the explosion, across Miller Road from the powerhouse, ground had been broken for the new DIG power plant. Construction crews worked diligently to finish the new plant, but it didn't become fully operational until 2001, and CMS Energy took

over the "co-generation" facility, which is fueled by both natural and blast furnace gas. Its generators produce 710 megawatts of energy, with up to 300 megawatts available to the Rouge Complex and the rest going to the metro Detroit power grid. DIG also produces 1.2 million pounds of industrial steam per hour. A bridge holding steam pipes and other conduits crosses over Miller Road, linking the DIG plant to the Rouge.

When the investigative team led by Dearborn fire marshal Richard Polcyn released its 89-page report later in 1999, it concluded that among the problems, there was no clear, written procedure for the employees to follow, and that communication "between all personnel was at best inadequate." The state blamed both Ford and UAW Local 600 for the safety lapses and inadequate training, though Sullivan maintained that until the powerhouse explosion, the union was never privy to all the information found in accident reports.

In September 1999, the state of Michigan and Ford reached a historic $7 million settlement. Ford paid a record $1.5 million civil penalty. The remaining money went into funding a number of safety

The point on the Dearborn Assembly line where the individual sheet metal components officially become a car and receive a vehicle identification number (VIN). Two autoworkers spot-weld the side panels onto the floorpan. *Ford Photomedia*

IN MEMORY
OF THOSE WE'VE LOST
UAW-FORD LOCAL 600

Glenn Zielinski '00

Above: Glenn Zielinski, a maintenance and construction painter at the Rouge, created this painting, *Powerhouse Memorial*, to commemorate the lives of the six men who died following the powerhouse explosion. The setting sun silhouettes the powerhouse and a kneeling worker, while the six stars overhead represent the men who died. *Glenn Zielinski Archives*

Right: In the aftermath of the powerhouse explosion, Ford Chairman William Clay Ford Jr. picked Tim O'Brien, director of the Environmental Quality Office, to meet with "green" architect William McDonough, whose ideas would radically change the shape of the Rouge. *Ford Photomedia*

and health programs, such as $1.5 million to create programs for power generation safety; $1 million to research industrial safety and health; $1.5 million for the treatment of burns and other critical care; a $1 million scholarship fund for the victims' survivors; and $500,000 for "potential third-party reimbursement."

"This historic agreement can never reclaim lost lives or restore injured bodies—but it can ease the suffering of the victims and their families by assuring a safer and healthier work environment for all Ford employees in the future," said Kathy Wilbur, then director of the Michigan Department of Consumer and Industry Services.

In the aftermath of the explosion, people expressed their grief in different ways. Glenn Zielinski of Canton, Michigan, who worked at the Rouge since hiring in at the Stamping Plant in 1973, picked up his paintbrush and went to work on a 30 x 36–inch canvas. Zielinski, a former marine, is officially classified as a maintenance and construction painter, a job he landed in 1985, and did his initial 90 days of training in the powerhouse. But the company began making use of his artistic talents after he painted a mural for the Dearborn Engine Plant in 1990.

As word got out of his abilities, he was chosen to paint murals for the Rouge Fitness Center and Dearborn Assembly. He was working on a mural at the Glass House when the blast occurred. "I knew several of the people who were killed in the explosion," Zielinski said. "I decided, after the tragedy happened, being an artist, I wanted to do something commemorating the tragedy and the lives lost."

The resulting painting, entitled *Powerhouse Memorial*, shows the silhouette of the power plant at sunset with a Ford worker, also in silhouette, kneeling, with his hard hat off, in prayer. Above are six stars, representing the six men who lost their lives. He completed the painting on his own accord for the first anniversary of the tragedy.

During the Rouge's time of mourning, during what seemed to be its darkest days, Bill Ford Jr. instructed Timothy O'Brien, director of Ford's Environmental Quality Office, and other Ford officers to meet with architect Bill McDonough and Michael Braungart, cofounder of the German Green Party, to determine if the company could economically and effectively apply any of the two men's philosophies.

"You sit back in your job and you say, 'Okay, I'll be happy to do it if Bill Ford wants me to,'" O'Brien said. "But you look at the people he got you to talk to, and one guy is this dean of the school of architecture at the University of Virginia, and it's not immediately apparent why that would be very helpful, and the other guy is a former founder of Greenpeace, and that's even less apparent as to how that's going to be helpful for this exercise. So, yeah, I went into it with mixed emotions."

O'Brien's doubts, however, evaporated after meeting with McDonough and Braungart, who espoused that the company should strive to be as clean as environmentally possible because it made economic sense, not because it should merely seek to do a little less damage than it had before.

On May 3, Bill Ford Jr. was the keynote speaker at a forum called the "National Town Hall Meeting on Sustainable Development" held at Henry Ford Museum & Greenfield Village. Ford surprised both O'Brien and McDonough (not to mention other Ford personnel in attendance) when he laid out a new vision for the redevelopment of the Rouge to be a "visible testament" to the company's commitment to environmental leadership.

"The original plans for the Rouge were not to make it into a concrete jungle, but was to make it into an industrial complex that was actually a pleasant place to work," Ford Jr. said. The Rouge would receive a new assembly plant, one with a "grass roof," Ford vowed, adding that significant "green space" would be incorporated into the complex, because it was at the "gateway for the Rouge River." These pronouncements dramatically altered the plans for the new Dearborn Truck Plant that would open in 2004.

By this time, nearly two decades after the EPA lawsuit against Detroit, rulings by Federal Judge John Feikens, and efforts by a grass-roots organization called "Friends of the Rouge," the waterway had come back to life. Limited fishing and canoeing were even being allowed again. Donn Werling, director of the Henry Ford Estate–Fair Lane on the University of Michigan-Dearborn campus, strongly advocated that tour boats run up and down the river from the estate to Greenfield Village and even down to the Rouge Complex, for those who wanted to engage in "industrial tourism."

Also attending the sustainable development meeting was Carl Valdiserri, Rouge Industries chairman and CEO, who also promised that the steelmaker would do what it could to help Ford out. Unfortunately, as Ford moved forward with its redevelopment on what it would call the "Ford Rouge Center," Rouge Steel's fortunes fell.

Ford's vision for redeveloping the old factory complex—often called a "brownfield"—was certainly unusual in an industry that normally prefers to build new auto assembly plants in "green fields," often uncontaminated farmlands.

In November 1999, the UAW and the Big Three completed a series of successful negotiations without a strike. The immediate big news that came out of the Ford contract was that the company had agreed to set up a number of social programs and family centers to support workers. In some ways, it was a reinvention of the old Sociological Department, except that the union had demanded it. Then it was revealed that in an effort to jump-start the company into the twenty-first century's "new economy," Ford would give away personal computers and printers to most of its 350,000 employees, along with Internet service at $5 a month.

Only half a year later did another provision of the contracts come to light, when the Big Three and the UAW revealed that they had jumped headlong into the United States "culture war" and would offer same-sex domestic partner benefits. Although other companies had

begun offering such programs, it was groundbreaking for the mostly conservative auto manufacturers to agree to the union's demands. Yet the provision was negotiated without any kind of debate by the union's rank and file or even a mention when the contract was voted on—the deal was a fait accompli.

By the dawn of the new millennium, the auto industry was facing a number of challenges beyond the Y2K scare or rumors that a mysterious Saudi named Osama bin Laden was planning a New Year's Eve terrorist attack in the United States. The industry had been shaken by the 1998 takeover of the Chrysler Corporation by Germany's Daimler-Benz AG. The takeover, called a "merger of equals," had taken the media by surprise, and the press began speculating that there were too many car companies in the world vying for too small a universe of car buyers. Who would merge next?

Ford would strike again in 2000, using its cash reserves to purchase the Land Rover sport utility line from Germany's BMW. Yet Ford's non-production costs swelled, and a number of disquieting trends became clear, despite the United States' nearly 17-million-unit car market. In February 2000, due to a design flaw in the 3.8-liter V-6's head gaskets, Ford launched an extended warranty program for hundreds of thousands of owners of select 1994 through 1995 Ford, Mercury, and Lincoln vehicles equipped with the engines. The program hurt Ford's bottom line.

Nasser set Ford on a course of investing in a wide range of enterprises, from auto service stores in Europe to its Internet presence just

This worker, with the nametag "Macho Man," appears to be setting a rubber seal in place, possibly for acoustical reasons, before the instrument panel is installed into this Mustang convertible. *Ford Photomedia*

Two workers install components into a metal shell that is beginning to look more and more like a Mustang. *Ford Photomedia*

words, if a group like the original 10 Whiz Kids existed within the company, one would automatically fail.

The idea, Nasser said, was to inspire employees to do better and to give the company a razor-edge focus. He added that no manager was forced to give out negative grades. General Motors, however, had tried a similar system in the 1980s, and it destroyed company morale while creating a distrust of upper management. Instead of replicating GE, Nasser's policies set Ford on track to follow GM. Many workers believed Nasser was targeting employees for automatic layoff when the next economic downturn occurred.

But the popular Explorer sent Ford's fortunes crashing. In February 2000, after a Houston television station reported that Explorers were rolling over after suffering a tire tread separation, the National Highway Traffic Safety Administration (NHTSA) launched an investigation. By late summer, as Ford showed off its next-generation Explorer to the media, the automaker and Bridgestone-Firestone were embroiled in a full-blown controversy that they tried to ease by recalling 6.5 million tires. NHTSA eventually linked the case to more than 270 deaths and 800 injuries.

The rollover controversy grew more intense when the automaker replaced an additional 13 million Firestone tires on its vehicles, leading the companies to sever their nearly 100-year relationship. At the time, Bill Ford Jr. said the Firestone crisis was personally troubling to him—his mother was a Firestone.

As the Explorer-Firestone controversy played out, the updates to the Dearborn Engine Plant were completed. Besides fresh paint and new lighting, the plant was equipped to manufacture Ford's new 1.8- to 2.3-liter, 16-valve I-4 engines. Using an extensive number of aluminum components, the new engine was 40 pounds lighter than the old Zetec I-4, offering better weight distribution and power-to-weight ratios for the 2001 Ranger pickup and the Escape SUV. Set up to make as many as 325,000 units per year, modular assembly equipment allowed the line at Dearborn Engine to quickly reconfigure the engines without delaying production.

Despite this good news on the manufacturing side, the worst wasn't over, as Ford lost $752 million in the second quarter of 2001, due mostly to Firestone tire replacement costs. (It also racked up a $692 million net loss in the third quarter of 2001, the first time in nearly a decade that Ford had consecutive losing quarters.) The company's relationship with its dealers and suppliers grew frayed, due to Nasser's policies; vehicle quality problems rose, delaying the launches of the 2001 Ford Escape and 2002 Ford Thunderbird; and employee morale continued to sink.

Taking a page from Henry Ford II's playbook, Bill Ford Jr. created the Office of the Chairman and CEO in July 2001, so he could review policies, strategy, and business proposals with Nasser. Ford also brought in Nick Scheele, chairman of Ford of Europe, promoting him

before the dot-com economy went bust. The U.S. Federal Reserve hiked interest rates to bring the "overheated" economy to a "soft landing," even though inflation was relatively low. Companies quietly froze hiring or reduced their workforces as everyone anticipated the inevitable downturn.

Inside Ford, the direction Nasser set was observed and followed. The work to instill the ideals of W. Edwards Deming into product planning and quality unraveled. The company paid attention to its "Premier Automotive Group," or PAG, which was to comprise Aston Martin, Jaguar, Volvo, Land Rover, and even (for a time) Lincoln. Not enough emphasis, it seemed, was placed on improving Ford's mass-market products.

Also adding to the internal distraction, Nasser instituted a new grading policy for white-collar employees. Inspired by General Electric's Jack Welch, the dictum instructed managers to rate only 10 percent of their workers as "high achievers" who would receive extra merit raises. Eighty percent would be ranked "average," and the lowest 10 percent were "underachievers" in danger of dismissal. In other to group vice president with responsibilities for overseeing product development, manufacturing, marketing, and sales of Ford brand vehicles in North America. Gone was the pretense that Ford would be a "caretaker chairman."

As the summer of 2001 drew to a close, the nation's economy was in the doldrums, with little hiring. But vehicle sales hadn't fallen much, and many business leaders were predicting an economic turnaround "next quarter."

Then, on a bright, warm morning in metropolitan Detroit, Dearborn Assembly plant workers were either returning from their breaks or going on them when their cell phones and fax pagers began going off about a plane striking one of the towers of the World Trade Center in New York City. At first, most thought it might have been a small plane, until word came in that the second tower had been struck too. Workers headed to the break rooms to watch TV when news came that a third plane had crashed into the Pentagon and a fourth had slammed into a Pennsylvania field.

Shocked as they were at the terrorist attacks, foremen told the workers to get back to the line—47 Mustangs an hour had to be completed. It

A man works on one of Ford's new 1.8- to 2.3-liter dual overhead cam (DOHC) inline four-cylinder engines (*above*). These engines use numerous aluminum components and are 40 pounds lighter than the old Zetec I-4 they replace. The plant was set up with modular assembly equipment (*left*), to permit reconfiguring the engine's features without delaying production. *Ford Photomedia*

Demise of the Ford Rouge Fire Department

Soon after the River Rouge Plant was created, the Ford Rouge Fire Department (FRFD) was formed.

For years, the firemen were incorporated into Harry Bennett's Service Department and were used in 1930 to turn their hoses on a riot by unemployed men and then in 1932 on the Hunger Marchers. Yet they mostly waited for fires to occur and checked the water mains, fire extinguishers, and hoses at the Rouge's factories and on Ford's ships. For years they also operated the plant's laundry service, providing thousands of sterilized towels to workers every day.

By 1920, the department had grown to 123 men and was located in Powerhouse No. 3, a small structure between the "B" Building and the Glass Plant. Its first fire engine is purported to have been a 1918 steam-powered model. After Ford acquired a newer fire truck, there were stories of firemen engaging in fistfights to find a position on the truck when an alarm sounded.

In the late 1930s, the FRFD moved into a more centrally located fire station, between the Glass Plant and the Spring and Upset Building (part of the Stamping Plant). When the United Auto Workers organized the Rouge, the Ford fireman joined the plant guards in forming Plant Protection Association 111.

During World War II, the department had about 110 men and operated a small fire station near the Naval Training School, with one truck and three firemen on each shift. Ironically, according to stories, the small station burned down.

The firemen were kept busy—blazes and mishaps could happen at any time in the vast complex—especially at the Ford steelworks. The years 1947 and 1948 appear to have been especially busy, with the fire that nearly destroyed the Dearborn Assembly Plant and blazes at the Administration Building and one of the foundries.

With the economic downturn of 1958, Ford cut its fire department in half, to about 60 firemen, with a fire chief, a deputy chief, six fire inspectors, three captains, and four lieutenants. At that time, the FRFD had a 1950 fire engine and a 1954 Class A, open-cab pumper.

The bulk of the firemen's work was recharging the portable fire extinguishers and testing fire hydrants. With an increased emphasis on the safety of workers, many new firemen received medical training, and Ford bought its first ambulance in 1970. Before that time, the department used a van to transport sick and injured workers to the Rouge's Medical Facility, located east of the fire station, near Dearborn Assembly, on Road 4.

A new Class A enclosed-cab pumper replaced the two 1950s trucks in 1973. After that vehicle was destroyed three years later by a train behind the Dearborn Stamping Plant, Ford bought a new pumper with a 500-gallon water tank.

As the country slid into recession in 1979, Ford cut the FRFD from 54 firefighters to 18. It was an ill-timed move—in November, after the last 10 firemen were laid off, one of the augers in the Pulverizer Building jammed, and the coal spontaneously combusted.

Ford Fire Department's new 1973 Ford Class A enclosed-cab pumper sits outside the Rouge firehouse. Due to the size of the Rouge complex and the number of factories, Ford established its own specialized fire department in 1918. At one time it numbered up to 123 men, but by 1958, it had been cut to 60. Its manpower was further slashed to 18 firefighters in 1979. *Kenneth Borg Archives*

When it seemed like the company was planning to disband the Rouge fire department altogether, the firefighters joined the International Association of Fire Fighters, chartering Local I-35 on March 7, 1980. Throughout the 1980s, with the future of the complex in doubt, the remaining firefighters were trained as emergency medical technicians (EMTs), and Ford replaced its 1976 pumper with a 1979 firefighting van. The department was split, three members going with Rouge Steel when it was sold off in 1989.

"As worker safety issues grew, we realized that we didn't have a lot of expertise in getting people who were trapped in machines out, so a 'press release' team was started at the Rouge," said former Ford fire captain Gary Dell. "What happened before was that it would take us 45 minutes or so to amass the right maintenance people that knew what to do with the machine. Some machines were designed so they couldn't go backwards, and that made it hard trying to get people out. This Stamping Plant group decided to get with the vendors to design the machines that could go in reverse and other things. Well, that program has really evolved."

The FRFD was also designated the "high-angle" and "confined-space" rescue team for not only the Rouge factories but also for Ford World Headquarters and the Ford research and engineering facilities in Allen Park and Dearborn. In 1998, the department handled 704 fire runs and 510 rescue runs, according to FRFD information. Despite its duties, Ford officials decided to reduce the depleted unit from "fire department" status to "fire brigade" in 2003, splitting its members among the automaker's five plants at the complex, even as it planned to reopen the Rouge to public tours.

"Times have changed," Ed Lewis of Ford Public Relations told *Detroit News* reporter Mark Truby. "We think they can be a more valuable resource inside the plants. This is all part of the twenty-first century renovation we are doing at the Rouge Center."

Ford's decision did not sit well with the Ford firefighters. Dearborn Fire Chief Michael Birrell was a bit more equivocal: "They are manning an ambulance on a round-the-clock basis and assigned the other firefighters to the buildings. They will be in charge of inspecting and maintaining the fire suppression systems, the alarm systems, and will also be available to respond to problems at other factories, riding golf carts with extinguishers, and others will be in pickup trucks."

The Dearborn Fire Department now responds to calls at the Rouge, but its personnel are no longer trained for the confined-space or high-angle rescues that may be required in the Ford factories, Birrell said. That responsibility falls to Ford.

A small overhead crane aids two men as they complete the assembly of the rear solid axle and differential for a 2004 Mustang. Both wear eye protection but no earplugs, even though this area of the plant can be pretty loud. *Ford Photomedia*

wasn't until 1 p.m., after word came that employees at Ford World Headquarters had been allowed to go home, that Rouge workers were also allowed to leave. At Rouge Steel, however, the furnaces were fired up—steel had to be poured, and workers remained on the job.

Because a large percentage of the Rouge Complex's workforce is of Arab descent, Ford issued new rules, imposing a "zero-tolerance policy" toward derogatory jokes or racially insensitive comments.

Also, over the years, the company has tried to crack down on sexual harassment at its factories. Since World War II, a growing number of women have worked in auto factories, but at the Dearborn Assembly Plant, the ratio has remained about 80 percent men to 20 percent women. "In paint, there's always been a lot of women, and there's a lot of women on the trim line," Penny Cauzillo said. "The final line and chassis have a lot of men. They do the harder jobs with a lot of heavy tires, engines, and the stuff underneath the car.

"Ford has a huge zero-tolerance policy, but most of the guys know where to stop with their comments. If someone says something that they're not supposed to, you tell them, 'You're in the red.' "

For Jac Nasser, life at Ford ended October 29, when his tenuous hold on his job finally slipped. Bill Ford Jr. told his CEO that it was time to step down. The Ford board of directors sanctioned the change early the next day, promoting Scheele to chief operating officer and giving him a seat on the board. That morning, Bill spoke to applauding employees at the Glass House, telling them that the automaker had lost

its way and it had to "focus on the basics of our business, which is building great product."

Nasser's ouster didn't surprise Wall Street, though not everyone was confident in the young Ford's abilities. Dominic Martillotti, an automotive analyst for Bear Stearns & Company of New York, said, "Ford needs to be more of a figurehead CEO and delegate duties to a quality team. That's not saying he is not a good leader, but in terms of actually knowing how things work in the auto business on an operational level, he needs strong warriors."

The sacking of Nasser was overdue, added Jay Woodworth, president of Woodworth Holdings, another Wall Street investment firm. The company's stock had declined more than any other auto company's from January 1999 until late 2001, while its market share had slipped badly in North America and was dreadful in Europe. It would take a lot of hard work to turn things around, especially with Toyota, Honda, and Nissan making strong comebacks.

No one lost sleep over Nasser's departure at Visteon either. Peter Pestillo, Ford's former head of human resources, had become chairman of the parts company when Ford spun it off as an independent enterprise in 1999. When he was interviewed in 2002 by the trade publication *Auto Interiors*, he said, "I think Ford has found its way back up from the bottom. It had faced, as one of my people characterized, a 'perfect storm' with the Firestone recall; the proliferation of competitors' new products, particularly trucks, that challenged them; costs that got out of line. Fortunately, the culture of meanness that was over there has now gone away."

With losses mounting to $3 billion by the end of 2001, Ford announced a restructuring program that would cut its workforce by 35,000 people worldwide, including 15,000 hourly, 5,000 salaried, and 1,500 temporary employees from its ranks in North America. Five factories would close, including Edison Assembly, Ontario Truck, St. Louis Assembly, Cleveland Aluminum Casting, and the Vulcan Forge Plant in Dearborn. Vulcan Forge was not part of the Rouge Complex but was nearby, on Dearborn's east city limit with Detroit. Layoffs occurred at 11 other factories, and line speed reductions at nine plants.

The budget cuts nearly derailed the renovations of the Rouge, including the grass roof and other environmental measures, but Ford Jr. held firm to his commitment that it must happen. By this time, Ford had announced that the Rouge's new "green" assembly plant would be called the "Dearborn Truck Plant" and would be able to build vehicles off three different platforms (chassis) and up to nine different body styles, giving it the flexibility to adapt to changing consumer tastes. The first vehicle produced at the new plant would be the next-generation Ford F-150 pickup, which was selling in excess of 800,000 units per year.

As the company's financial situation looked grimmer, Ford Jr. turned toward an experienced retiree who held clout on Wall Street, bringing Allan Gilmour back to his old post as chief financial officer in May 2002.

The UAW was also hurt by the layoffs, not only at Ford but also at DaimlerChrysler, which had gotten into financial trouble six months before Ford, and at General Motors. As older workers retired, they were not necessarily replaced. Union membership plunged from 701,818 members in 2001 to 624,585 by the end of 2003, its lowest total since 1941 and a far cry from its high point of nearly 1.5 million in 1979. While the Big Three declined, the union had been unable to organize the North American factories of Toyota, Honda, Nissan, Mercedes, or BMW. Another reason for the union's decline was that more than 130,000 of its Canadian members split off in October 1984 to form the Canadian Auto Workers union, amid feelings that the American-based UAW was shortchanging them.

By 2003, the year of its centennial, Ford Motor Company had lost $6.4 billion in the previous two years, while its stock had plunged to a 10-year low of $6.90 per share. Some Wall Street pundits claimed that Ford should declare bankruptcy.

Yet the company continued with its restructuring program and held its hundredth birthday bash from June 12 to 16. The 152 acres of the Ford World Headquarters complex were turned into a vast amusement park, drawing nearly 225,000 people. One highlight was the tour of the still unfinished Dearborn Truck Plant rising next to the old Dearborn Assembly Plant.

Renovations to the venerable Dearborn Stamping Plant were completed in 2003. The factory, with sections that dated back to 1936, was ready to start making doors and hoods for the new-generation F-150. The pickup came out that year as a 2004 model and was built at Ford's Norfolk and Kansas City plants. (When Dearborn Truck started up, it was not expected to take production away from the other two truck assembly plants, because it replaced the Oakville, Ontario, factory that was shuttered by the end of 2004.)

Among its renovations, the Stamping Plant received an enormous 7.4-million-pound Schuler five-station crossbar transfer press that is nearly three-quarters of a football field in length and about as high as a two-story house. The press can make 700 parts per hour. Automated guided vehicles (AGVs) bring steel blanks up from the plant's basement, and a forklift driver loads the blanks into a cart that feeds the massive machine. Once the parts are stamped, the press feeds them into a rack, and an elevator takes them to the basement, where they are loaded into an AGV. Despite Schuler press' size, dies for it can be changed within 12 minutes (a far cry from half day or more for older presses).

The old Frame Plant changed identities, too, in June 2003, when it was renamed the Dearborn Diversified Manufacturing (DDM) Plant. Frames for the F-150 would be produced at a Dana Corporation facility and shipped in by rail, so DDM would assemble chassis and rear-axle-related components for the F-Series pickup truck.

The stage was set for the new Dearborn Truck Plant to open.

Above: A conveyor brings five-spoke aluminum wheels to the line for workers to attach to fortieth-anniversary Mustangs. *Ford Photomedia*

Right: Plants play another role in sustainable development at the Rouge—cleansing the soil of contaminants. Michigan State University students planted a 1.6-acre plot of land near the closed coke ovens in 2002. The flowers, bushes, and trees were chosen because they can remove polyaromatic hydrocarbon (PAH) contamination from the soil and break it down into safe, organic compounds. In the background to the left is the old powerhouse, with demolition crews removing the smokestacks. To the right, the white building on the other side of Miller Road is the new Dearborn Industrial Generation (DIG) plant. *Ford Photomedia*

Epilogue

An Icon for the Twenty-First Century

"No man can say anything of the future. We need not bother about it. The future has always cared for itself in spite of our well-meant efforts to hamper it. If today we do the task we can best do, then we are doing all that we can do."

—Henry Ford, Today and Tomorrow, 1926

When the River Rouge Plant took shape in 1919, Ford Motor Company was on its way to dominating the American auto industry through most of the 1920s. Although some 266 different makes of gasoline-powered automobiles were available in the United States, Ford made 750,000 of the 1,974,000 vehicles sold in 1919, or about 37.9 percent of the market. At the time, the Highland Park Plant was more famous, but the Rouge grew to eclipse it.

The concept for the Rouge was that it would become one vast plant, taking in raw materials at one end and rolling finished cars out the other. Henry Ford and his company surmounted a number of challenges before that idea became reality in December 1927, when the first production Model A was finished.

"That's what made Henry Ford a pioneer—doing things before they were commonly done," said Jay Richardson, manager of Ford's Heritage Project for the Rouge. "And I think that's what makes the new Ford Rouge Center interesting as well. We've built on his vision and are doing things here that are not typically done in the industrial world. We are really redefining what industrial leadership is all about."

Vertical integration was a way of life at Ford for many years, noted Dr. David Cole, president of the Ann Arbor–based Center for Automotive Research and a well-known auto analyst.

"Henry Ford had the philosophy that he wanted to make everything except fuels and lubricants. His idea was to control the total value chain, and it worked," Cole said. "Ford, though, ended up losing its market position to General Motors because of the rigidity of Henry Ford's car design philosophy—epitomized by the slogan 'You can have a Ford car in any color you want, as long as it's black.'"

In the early days of the American auto industry, both Ford and GM faced a supply base that was in rough shape, so vertical integration allowed them to develop and improve the quality of their cars. By the 1970s, however, as General Motors, Ford, and Chrysler faced increased foreign competition, they compared their operations to outside firms and found that many of their captive parts plants had become inefficient.

Vertical integration had broken down at the Rouge, though with the new Dearborn Truck Plant in operation, the Stamping and Diversified Dearborn Diversified Manufacturing (DDM) plants would at least make some of the F-Series pickup trucks' components.

"Although Dearborn Engine will not be making engines for the F-150, they will be coming either from Windsor [Ontario] or Romeo [Michigan], so they aren't very far away," said James Padilla, then president of Ford North America and South America Operations, when interviewed in January 2004. "Several Visteon facilities in the area will be supplying components, instrument panels and the like. And we will be bringing a lot of components, such as other stampings, from Woodhaven, from fairly local arrangements. So everything will be pretty close to just-in-time delivery."

The Rouge declined at Ford because it started to "capture the essence of what was out of date and old and did not fit the contemporary world," Cole said. "And Ford's attention was elsewhere, investing in a lot of other areas and overseas. . . . Eventually, management realized they had to do something with this huge manufacturing complex—either throw it away or make it into a showplace for twenty-first-century manufacturing."

The success of the Rouge will not make or break Ford, Cole added. The critical issue will be whether Ford is able to develop and successfully build good products that buyers want.

Another factor that will determine Ford's success or failure is how fast it can take waste out of its entire manufacturing system, said James P. Womack, president and founder of the Lean Enterprise Institute in Massachusetts. Womack is former director of research for Massachusetts Institute of Technology's International Motor Vehicle Program. He also coauthored several books on lean production, including *The Machine That Changed the World*, a famed study of vehicle assembly plants that contrasted the "Toyota Production System" with traditional mass-production methods.

Womack points out that in its financial crisis during 2001 and 2002, when it lost $6.4 billion, Ford went back to its tried-and-true

The Rouge Plant, photographed from the Melvindale side of the Rouge River in 1941. The factory complex was built to be a showcase of vertical integration. *Ford Photomedia*

An overhead clamp-shell conveyor takes the body of this F-150 from the trim line to the final assembly line.
Ford Photomedia

tactics of squeezing its suppliers for cost reductions and "decontenting" vehicles—i.e., removing standard equipment. The problem was that many suppliers, like Visteon, didn't have any margins (profits) left to cut, and customers soon realized they weren't getting the cars they thought they were buying.

"What's left is the lean, hard stuff of actually trying to take waste out of the system, as opposed to taking value out," Womack said. "I wish Ford

the best, but that organization only knows how to squeeze and decontent. They really don't know anything about how to optimize their value stream to maximize value to the consumer and minimize costs. I've had some painful personal experience of trying to help Ford over the years and gotten nothing for my efforts. Well, today is a new day."

Ford's new Dearborn Truck Plant (DTP), the first new vehicle assembly plant built in metropolitan Detroit since Chrysler Jefferson

Two workers install a section of sedum roof on top of the new Dearborn Truck Plant in 2002. While it looks like sod, the succulent plants are actually on a type of industrial mat with several layers *(below)*. Below the sedum are a semi-organic layer of soil with shale, sand, peat, and compost; a fleece mat that holds water; a drainage layer to remove excess water from the roof; and a waterproof layer, to protect the metal roof of the factory below. *Ford Photomedia*

North opened in 1992, may be one of the hard steps the company has to take to prosper. Only with the guidance of Bill Ford Jr. and a few other executives did it survive the company's severe budget cuts. DTP was built with the idea of being "green," lean, and flexible, Jay Richardson said.

Ford's truck factory is actually three interconnected buildings—the final-assembly building with its "grass" roof, the 800,000-square-foot Body Shop, and the Paint Shop—with a total of 2.3 million square feet. Traditionally, Ford made any environmental decisions much later in the construction processes, and they were much narrower in scope, such as figuring out what state and federal permit requirements and emission controls were needed, O'Brien said. Bill Ford Jr.'s decision to make the truck plant a model of sustainable development—to have a positive impact on the environment—changed the ultimate design of the factory before the November 2000 groundbreaking.

The *Guinness Book of World Records* lists the truck plant as having the "World's Largest Living Roof." When Ford announced the plan for the "grass roof," the media speculated that it might be a rooftop garden and wondered how many tons of soil would be spread up there. Actually, the living part of the roof has several varieties of a drought-resistant perennial plant called sedum. Instead of being

The main building of the Dearborn Truck Plant has the world's largest habitat roof as part of a natural storm-water drainage system, plus 10 roof monitors and 36 smaller skylights to provide extensive natural light inside.
Ford Photomedia

benefit is that the sedum mats provide a layer of natural insulation. This will reduce heating and cooling costs, and help the factory's "intelligent" heating and cooling system, which recirculates heat generated by the machinery in the wintertime and brings in cool air at ground level during the summer.

As DTP was built, the habitat roof was grown on a 10-acre patch of Ford's nearby Allen Park Clay Mine Landfill, which itself was in the process of being closed down for reuse as the site of a future shopping center that will employ some of the same environmental features as the Rouge.

Hearkening back to the days when Rouge factories had vast skylights, DTP's final assembly building has 10 "roof monitors"—skylights enclosed by glass boxes that are 115 feet long, 25 feet wide, and 22 feet tall and are glazed with energy-efficient glass—plus 36 smaller skylights. The Body Shop has an additional 24 skylights. Together, these windows to the sky should reduce the need for artificial lighting on sunny days and make the factory's interior brighter and airier.

Another part of the natural storm-water management system can be seen along the 1.5-mile stretch of Miller Road that runs along the eastern edge of the Rouge. Ford undertook a $10 million facelift of the historic road, which included rebuilding a one-third-size replica of the famed Gate 4 overpass, along with a new entry arch of red brick and gray limestone, reminiscent of the old entranceway. Just inside the gate is a memorial to the six men who died in the 1999 powerhouse explosion.

Miller Road also features a green belt of 85,000 flowering plants, 20,000 shrubs, and hundreds of trees (including two varieties of Hawthorne, which were a favorite of Henry Ford's) on either side of the six-lane boulevard. The greenery not only looks attractive, it cuts down on pollution. Many of the plantings were chosen because they trap airborne dust. In the boulevard's median are "wetland ditches," called swales, that are part of the Rouge's natural storm-water management system. The swales feature grasses, sand, and gravel that filter the water before it seeps into the Rouge River.

The storm-water management system includes experimental porous pavement placed on top of one of Dearborn Assembly's vehicle shipping lots in 2000. Water seeps through the pavement's tiny holes and enters a filtration system of rock storage beds that channels it to the swales. The porous paving was such a success that Ford used it for DTP's new 16-acre shipping lot.

Plants play another role of sustainable development at the Rouge: cleansing the soil of contaminants. A 1.6-acre plot of trees, cardinal flowers, bulrush, monkey flower, cordgrass, red bud, and hickory was planted near the closed coke ovens and the small gas tower in 2002. Using a biological process called "phytoremediation," the plants remove polyaromatic hydrocarbon (PAH) contamination, a byproduct of years of steel manufacturing, from the soil and break it down into safe, organic compounds.

planted in soil, a more "industrial" approach was taken. The sedum grows in thin, four-layer mats called "Xero Flor" that include an organic layer, with a mixture of shale, sand, peat, compost, and dolomite; a layer of mineral wool; a drainage layer; and finally, a root-resistant membrane to protect the factory's traditional tar-covered steel roof.

The depth of the mats was engineered to prevent large, non-native plants from springing up on the roof (the idea was to create a garden that didn't require a lot of care and attention), and the structural steel was strengthened to support a roof that weighed up to 25 pounds per square foot (although the sedum mats, when fully saturated, are expected to weigh only 15 pounds per square foot).

While the habitat roof sounds expensive, its design and other improvements around the complex actually saved Ford $35 million, compared to constructing a traditional sewer and water-treatment system, O'Brien said. "The habitat roof . . . will capture storm water off the 10.4-acre final assembly building and allow it to be cleaned or evaporated naturally, as opposed to an engineered approach," O'Brien explained, "which is a big system of sewers and pipes and catchment basins and treatment systems."

The green roof is also expected to extend the life of the factory's roof up to 30 years, because it will mitigate the extremes of the freeze-thaw cycle that cause traditional flat roofs to crack and leak. Another

With all the flowering plants, Ford embarked on project to pollinate them by bringing in three queen bees and 20,000 honey bees, set up in three hive boxes near the Visitors Center.

The Dearborn Truck Plant is a large step forward for Ford in terms of manufacturing and environmental issues, Padilla said. With the factory able to build vehicles on up to three different architectures and nine different body styles, the company has much more flexibility to respond to consumer demand. The environmental aspects of the plant, including its natural rainwater management techniques, will be studied to see if they can be applied at other Ford plants.

DTP's design offers lessons for worker safety too. "One of the most pressing challenges is worker safety on a shop floor, particularly with Hi-Los moving around," Padilla said. "By and large, we are going to make [DTP] into a Hi-Lo–free factory. And when workers have to do any of their support activities—training, cafeteria, and locker rooms—it will be upstairs on the mezzanine level, off the factory floor. So we have moved the traffic flow away from the equipment and machinery."

The truck plant will have about two hours' worth of parts "line-side" and another 10 hours of parts "off-line." By contrast, in 2003, Dearborn Assembly kept four hours of parts line-side, while many other auto factories might have inventory for two days or more. To make sure the factory has enough parts, computers connect it to nearby suppliers, ordering components as needed.

Because the factory will thus handle about 500 deliveries and some 200 shipments a day, the state of Michigan reconstructed the nearby I-94 and Schaefer Road interchange to handle the truck traffic. Reminiscent of the manner in which Clare Snider choreographed the timing of ore freighters entering the boat slip, the trucks will enter a staging area on the west side of the complex. After a brief wait, they will enter the receiving docks, offload, and get back onto the freeway, to avoid unnecessary delays.

The most challenging aspects of building DTP were space constraints, O'Brien said. Compromises had to be made on where to locate the Body Shop, where to build the Paint Shop, and how to configure the buildings to allow trucks to get in and out of the site. Yet it was rare to have enough land to build a new vehicle assembly plant on such a site before the old factory was decommissioned.

Above: The plantings outside the Rouge office building, which housed offices for Ford and Rouge Steel, look attractive but were also chosen for their ability to cut down on airborne dust. *Ford Photomedia*

Right: An F-150 frame produced by Dana Corporation of Toledo, Ohio, enters the Dearborn Truck Plant's final assembly area via a conveyor. The frame is upside down so the axle can be put in place. After some of the bottom components are attached, it will be flipped over. *Ford Photomedia*

DTP's assembly line uses entirely different technology than Dearborn Assembly. Instead of a visible chain that hauls the chassis along, the F-Series pickup trucks will, for the most part, ride on "skillets" that stay flush with the factory floor as they move. The skillets have wooden platforms, because wood is far better for the human foot to stand on than concrete or metal, even with rubberized mats. Skillets are not new to the automotive industry, but DTP is probably the first to use them so extensively.

"We probably have upwards of around 250 skillets," said Dennis Profitt, who was the director and construction site manager. "One type is called a 'smart' skillet, because it goes up and down automatically, adjusting the job to the workers' heights to eliminate bending and stretching."

The truck line is also shorter than the Mustang line at the old Dearborn Assembly Plant, with 40 percent fewer workstations. These stations are also flexible, with tools and robots that can be quickly changed over to make different vehicles. The level of automation, however, depends on the different departments. The new factory will also be quiet compared to the old Dearborn Assembly, because workers use lighter and less bulky direct current (DC) electric tools rather than pneumatic tools.

"In the Body Shop, because of the way the tools are designed, the vast majority of the welds are automated robotically," Jay Richardson said. "Actually, it will have less automation than some other plants in the Ford system, and we've done that to make sure we maintain flexibility."

A high level of automation limits a factory's ability to make multiple models. In the final assembly area, flexibility comes from the people who work in teams to take control of quality on the shop floor, not the machines, Richardson said.

One of those people is Penny Cauzillo, who was a team leader at Dearborn Assembly before it closed. "In the team leader role, I'm getting more involved with quality issues and problem solving, which I do together with my team," she said. "I have seven people that I stock, and back up the others when they have to go to the bathroom. And there may be some opportunities to get off the line and do some additional training."

Every Monday the team leaders meet, bringing together people from the body and trim shops, engineers, managers, quality inspectors, and pre-delivery people to discuss quality problems—such as loose rocker panels or squeaks and rattles. Using a worksheet, they try to fix

One of Ford's beekeepers checks on the three beehives set in a grove of young trees just south of the Rouge Visitors Center. The approximately 20,000 honeybees in these hives will pollinate all the plantings that spruce up the 85-year-old factory complex. They will also produce "Rouge Honey"—but that edible delight may not end up on store shelves.
Ford Photomedia

The Dearborn Truck Plant has only two hours' worth of parts in storage racks like these along the line. By and large, the factory will be forklift-free, to reduce the chances of accidents. *Ford Photomedia*

the problems by figuring out how they were caused. "It does work to some extent, but it's hard to get everyone involved on the same page," Cauzillo said. "Fortunately, a lot of the salary people are willing to talk to the hourly person, because they know that we're the ones on the job every day and see the problems."

The worker team concept doesn't sit too well with some UAW retirees, such as Samuel Cain and Albert Stevenson, who view it as a threat to unionism, because it might allow management to once again manipulate individual workers while giving them the illusion of camaraderie.

But nearly every Ford plant has worker teams operating in them, Padilla noted. The teams focus on safety, quality, delivery, cost, morale, and environmental issues, represented by the acronym "SQDC & ME." "We have team boards that address those issues, to get help where it's needed, so they can regulate their own work environment," Padilla said.

With workers controlling quality, Ford expects most vehicle flaws to be discovered and fixed on the line, as they are in Toyota plants. As a result, the pre-delivery garage, where the pickup trucks will be tested on

The assembly line at the Dearborn Truck Plant uses skillet conveyors—special platforms on which the vehicle chassis rides down the line, flush with the plant floor (left). Several types of skillets are used in different areas of the plant, some capable of raising or lowering the trucks, thus adjusting to the workers' heights and eliminating excess bending and stretching. The idea for skillets is not entirely new, as can be seen from the photo of convertible tops being built at Highland Park in 1949 (below). Of course, these workers were building a component, not an entire vehicle. *Ford Photomedia*

dynamometers and tested for water leaks, will be one-third the space normally allocated.

By the latter half of 2003, the first few teams of workers had transferred to DTP (and trained in other nearby buildings) to learn their new jobs and the best way to build the F-150s. By spring 2004, DTP began building a limited number of pre-production F-150s. Before DTP could become fully operational, however, Dearborn Assembly had to shut down.

Even as DTP was under construction, it hosted a number of special events, including four days of media briefings in December 2002 regarding the specifications of the 2004 F-150. The briefings—one-day meetings for four "waves" of nearly 100 reporters and auto analysts—were held in one of the receiving docks, even as construction workers were laying the concrete floor elsewhere.

Bill Ford Jr. led off the first day's briefing on December 3. Both the Rouge and the F-150 represented the "heart and soul" of Ford Motor Company, Ford said. Although the Rouge was known for vertical integration, the new truck plant would become the icon for twenty-first-century manufacturing.

The F-Series pickup truck, which started with the first F-1 that debuted in 1947 and was briefly built on an assembly line at "B" Building,

An employee works on a door before it's attached to an F-150 pickup truck in December 2003. Instead of using pneumatic tools, which were common at the old Dearborn Assembly Plant, he uses an electric screwdriver, which is much quieter. *Ford Photomedia*

has sold an average of 800,000 units per year. For nearly 20 of the past 27 years, it has been America's bestselling truck and the bestselling vehicle in the United States.

The Ford pickup was completely revamped for 2004, offering either the 4.6- or 5.8-liter Triton V-8, producing 231 and 300 horsepower, respectively. Initially, five different interior styles were available, from the workhorse XT to the luxurious Lariat. (The leather-clad King Ranch version was added for 2005.) It offered three cabs, from the two-seat version to two full rows of seats in the CrewCab, and pickup beds from 5½ to 8 feet long.

The incomplete truck plant hosted another unusual (and historic) event—a black-tie dinner dance to raise funds to preserve the Henry Ford Estate–Fair Lane. Normally, the dances were held in the Ritz Carlton–Dearborn's glitzy ballrooms, but the party was held instead on the assembly line floor, on April 12, 2003, with $1 million worth of Cartier jewelry on display.

DTP took its official bow with the beginning of the first public Rouge factory tours in 24 years. When Ford ended public tours of the Rouge in 1980, a part of the Motor City had died with them. Although Ford officers were no longer proud of the complex, the Detroit Regional Chamber of Commerce reported that auto factory tours were the top requests of the area's 16.9 million annual visitors.

Ford responded by opening the $25 million Spirit of Ford, a company-owned attraction in Dearborn, across the street from the Henry Ford Museum & Greenfield Village on May 28, 1999. This facility offered a "virtual tour"—a movie—of auto production, along with other displays reminiscent of the old Rotunda. Mounted on an exterior wall was the salvaged stone from the old Administration Building with the Ford name etched in it. Yet Spirit of Ford failed after nine months, when it drew only a fraction of the expected attendance. Ford turned the oval-shaped building into a conference center.

With the construction of the new DTP, Ford came up with a better idea. The car company teamed with the Henry Ford Museum & Greenfield Village, which had the marketing expertise to draw more

A worker uses a robotic arm to help guide an instrument panel module into the cab of an incomplete F-150 Crew Cab. The Dearborn workers decided that the truck bodies should arrive with their doors off, unlike at other Ford truck plants, because it makes it easier to install the interior components. *Ford Photomedia*

The last Mustang has galloped off the line of the 86-year-old Dearborn Assembly Plant at 1:07 p.m., May 10, 2004. Throngs of workers gathered for the celebration, knowing their jobs were secure and that they would cross the parking lot to the new truck plant. The man in the tan sports jacket next to the passenger door is Oscar "Oz" Hov-sepian, who drove the first Mustang off the assembly line in 1964.
Ford Photomedia

than a million visitors a year, to recast the entire factory-tour concept for the twenty-first century.

The Henry Ford Museum (the old Edison Institute) had gone through its own lean times during the 1980s and 1990s. Despite this, it added an IMAX theater and shut down Greenfield Village for half a year to reconstruct its aging infrastructure in time for Ford Motor Company's centennial celebration in 2003. The organization also renamed itself "The Henry Ford."

The public tours returned on May 3, 2004, to a sold-out crowd. In fact, the factory tour was reportedly sold out for the next two months. Visitors hopped on motor coaches at The Henry Ford for a 15-minute ride to the specially constructed, 30,000-square-foot

Visitors Center, near the Miller Road T-bridge at the northeast corner of the Ford Rouge Center. The center is equipped with solar panels and a 12,500-gallon cistern to collect rainwater, to irrigate the plants outside.

Inside is a mural by John Watkiss, the Los Angeles artist known for comic book series such as "Dark Knight" and "Conan" and the Disney feature films *Tarzan* and *Atlantis*. Visitors then view the *Legacy* film that highlights the Rouge's history, while the Art of Manufacturing theater offers a true multisensory experience. Visitors sit in chairs that swivel 360 degrees as they are bombarded by images of steel being made into cars. Heat thrown off by multiwatt light bulbs simulates the heat of molten steel being poured into molds. Scents of new metal and even

From the Model As that rolled off the assembly line in 1927 (*below*) to the first pre-production F-150 pickup truck (*left*), finished on September 30, 2003, the Rouge has manufactured many of Ford Motor Company's key products. With the new Dearborn Truck Plant, the complex is set to build vehicles well into the twenty-first century.
Ford Photomedia

mist fall from the ceiling. It is the closest visitors on this modern Rouge tour will get to the nearby steel mills.

From the theaters, the tourists ride an elevator to the observation deck, 81 feet off the ground, where they can look over the truck plant's grass roof and learn more about the Rouge and its environmental features. An enclosed overpass then takes them to the mezzanine level, above the assembly plant floor. Although separated from the action below, they are spared from potential hazards while having a bird's-eye view of the assembly process.

The tour concludes back at the Visitors Center, which features a gallery of legendary vehicles manufactured at the Rouge. During the recent renovation, parts of old Eagle Boat submarine chasers, such as propeller blades, were found buried and may be added to the gallery.

Rouge Steel under New Management

In the aftermath of the 1999 powerhouse explosion, Rouge Industries faced one disaster after another, while foreign competition grew ever more intense.

In late 2001, a fire all but destroyed the Double Eagle Steel Coating plant on Miller Road, across the street from where Ford had broken ground on its new truck factory. Although Double Eagle was a joint-venture facility with U.S. Steel, it knocked out Rouge Steel's electro-galvanizing line for nine months.

When a massive blackout struck the eastern United States and Canada on June 21, 2003, the dust catcher on the "C" blast furnace exploded, causing significant damage to the furnace. Then, on September 16, an oxygen tank exploded outside one of Rouge Industries' plants, charring dozens of cars in a parking lot. On top of these calamities, the steelmaker faced ever-rising coke and natural gas prices.

Since 1998, about 35 American steelmakers had filed for bankruptcy in a desperate effort to restructure. In March 2002, the Bush administration imposed tariffs that were supposed to last until 2005, in an effort to give steel companies a chance to reform their operations. However, as the tariffs drove steel prices up in the United States, auto manufacturers and suppliers raised a hue and cry. In November 2003, the World Trade Organization ruled that the tariffs violated international treaties, forcing the United States to drop them or risk a trade war with the European Union. But by that time, Ford's former steelworks had gone under.

Between 1999 and the end of 2003, Rouge Industries had lost $360 million. Then, in the summer of 2002, there were rumors that both OAO Severstal, Russia's second largest steelmaker, and U.S. Steel, America's largest steel corporation, were looking at buying Rouge Industries. They had their chance to fight over the remains of Henry Ford's steel company after Rouge Industries filed for Chapter 11 bankruptcy protection on October 24, 2003.

On December 23, Severstal won the bidding war against U.S. Steel in bankruptcy court when it raised its offer from $215 million to $285.5 million. The Russians, though, had a powerful ally—UAW Local 600 backed their bid rather than the uncertainties of ownership by the American company. The union feared that U.S. Steel, which had its own excess manufacturing capacity, would shut the Rouge down. The Russians, on the other hand, offered the UAW a seat on their board of directors and promised to reinvest in the Rouge, saving most of its 2,600 employees.

With the court's decision, Rouge Industries became part of Severstal North America. Some 700 hourly workers retained the right to transfer back to Ford, while Severstal soon indicated that it might cut 400 jobs at the Rouge.

According to steelworkers at the Rouge and reports by Interfax Information Services, the European-based news service, Severstal proposed to introduce new technology to the Rouge, to increase its output from 2.5 million to 3.2 million metric tons. There was speculation, however, that Severstal would close the Rouge's two remaining blast furnaces and send steel slabs from its plants in Russia for the Rouge's mill to finish. Such a decision would mark the end of yet another era at the Rouge, making its storage bins and boat slip operations superfluous.

As this book was being completed, Severstal had begun demolition of the Rouge's old coke ovens, and it is likely that the rusting small gas tower, an icon since the 1930s, will also be scrapped.

Rouge Steel's fate had a number of ironic twists. For decades, until it decided to sell off its steel division in the 1980s, Ford Motor Company had proudly proclaimed itself the only major automaker that owned its own integrated steel company. Severstal might not be a major automaker, but it does have its own car and engine factories. Also, Henry Ford had invested in the Soviet Union in the 1930s, building upward of 1,000 factories, so it seemed fitting that the Russians would come back to rescue a part of the Rouge.

This photo shows the exterior of the Rouge Steel Hot Strip Mill in 1994, taken near the Schaefer Road and Interstate 94 interchange. *AP/Wide World Photos*

The Henry Ford projects that the new Rouge tour will draw about 300,000 people annually—50,000 more per year than the old tours drew before their demise.

One week after DTP opened for public tours, a ceremony called the "Last Stampede" saw the last Mustang come off the line at the 86-year-old Dearborn Assembly Plant. Sales of the last of the fourth-generation Mustangs, which coincided with the pony car's fortieth anniversary, had been surprisingly swift, according to Ford officials, thanks to a sales promotion enticing customers to buy a Mustang for "$5 a day" (after the down payment). It was a gimmick Henry Ford would have loved.

"Mustang . . . is the number-one car in its segment because of the workers who assemble the car in this plant—which means when we go to the new truck plant, we expect the F-150 also to be the best truck in this segment, because it will be Rouge tough," said Jerry Sullivan, UAW Local 600 president.

At its end, Dearborn Assembly ran at 40 units an hour. On its last day, Ford brought back retiree Oscar "Oz" Hov-sepian, 79, who had driven the first Mustang off the line. Joining Hov-sepian on Dearborn Assembly's final day was Fred Galicki, an employee with 32 years of service who was selected by his fellow workers to drive the car.

Hov-sepian was born and raised in Detroit's Delray neighborhood. He started working at the Rouge in January 1943 and retired in June 1980. "I came in here right out high school, knowing that I was going to be drafted in the service," Oz said. "I [worked] next door at the Dearborn Stamping Plant in a unit there that they called 'spring and upset.' I stayed there for about four months and then was drafted."

After World War II, Hov-sepian returned to his job at the Stamping Plant before being transferred to Dearborn Assembly, but his first day was December 16, 1948, the day after a fire destroyed one-third of the factory. Not knowing of the blaze the night before, he reported for work and saw that a whole side of the building was gone.

During the next decade, he became an engineer/supervisor and came to be in charge of 40 to 50 inspectors on the final line. He was therefore in the right place to drive the first 1964½ Mustang off the line.

"They keep trying to persuade me that the white convertible was first. I don't believe it was the white convertible. Just realistically, the convertible just wasn't ready," Hov-sepian said. "And I've never said that I drove the first one off the line—you have to give that credit to Henry Ford [II] or Iacocca. I drove the first 'unit' off."

Watching the ceremony was Jim Paglino, the vehicle manager, who had been working 10-hour days, six days a week for more than a year as Dearborn Assembly wrapped up its production. Paglino's grandfather, Vincenzo, had started at the Rouge's iron foundry back in 1917, and Paglino wears his retirement watch. Additionally, his father worked at the complex from 1941 until 1985.

"I had owned a used '65 Mustang in 1972, before I started working at Ford," Paglino said. "I never thought my career would bring me to this place to build Mustangs. This place has been great for my family, and it's brought a lot of people together.

Hundreds of employees waited for the last car to come off the line. Some started chanting, "D-A-P, D-A-P, D-A-P" before the loudspeakers started playing Wilson Pickett crooning the song "Mustang Sally."

The final Mustangs coming down the line were all white. Then, at 1:07 p.m. May 10, 2004, the last one appeared. It was a crimson GT convertible driven by Galicki, with Hov-sepian in the front passenger seat. The car pulled to a roped-off area where the first Mustang, the white convertible now owned by The Henry Ford, was parked. Nearby sat a silver pre-production 2005 pony car. Even before Galicki turned off the engine, a crowd of workers swarmed forward.

Ford had built 8.3 million Mustangs when 2004 model production came to a close. Of that number, some 6.7 million of the pony cars had been built at Dearborn Assembly. There was a great deal of speculative reporting about what would happen with the DAP, but as this book is completed, no decisions have been made. In the DTP Visitors Center hangs a diagram of the Ford Rouge Center, showing how it may look in the future, with the outline of Dearborn Assembly removed from the map. Company spokespersons, however, have said that Ford wants to preserve a portion of the factory—possibly the remains of "B" Building—for historical purposes.

The DAP's 2,000 workers are now working in the DTP. As this book goes to press, "Job 1" of the production version of the F-150 is scheduled to come off the line on June 7, 2004. As the workers get used to building pickup trucks instead of cars, production will be ramped up, and future products, such as the 2006 Lincoln Mark LT truck, will be added to the line.

The Stamping, Diversified Products (Frame), Engine, and even the old Glass Plant have all been rejuvenated. Yet the future of the Rouge's steelmaking operations remains cloudy. Still, the tradition of work at the Rouge has survived for another day and, maybe, so has the promise of prosperity for the future.

The Dearborn Truck Plant is the culmination of Bill Ford Jr.'s vision for a new Rouge Center and for how worker and environmental concerns can be made compatible with heavy industry. The automaker went through a step-by-step process to set key business goals, understand the environmental aspects, and set its objectives for improvement. The basic idea, hearkening back to Henry Ford's goals, is that if manufacturing waste is eliminated, so too are air, water, and solid waste issues. The company has built on its founder's vision and is set to redefine industrial leadership. The Rouge will once again serve as a model for truly modern manufacturing.

Resources

Books

Abodaher, David. *Iacocca*. New York: Macmillan, 1982.

Babson, Steve, with Ron Alpern, Dave Elsila, and John Revitte. *Working Detroit: The Making of a Union Town*. Detroit: Wayne State University Press, 1986 (originally published by Adama Books, 1984).

Bradsher, Keith. *High and Mighty: SUVs—The World's Most Dangerous Vehicles and How They Got That Way*. New York: PublicAffairs, 2002.

Brecher, Jeremy. *Strike!* New York: Fawcett Publications, 1974.

Brinkley, Douglas. *Wheels for the World: Henry Ford, His Company, and a Century of Progress*. New York: Viking, 2003.

Bryan, Ford R. *Beyond the Model T*. Detroit: Wayne State University Press, 1990.

———. *Rouge: Pictured in Its Prime*. Detroit: Wayne State University Press, 2003.

Byrne, John A. *The Whiz Kids*. New York: Doubleday, 1993.

Chafets, Ze'ev. *Devil's Night: And Other True Tales of Detroit*. New York: Random House, 1990.

Chrysler, Walter P., with Boyden Sparkes. *Life of an American Working Man*. New York: Dodd, Mead & Co., 1950 (originally published by The Curtis Publishing Co., 1937).

Coffey, Frank, and Joseph Layden. *America on Wheels: The First 100 Years, 1896–1996*. Los Angeles: General Publishing Group, 1998.

Collier, Peter, and David Horowitz. *The Fords: An American Epic*. New York: Simon & Schuster, 1987.

Dayton, Eldorous L. *Walter Reuther: The Autocrat of the Bargaining Table*. New York: The Devin-Adair Co., 1958.

Dearborn: Fifty Years of Progress. Dearborn: Mich.: Dearborn Historical Museum, 1979.

Eaton, Eleanor. *Dearborn: A Pictorial History, Rev. ed*. Virginia Beach, Va.: The Donning Co., 1990.

Faulkner, Harold U., and Mark Starr. *Labor in America*. New York: Oxford Book Co., 1955.

Ford, Henry, with Samuel Crowther. *Today and Tomorrow*. Cambridge, Mass.: Productivity Press, 1988 (originally published by Doubleday, Page & Co., 1926).

Good, David L. *Orvie: The Dictator of Dearborn*. Detroit, Mich.: Wayne State University Press, 1989.

Gunnell, John A., and Brad Bowling. *Mustang: America's Favorite Pony Car, 2nd ed*. Iola, Wis.: Krause Publications, 2001.

Halberstam, David. *The Reckoning*. New York: Avon Books, 1986.

Hickerson, J. Mel. *Ernie Breech*. New York: Meredith Press, 1968.

Ingrassia, Paul, and Joseph B. White. *Comeback: The Fall & Rise of the American Automobile Industry*. New York: Simon & Schuster, 1994.

Kenna, Michael, with Lee R. Kollins. *The Rouge*. Santa Monica, Calif.: Ram Publications, 1995.

Kidder, Warren Benjamin. *Willow Run: Colossus of American Industry*. Lansing, Mich.: KFT Publishers, 1995.

Kollins, Michael J. *Pioneers of the U.S. Auto Industry, Vol. 1, The Big Three*. Warrendale, Pa.: Society of Automotive Engineers, 2002.

Lacey, Robert. *Ford: The Men and the Machine*. New York: Little, Brown & Co., 1986.

Lasky, Victor. *Never Complain, Never Explain: The Story of Henry Ford II*. New York: Richard Marek Publishers, 1981.

Marcus, Sheldon. *Father Coughlin: The Tumultuous Life of the Priest of the Little Flower*. Little, Brown & Co., 1973.

Nevins, Allan, and Frank Ernest Hill. *Ford: Expansion and Challenge, 1915–1933*. Charles Scribner's Sons, 1957.

———. *Ford: Decline and Rebirth, 1933–1962*. Charles Scribner's Sons, 1963.

Novak, William, and Lee Iacocca. *Iacocca: An Autobiography*. New York: Bantam Books, 1983.

Olsen, Byron, and Joseph Cabadas. *The American Auto Factory*. St. Paul, Minn.: MBI Publishing, 2002.

Petersen, Donald E., and John Hillkirk. *A Better Idea: Redefining the Way Americans Work*. New York: Houghton Mifflin, 1991.

Pitrone, Jean Maddern. *Tangled Web: Legacy of Auto Pioneer John F. Dodge*. Hamtramck, Mich.: Avenue Publishing, 1989.

Reuther, Victor G. *The Brothers Reuther*. New York: Houghton Mifflin, 1976.

Snider, Clare J., and Michael W. R. Davis. *The Ford Fleet*. Cleveland: Freshwater Press, 1994.

Werling, Donn P. *Henry Ford: A Hearthside Perspective*. Warrendale, Pa.: Society of Automotive Engineers, 2000.

Womack, James P., Daniel T. Jones, and Daniel Roos. *The Machine That Changed the World*. New York: HarperCollins, 1990.

Woodford, Frank B., and Arthur M. Woodford. *All Our Yesterdays: A Brief History of Detroit*. Detroit, Mich.: Wayne State University Press, 1969.

Periodicals

Baird, Dwight G. "Industrious Application of Inventive Genius to the Natural Resources of the Earth is the Groundwork of Prosperous Civilization," *American Business*, September 1948.

Byrne, Jack. "Steel Was Gold to Ford, '46 to '50." *Ford Facts*, November 27, 1954.

Connelly, Mary. "Where Jacques Nasser Went Wrong." *Automotive News*, October 15, 2001.

Eberwein, Cheryl. "Rouge Plant: Aging Giant." *Dearborn Press & Guide*, April 9, 1987.

"Ex-Wrestler Big Daddy to Diesels." *Ford World*, August 26, 1966.

Flint, Jerry. "Revolution Needed at Ford." *Forbes*, May 27, 2002.

King, R. J., and Mark Truby. "New Rouge Plant: Best of Both Worlds." *Detroit News*, December 4, 2002.

Lewis, David L. "Ford Country" column. *Cars & Parts*, various issues.

———"Harry Bennett, Ford's Tough Guy." *Detroit*, June 18, 1973.

———"Henry Ford's Anti-Semitism and Its Repercussions." *Michigan Jewish History*, January 1984.

Meyer, Agnes E. "The Real Edsel Ford: Efficiency Made an Art at Huge Willow Run Bomber Plant." *Washington Post*, March 5, 1943.

Miller, John. "Making the Ford Fleet Shipshape for Spring." *Ford World*, March 4, 1965.

Morris, Betsy. "Idealist on Board: This Ford Is Different." *Fortune*, April 3, 2000.

Philips, David. "Half a Century Out Front at Dearborn Iron Foundry." *Ford World*, December 8, 1970.

Rosenblatt, Roger. "The Man Who Wants Buildings to Love Kids." *Time*, February 15, 1999.

"Steel Ships Take Iron Men." *Ford World*, November 20, 1970.

Taylor, Alex III. "The Fight at Ford: Behind Bill's Boardroom Struggle." *Fortune*, April 3, 2000.

Truby, Mark. "Rouge Fire Crew Battles to Keep 80-Year Tradition." *Detroit News*, February 28, 2003.

"Walter Shaw Leaves Ford's—with a Pension." *United Automobile Worker*, March 1950.

Detroit Free Press, various issues.
Detroit News, various issues.
Ford Facts, Ford Local 600 UAW, various issues.
Ford Rouge News, Ford Motor Company, various issues.
Ford World, Ford Motor Company, various issues.
U.S. Auto Scene, various issues.

Pamphlets/Speeches

Albert Kahn Associates. *100th Anniversary Brochure*. 1995.
———. *AIA Gold Metal Submittal*, circa 1995.
Snider, Clare J. "Speech of Marine Operations at Ford to Marine Historical Society," November 19, 1959.

———. "Marine Operations, 1917–1975: A History of Marine Operations—Ford Motor Company," date unknown.
Steel by Ford. Ford Motor Company, circa 1974.
Welcome to: Power & Utility Operations. Ford Motor Company/United Auto Workers, circa late 1980s.

Web Sites

Auto Channel. www.autochannel.com.
Dressel, Judith. "Edsel Ford, Modernist." Detroit Area Art Deco Society. www.daads.org, 2000.
Ford Fire Department at Rouge Complex. www.fordfire.com.
Hemmings Motor News. www.hemmings.com.
Public Broadcasting System. www.pbs.org.

Index